PATHWAYS

Reading, Writing, and Critical Thinking

4

Laurie Blass   Mari Vargo   Keith S. Folse, Series Consultant

NATIONAL GEOGRAPHIC LEARNING | HEINLE CENGAGE Learning

Australia • Brazil • Japan • Korea • Mexico • Singapore • Spain • United Kingdom • United States

Pathways 4
Reading, Writing, and Critical Thinking
Laurie Blass and Mari Vargo
Keith S. Folse, Series Consultant

Publisher: Andrew Robinson

Executive Editor: Sean Bermingham

Associate Development Editor: Ridhima Thakral

Contributing Editor: Karen Davy

Director of Global Marketing: Ian Martin

International Marketing Manager:
 Caitlin Thomas

Director of Content and Media Production:
 Michael Burggren

Senior Content Project Manager: Daisy Sosa

Manufacturing Buyer: Marybeth Hennebury

Cover Design: Page 2, LLC

Cover Image: Alaska Stock Images/
 National Geographic Creative

Interior Design: Page 2, LLC

Composition: Page 2, LLC

For permission to use material from this text or product, submit all requests online at **cengage.com/permissions**
Further permissions questions can be emailed to **permissionrequest@cengage.com**

International Student Edition:

ISBN-13: 978-1-133-31706-7

U.S. Edition:

ISBN-13: 978-1-133-31686-2

National Geographic Learning
20 Channel Center Street
Boston, MA 02210
USA

Cengage Learning is a leading provider of customized learning solutions with office locations around the globe, including Singapore, the United Kingdom, Australia, Mexico, Brazil, and Japan. Locate your local office at: **ngl.cengage.com**

Cengage Learning products are represented in Canada by Nelson Education, Ltd.

Visit National Geographic Learning online at **ngl.cengage.com**
Visit our corporate website at **www.cengage.com**

Printed in the United States of America
2 3 4 5 6 7 8 19 18 17 16 15 14

Contents

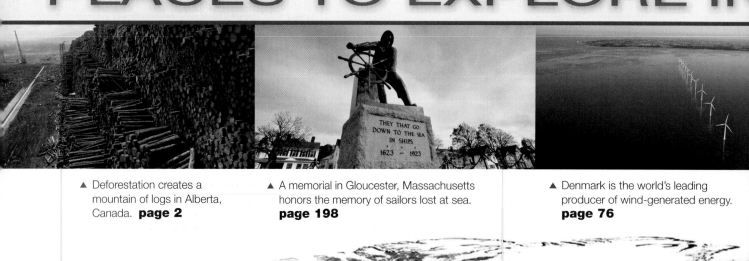

▲ Deforestation creates a mountain of logs in Alberta, Canada. **page 2**

▲ A memorial in Gloucester, Massachusetts honors the memory of sailors lost at sea. **page 198**

THEY THAT GO
DOWN TO THE SEA
IN SHIPS
1623 — 1923

▲ Denmark is the world's leading producer of wind-generated energy. **page 76**

In the seas east of Yucatan peninsula, Mexico, a school of sardines uses swarm techniques to defend against a sailfish attack. **page 102**

PATHWAYS

▲ Communities on Ikaria, Greece are some of the longest-living in the world. **page 175**

▲ Tigers in the jungles of Sumatra, Indonesia face an uncertain future. **page 30**

▲ The unearthly landscape in Reed Flute Cave in Guilin, south east China is one of the natural wonders of the world. **page 52**

Rice is an important part of the economy for the Betsileo people of Madagascar. **page 148**

Scope and Sequence

Unit	Academic Pathways	Vocabulary
 **1** **Our Human Impact** *Page 1* **Academic Track:** Interdisciplinary	**Lesson A:** Understanding cohesion (I) Analyzing arguments **Lesson B:** Reviewing essay writing Writing a cause-effect essay	Understanding meaning from context Using vocabulary to complete definitions Applying vocabulary in a personalized context **Word Link:** *equi-*
 **2** **Conservation and Protection** *Page 25* **Academic Track:** Environmental Science/Life Science	**Lesson A:** Understanding appositives Analyzing text organization **Lesson B:** Reviewing the thesis statement Writing a persuasive essay	Understanding meaning from context Using vocabulary to complete definitions Applying vocabulary in a personalized context **Word Partners:** *priority; intrinsic*
3 **Beautiful** *Page 47* **Academic Track:** Sociology/Aesthetics	**Lesson A:** Using a concept map to identify supporting details Applying ideas **Lesson B:** Supporting a thesis Writing an evaluative essay	Understanding meaning from context Using vocabulary to complete definitions Applying vocabulary in a personalized context **Word Partners:** *proportion*
 **4** **Powering Our Planet** *Page 71* **Academic Track:** Interdisciplinary	**Lesson A:** Recognizing a writer's tone Understanding figurative language **Lesson B:** Avoiding plagiarism Writing a summary essay	Understanding meaning from context Using vocabulary to complete definitions Applying vocabulary in a personalized context **Word Partners:** *prospect; on behalf* **Word Link:** *auto-*
 **5** **Working Together** *Page 95* **Academic Track:** Life Science/ Sociology	**Lesson A:** Identifying subjects in complex sentences Evaluating sources **Lesson B:** Organizing a comparative essay Writing a comparative essay	Understanding meaning from context Using vocabulary to complete definitions Applying vocabulary in a personalized context **Word Usage:** *complementary*

Reading	Writing	Viewing	Critical Thinking
The Human Age By Elizabeth Kolbert (argumentative essay) Identifying main ideas and key details Understanding infographics Skill Focus: Understanding cohesion (I)	Goal: Writing a cause-effect essay about human impacts Language: Using cohesive devices Skill: Essay writing (review)	Video: *Man-Made Earthquakes* Viewing to confirm predictions Viewing for general understanding and specific information Relating video content to reading texts	Evaluating causes and effects Inferring meaning from context Synthesizing information to make connections Evaluating thesis statements Analyzing a model essay CT Focus: Analyzing arguments
A Cry for the Tiger By Caroline Alexander (explanatory/persuasive report) Identifying main ideas Scanning for key details (numbers) Identifying reasons and solutions Skill Focus: Understanding appositives	Goal: Writing a persuasive essay about a problem and a possible solution Language: Using appositives Skill: Writing a thesis statement (review)	Video: *Tigers in the Snow* Viewing to confirm predictions Viewing for general understanding and specific information Relating video content to reading texts	Analyzing and evaluating text organization Inferring meaning from context Synthesizing information to make a comparison Evaluating thesis statements Justifying an opinion Analyzing a model essay CT Focus: Analyzing text organization
Images of Beauty By Annie Griffiths (expository/classification article) Identifying main ideas and key details Skill Focus: Using a concept map to identify supporting details	Goal: Writing an evaluative essay about a visual art form Language: Using nonrestrictive adjective clauses Skill: Supporting a thesis	Video: *Oregon Coast* Activating prior knowledge Viewing for general understanding and specific information Relating video content to reading texts	Applying ideas to other contexts Reflecting on a writer's opinion Synthesizing information to apply criteria Analyzing a thesis statement and supporting ideas Analyzing a model essay CT Focus: Applying ideas to new contexts
Our Energy Challenge By Bill McKibben (argumentative/persuasive essay) Identifying main ideas and key details Interpreting charts Understanding a process Skill Focus: Recognizing a writer's tone	Goal: Writing a summary essay about energy Language: Avoiding plagiarism Skill: Writing a summary	Video: *Powering Cities* Viewing to confirm predictions Viewing for general understanding and specific information Relating video content to reading texts	Evaluating reasons Synthesizing information to make a judgment Evaluating summaries Analyzing a model essay CT Focus: Interpreting figurative language
The Smart Swarm By Peter Miller (explanatory article) Identifying main ideas and purpose Summarizing key details Skill Focus: Identifying subjects in complex sentences	Goal: Writing a comparative essay about two types of collaboration Language: Using parallel structure Skill: Organizing a comparative essay	Video: *Locust Swarm* Viewing to confirm predictions Viewing for general understanding and specific information Relating video content to reading texts	Analyzing information Synthesizing information to make hypotheses Analyzing essay notes Analyzing a model essay CT Focus: Evaluating sources

Scope and Sequence

Unit	Academic Pathways	Vocabulary
 **6** **Language and Culture** *Page 119* **Academic Track:** Interdisciplinary	**Lesson A:** Inferring an author's attitude Understanding verbal phrases **Lesson B:** Writing introductions and conclusions Writing a personal opinion essay	Understanding meaning from context Using vocabulary to complete definitions Applying vocabulary in a personalized context **Word Link:** *ir-; con-; crypt*
 **7** **Resources and Development** *Page 141* **Academic Track:** History/Economics	**Lesson A:** Identifying a writer's point of view Understanding cohesion (II) **Lesson B:** Researching and note-taking Writing an expository essay	Understanding meaning from context Using vocabulary to complete definitions Applying vocabulary in a personalized context **Word Partners:** *tension*
 **8** **Living Longer** *Page 165* **Academic Track:** Health and Medicine	**Lesson A:** Predicting a conclusion Asking questions as you read **Lesson B:** Planning a research paper Writing an argumentative research paper	Understanding meaning from context Using vocabulary to complete definitions Applying vocabulary in a personalized context **Word Link:** *struct; uni-*
9 **Memorable Experiences** *Page 189* **Academic Track:** Interdisciplinary	**Lesson A:** Making inferences Analyzing a personal narrative **Lesson B:** Using sensory details Writing an extended personal narrative	Understanding meaning from context Using vocabulary to complete definitions Applying vocabulary in a personalized context **Word Usage:** *ensure/insure* **Word Partners:** *assumption*
 **10** **Imagining the Future** *Page 211* **Academic Track:** Interdisciplinary	**Lesson A:** Reading literature critically Identifying literary elements **Lesson B:** Writing critically about literature Writing an analysis of fiction excerpts	Understanding meaning from context Using vocabulary to complete definitions Applying vocabulary in a personalized context **Word Link:** *liter* **Word Partners:** *flee/fled*

Reading	Writing	Viewing	Critical Thinking
The Secret Language By Daisy Zamora (autobiographical essay) Identifying main ideas and key details **Skill Focus:** Understanding verbal phrases	**Goal:** Writing a personal opinion essay about language learning **Language:** Adding information with verbal phrases **Skill:** Writing introductions and conclusions	**Video:** *Kenyans in New York* Viewing to confirm predictions Viewing for general understanding and specific information Relating video content to reading texts	Analyzing types of language Personalizing an author's experience Synthesizing to make a comparison Analyzing an introduction and a conclusion Analyzing a model essay **CT Focus:** Inferring an author's attitude
The Shape of Africa By Jared Diamond (expository/persuasive essay) Identifying chronology Identifying main ideas and key details **Skill Focus:** Understanding cohesion (II)	**Goal:** Writing an expository essay about a country or region's development **Language:** Referring to sources **Skill:** Researching and note-taking	**Video:** *The Encroaching Desert* Activating prior knowledge Viewing for general understanding and specific information Relating video content to reading texts	Evaluating a writer's text organization Synthesizing to make an interpretation Evaluating and applying research information Analyzing a model essay **CT Focus:** Identifying a writer's point of view
Beyond 100 By Stephen S. Hall (explanatory scientific article) Identifying main ideas and key details identifying supporting examples Understanding infographics **Skill Focus:** Asking questions as you read	**Goal:** Writing an argumentative research paper about longevity **Language:** Explaining the significance of evidence **Skill:** Planning a research paper	**Video:** *Secrets of a Long Life* Viewing to confirm predictions Viewing for general understanding and specific information Relating video content to reading texts	Making inferences from an infographic Synthesizing to make inferences Evaluating research topics and evidence Analyzing a model essay **CT Focus:** Predicting a conclusion
Welcome Stranger By Sebastian Junger (personal narrative) Identifying purpose and structure Identifying key details **Skill Focus:** Analyzing a personal narrative	**Goal:** Writing an extended personal narrative about a past experience **Language:** Reviewing past forms **Skill:** Using sensory details	**Video:** *Frontline Diary* Viewing to confirm predictions Viewing for general understanding and specific information Relating video content to reading texts	Personalizing an author's experience Synthesizing to make hypotheses Analyzing an author's sensory details Applying information Analyzing a model essay **CT Focus:** Making inferences about a text
My Mars and extracts from **The Martian Chronicles** By Ray Bradbury (autobiographical essay/fiction extracts) Identifying main ideas and key details **Skill Focus:** Identifying literary elements	**Goal:** Writing an analysis of fiction excerpts **Language:** Using a variety of sentence types **Skill:** Writing critically about literature	**Video:** *Mission: Mars* Viewing to confirm predictions Viewing for general understanding and specific information Relating video content to reading texts	Interpreting figurative language Inferring motivation and purpose Synthesizing to make hypotheses Evaluating analysis topics and evidence Analyzing a model essay **CT Focus:** Reading literature critically

EXPLORE A UNIT

Each unit has two lessons.

Lesson A develops academic reading skills and vocabulary by focusing on an important contemporary theme. The language and content in these sections provide the stimulus for a guided writing task (Lesson B). A video section acts as a content bridge between Lessons A and B.

UNIT

Our Human Impact

ACADEMIC PATHWAYS

Lesson A: Understanding cohesion
Analyzing arguments
Lesson B: Reviewing essay writing
Writing a cause-effect essay

Think and Discuss

1. In what ways have humans changed the planet?
2. What are some of the positive and negative effects of the changes humans have made on the planet?

▲ Terraced rice paddies have transformed the rural landscape in Yunnan Province, China.

The **unit theme** focuses on an academic content area relevant to students' lives, such as Health Science, Business and Technology, and Environmental Science.

Academic Pathways highlight the main academic skills of each lesson.

Exploring the Theme provides a visual introduction to the unit. Learners are encouraged to think critically and share ideas about the unit topic. Authentic charts, maps, and graphics from National Geographic help learners comprehend key ideas and develop visual literacy.

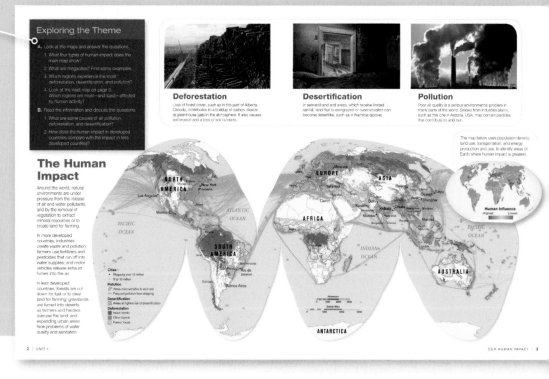

Exploring the Theme

A. Look at the maps and answer the questions.

1. What four types of human impact does the main map show?
2. What are megacities? Find some examples.
3. Which regions experience the most deforestation, desertification, and pollution?
4. Look at the inset map on page 3. Which regions are most—and least—affected by human activity?

B. Read the information and discuss the questions.

1. What are some causes of air pollution, deforestation, and desertification?
2. How does the human impact in developed countries compare with the impact in less developed countries?

Deforestation
Loss of forest cover, such as in this part of Alberta, Canada, contributes to a buildup of carbon dioxide (a greenhouse gas) in the atmosphere. It also causes soil erosion and a loss of soil nutrients.

Desertification
In semiarid and arid areas, which receive limited rainfall, land that is overgrazed or overcultivated can become desertlike, such as in Namibia (above).

Pollution
Poor air quality is a serious environmental problem in many parts of the world. Smoke from industrial plants, such as this one in Arizona, USA, may contain particles that contribute to acid rain.

The Human Impact

Around the world, natural environments are under pressure from the release of air and water pollutants, and by the removal of vegetation to extract mineral resources or to create land for farming.

In more developed countries, industries create waste and pollution; farmers use fertilizers and pesticides that run off into water supplies; and motor vehicles release exhaust fumes into the air.

In less developed countries, forests are cut down for fuel or to clear land for farming; grasslands are turned into deserts as farmers and herders overuse the land; and expanding urban areas face problems of water quality and sanitation.

The map below uses population density, land use, transportation, and energy production and use, to identify areas of Earth where human impact is greatest.

Cities
- Megacity, over 10 million
- 5 to 10 million

Pollution
- Areas most sensitive to acid rain
- Frequent pollution from shipping

Desertification
- Areas at highest risk of desertification

Deforestation
- Intact forests
- Other forests
- Former forest

Human Influence
Highest   Lowest

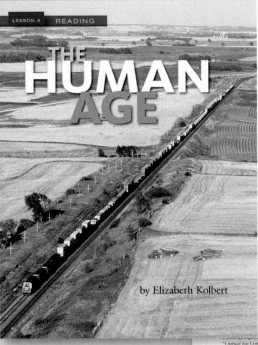

B | **Building Vocabulary.** Complete the sentences with the words from the box.
Use a dictionary to help you.

| compound | concept | criteria | incorporate | register | shifting |

1. As a result of global warming, some bird species are moving to new places. For example, the North American warbler is _____ its habitat 65 miles to the north.
2. One of the _____ for naming a new animals species is that the name must be easy to remember.
3. Researchers have recently discovered that a combination of chemicals in a common weed killer, a _____ called POE-15, can have a serious effect on human health.
4. If you _____ an invention with the patent office, your idea will go into an official record, and it will be protected so that it cannot be copied.
5. A basic scientific _____ is cause and effect—the idea that an event is caused by or affected by another event.
6. To _____ something means to include it within something that already exists.

▲ An endangered golden-cheeked warbler

In **_Preparing to Read_**, learners are introduced to key vocabulary items from the reading passage. Guided pre-reading tasks and strategy tips encourage learners to think critically about what they are going to read.

LESSON A   READING

THE HUMAN AGE

by Elizabeth Kolbert

Human beings have altered the planet so much in just the past century or two that we now have a new name for a new epoch: the Anthropocene.

THE WORD *ANTHROPOCENE* was coined by Dutch chemist Paul Crutzen about a decade ago. One day Crutzen, who shared a Nobel Prize for discovering the effects of ozone-depleting **compounds**, was sitting at a scientific **conference**. The conference chairman kept referring to the Holocene, the epoch that began at the end of the last ice age, 11,500 years ago, and that—officially, at least—continues to this day.

"Let's stop it," Crutzen recalls blurting out. "We are no longer in the Holocene. We are in the Anthropocene." It was quiet in the room for a while. When the group took a coffee break, the Anthropocene was the main topic of conversation. Someone suggested that Crutzen copyright the word.

Way back in the 1870s, an Italian geologist named Antonio Stoppani proposed that people had introduced a new era, which he labeled the Anthropozoic. Stoppani's proposal was **ignored**; other scientists found it unscientific. The Anthropocene, by contrast, struck a chord. Human impacts on the world have become a lot more obvious since Stoppani's day, in part because the size of the population has roughly quadrupled,[1] to nearly seven billion. "The pattern of human population growth in the 20th century was more bacterial than primate," biologist E. O. Wilson has written. Wilson calculates that human biomass[2] is already a hundred times larger than that of any other large animal species that has ever walked the Earth.

In 2002, when Crutzen wrote up the Anthropocene idea in the journal *Nature*, the **concept** was immediately picked up by researchers working in a wide range of disciplines. Soon it began to appear regularly in the scientific press. "Global Analysis of River Systems: From Earth System Controls to Anthropocene Syndromes" ran the title of one 2003 paper. "Soils and Sediments in the Anthropocene" was the headline of another, published in 2004.

[1] *quadruple* **quadruple.** Units increase by a factor of four.
[2] **Biomass** refers to the total amount of living matter in an area.

◀ **Western Minnesota:** Vast wheat fields and long train lines have created a distinctive human landscape in the Midwestern United States.

The **_Reading_** passage is an authentic text related to the unit theme. Reading texts include magazine articles, book extracts, and passage from literature. Each reading passage is recorded on the audio program.

LESSON A   READING

IF WE HAVE INDEED entered a new epoch, then when exactly did it begin? When did human impacts rise to the level of geologic significance?

William Ruddiman, a paleoclimatologist at the University of Virginia, has proposed that the invention of agriculture some 8,000 years ago, and the deforestation that resulted, led to an increase in atmospheric CO_2 just large enough to stave off what otherwise would have been the start of a new ice age. In his view, humans have been the dominant force on the planet practically since the start of the Holocene. Crutzen has suggested that the Anthropocene began in the late 18th century, when, ice cores show, carbon dioxide levels began what has since proved to be an uninterrupted rise. Other scientists put the beginning of the new epoch in the middle of the 20th century, when the rates of both population growth and consumption accelerated rapidly.

Zalasiewicz now heads a working group of the International Commission on Stratigraphy (ICS) that is tasked with officially determining whether the Anthropocene deserves to be **incorporated** into

the geologic timescale. A final decision will require votes by both the ICS and its parent organization, the International Union of Geological Sciences. The process is likely to take years. As it drags on, the decision may well become easier. Some scientists argue that we've not yet reached the start of the Anthropocene—not because we haven't had a dramatic impact on the planet, but because the next several decades are likely to prove even more stratigraphically significant than the past few centuries. "Do we decide the Anthropocene's here, or do we wait 20 years and things will be even worse?" says Mark Williams, a geologist and colleague of Zalasiewicz's at the University of Leicester in England.

Crutzen, who started the debate, thinks its real value won't lie in revisions to geology textbooks. His purpose is broader: He wants to focus our attention on the consequences of our collective action—and on how we might still avert the worst. "What I hope," he says, "is that the term *Anthropocene* will be a warning to the world."

▼ **Trotternish, Isle of Skye:** Millions of years of history are recorded in the rocks of Scotland. Are we creating a new chapter in Earth's geologic history?

"I noticed that Crutzen's term was appearing in the serious literature, without quotation marks and without a sense of irony," he says. In 2007, Zalasiewicz was serving as chairman of the Geological Society of London's Stratigraphy Commission. At a meeting, he decided to ask his fellow stratigraphers what they thought of the Anthropocene. Twenty-one of 22 thought the concept had merit.

Their answer prompted him to look at it as a formal problem in geology. Would the Anthropocene satisfy the criteria used for naming a new epoch? In geology, epochs are generally marked off by changes in the type of life-forms that prevail. The end of one epoch and the start of the next is often indicated by the appearance and disappearance of different types of fossils in **sedimentary rocks**[4]—the emergence of one type of commonly fossilized organism, say, or the disappearance of another.

The rock record of the present doesn't exist yet, of course. So the question was: When it does, will human impacts show up as "stratigraphically significant"? The answer, Zalasiewicz's group decided, is yes—though not necessarily for the reasons you would expect.

[3] **Stratigraphy** is a branch of geology concerned with the study of rock layers.
[4] **Sedimentary rocks** are formed from sediment—solid material that settles at the bottom of a liquid, especially earth and pieces of rock that have been carried along and then left somewhere by water, ice, or wind.

	Era	Period		Epoch	Millions of Years
	Cenozoic	Quaternary		Holocene	
				Pleistocene	
		Neogene		Pliocene	1.5
				Miocene	2.3
		Paleogene		Oligocene	
				Eocene	
				Paleocene	65
	Mesozoic	Cretaceous			
		Jurassic			
		Triassic			250
	Paleozoic	Permian			
		Carboniferous	Pennsylvanian		
			Mississippian		
		Devonian			
		Silurian			540
		Ordovician			
		Cambrian			
	Precambrian	Proterozoic			2500
		Archean			3800
		Hadean			4600

start of the Anthropocene?

▲ **Humboldt County, California:** The effects of timber logging are clearly visible from the air above Maple Creek, near Redwood National Park.

PROBABLY THE MOST OBVIOUS way humans are altering the planet is by building cities, which are essentially vast stretches of man-made materials—steel, glass, concrete, and brick. But it turns out most cities are not good candidates for long-term preservation for the simple reason that they're built on land, and on land the forces of erosion tend to win out over those of sedimentation. From a geologic **perspective**, the most plainly visible human effects on the landscape today "may in some ways be the most transient."[5] Zalasiewicz has observed.

Humans have also transformed the world through farming; something like 38 percent of the planet's ice-free land is now **devoted to** agriculture. Here again, some of the effects that seem most significant today will leave behind only subtle traces at best.

Fertilizer factories, for example, now take more nitrogen from the air—converting it to a biologically usable form—than all the plants and microbes on land; the runoff from fertilized fields is triggering life-threatening blooms of algae[6] at river mouths all over the world. But this global perturbation[7] of the nitrogen cycle will be hard to detect because synthesized nitrogen is just like its natural **equivalent**. Future geologists are more likely to grasp the scale of 21st-century industrial agriculture from the pollen[8] record—from the monochrome[9] stretches of corn, wheat, and soy pollen that will have replaced the varied record left behind by rain forests or prairies.

[5] **Transient** describes a situation that lasts only a short time or is constantly changing.
[6] **Algae** are organisms with no stems or leaves that grow in water or on damp surfaces.
[7] A **perturbation** is a small change to something, especially an unusual change.
[8] **Pollen** is a fine powder produced by flowers; it fertilizes other flowers of the same species so that they produce seeds.
[9] Something is **monochrome** if it is all one color.

UNDERSTANDING THE READING

A | Identifying Main Ideas. Write answers to the questions.

1. What is the purpose of Kolbert's article? Complete the main idea.

   Kolbert's purpose is to present the idea of a new _____ and to show how our human impact will be noted in the future.

2. What does "Anthropocene" mean? Explain it in your own words.

   _____
   _____

3. The reading passage has three main parts. Where could you place each of these section heads? Write paragraph letters: A, B, and D.

Section Head	Before Paragraph . . .
How We Are Changing the Planet	_____
Tracing the Origins of the Anthropocene	_____
A New Perspective on Earth's History	_____

4. What four main areas does Kolbert examine for signs of human impact?

   cities, _____

B | Identifying Key Details. Write answers to the questions.

1. When was the idea of a new era first proposed? What was it called?

   _____

2. What do cities basically consist of, according to Kolbert? Why might cities not be visible in the future?

   _____
   _____

3. How do fertilizers and industrial farming affect the environment?

   _____
   _____

Guided comprehension tasks and reading strategy instruction enable learners to improve their academic literacy and critical thinking skills.

Critical Thinking tasks require learners to analyze, synthesize, and critically evaluate the ideas and information in the reading.

LESSON A   UNDERSTANDING THE READING

C | Critical Thinking: Evaluating. Use your answers to exercise **B** to complete the chart summarizing the human impact. Then discuss this question in a small group: Of the four kinds of human impact, which do you think will leave the most obvious record in the future? Why?

	The Human Effect	Will It Leave a Trace? Why, or Why Not?
Cities	by building _____ structures	No—structures built on lands _____ may make them disappear
Farming	by using fertilizers	_____—but only from the _____ record of the shift from a variety of plants to a few types
Forests	by _____	Maybe—sedimentation and _____ may be noticed
Atmosphere	by _____ the atmosphere	Most likely—shifts in habitat range will leave traces in _____; _____ of the world's oceans and corals will cause _____

D | Understanding Infographics. Look at the infographic on page 10 and answer the questions. Then discuss your answers with a partner.

1. What is the main purpose of the infographic? Circle the best answer.

   a. to show the importance of changes in human technology since 1900
   b. to show how different factors have contributed to our human impact
   c. to show how population growth has risen faster than affluence

2. Look at the "I=PAT" formula. What does it mean? Explain it in your own words.

   _____
   _____

3. Describe how the following factors have increased since 1900.

   population: _____

   GDP (affluence): _____

   technology: _____

CT Focus: Analyzing arguments

An argument usually presents a debatable issue and includes evidence that supports the issue. When you read a passage that presents an argument, first identify the issue—the writer's argument. Then analyze the writer's evidence. Is it fully developed? Is it accurate? Is it detailed? Is it current? How do you know?

E | Critical Thinking: Analyzing Evidence. In the reading on pages 6–12, what evidence does the writer present in support of either side of the main issue? Take notes in the chart. Then discuss answers to the questions below with a partner.

Issue: Our impact on the planet is so great that we are now living in a new epoch.

Arguments For	Arguments Against

1. Are the arguments on both sides equally balanced, or is there more evidence for one side than the other?

2. Are we at the start of a new epoch? Should we name the current period "Anthropocene"? Why, or why not?

F | Identifying Meaning from Context. Find and underline the following words and expressions in the reading passage. Use context to guess their meanings. Then match the sentence parts.

1. _____ Paragraph A: If a word is **coined by** someone,
2. _____ Paragraph C: If an idea **struck a chord**,
3. _____ Paragraph D: If a concept is **picked up**,
4. _____ Paragraph J: If something is **life-throttling**,
5. _____ Paragraph M: If a consequence is **discernible**,
6. _____ Paragraph O: If you **stave off** an event,
7. _____ Paragraph P: When something **drags on**,

a. it moves slowly.
b. you can detect it.
c. other people thought it sounded logical.
d. you prevent it from happening.
e. people decide to adopt it.
f. it was invented by that person.
g. it causes things to die.

Reading Skill: Understanding Cohesion

Cohesion is the way that ideas are linked in a text. Writers use certain techniques (sometimes called "cohesive devices") to refer to ideas mentioned elsewhere in the passage. Some of these techniques include pronouns (one[s], another, the other), demonstratives (this, that, these, those), and synonyms.

Look at these examples from "The Human Age."

In 2002, when Crutzen wrote up the Anthropocene idea in the journal Nature, the concept was immediately picked up by researchers working in a wide range of disciplines.

The writer uses a synonym, *the concept*, to refer to *the idea* in the first part of the sentence.

Wilson calculates that human biomass is already a hundred times larger than that of any other large animal species that has ever walked the Earth.

In this example, the writer uses *that* to refer to *biomass*.

Note: The referent—the word or idea that is referred to—is not always close to the cohesive device. It may be in a different part of the sentence, or in a different sentence or section of the text.

A | Analyzing. Circle the word or idea that each underlined word in these extracts refers to.

1. Paragraph D: "Global Analysis of River Systems: From Earth System Controls to Anthropocene Syndromes" ran the title of one 2003 paper. "Soils and Sediments in the Anthropocene" was the headline of another, published in 2004.

   a. title   b. paper   c. river system

2. Paragraph H: But it turns out most cities are not good candidates for long-term preservation for the simple reason that they're built on land, and on land the forces of erosion tend to win out over those of sedimentation.

   a. forces   b. cities   c. candidates

B | Analyzing. Find the following excerpts in "The Human Age." Write the words or ideas that each underlined words or phrases refer to.

1. Paragraph E: At first, most of the scientists using the new geologic term were not geologists.

2. Paragraph F: The boundaries between epochs are defined by changes preserved in sedimentary rocks—the emergence of one type of commonly fossilized organism, say, or the disappearance of another.

3. Paragraph L: Probably the most significant change, from a geologic perspective, is one that's invisible to us—the change in the composition of the atmosphere.

4. Paragraph M: The most recent one, which is believed to have been caused by the impact of an asteroid, took place 65 million years ago, at the end of the Cretaceous period.

Viewing tasks related to an authentic National Geographic video serve as a content bridge between Lessons A and B. (Video scripts are on pages 235–242.)

VIEWING Man-Made Earthquakes

Before Viewing

A | Using a Dictionary. Here are some words you will hear in the video. Match each one with the correct definition. Use a dictionary to help you.

| excavation | extract | induced | perturb | stress (v.) |

1. _____ disturb greatly
2. _____ the act of digging in the earth
3. _____ put pressure on
4. _____ caused; triggered
5. _____ take out; remove

B | Thinking Ahead. Discuss these questions with a partner: What are some examples of materials that are mined? What are some possible positive and negative effects of mining?

While Viewing

B | Read the questions (1–5). Think about the answers as you view the video.

1. Where did the earthquake described in the video occur?
2. What were the effects of this earthquake?
3. What was a possible cause of the earthquake?
4. What are "pre-existing conditions"? How do earthquakes affect them?
5. What percentage of earthquakes around the world may be caused by mining?

After Viewing

A | Discuss the answers to the questions in exercise **B** in "While Viewing" with a partner.

B | Critical Thinking: Synthesizing. How does mining contribute to the human impact on the planet?

▼ Gold miners at Serra Pelada Mine, Brazil

OUR HUMAN IMPACT | 17

EXPLORE A UNIT

The **Goal of Lesson B** is for learners to relate their own views and experience to the theme of the unit by completing a guided writing assignment.

Integrated **grammar practice and writing skill development** provides scaffolding for the writing assignment.

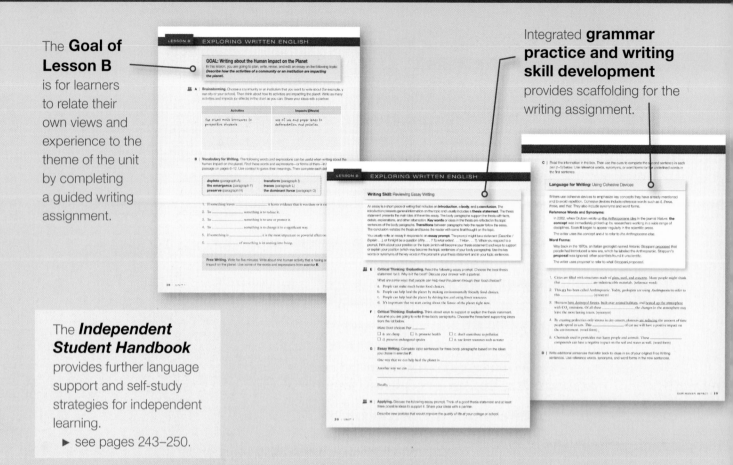

The **Independent Student Handbook** provides further language support and self-study strategies for independent learning.
▶ see pages 243–250.

Resources for *Pathways* Level 4

Video DVD with authentic National Geographic clips relating to each of the ten units.

Teacher's Guide including teacher's notes, expansion activities, rubrics for evaluating written assignments, and answer keys for activities in the Student Book.

Audio CDs with audio recordings of the Student Book reading passages.

A **guided process approach** develops learners' confidence
in planning, drafting, revising, and editing their written work.

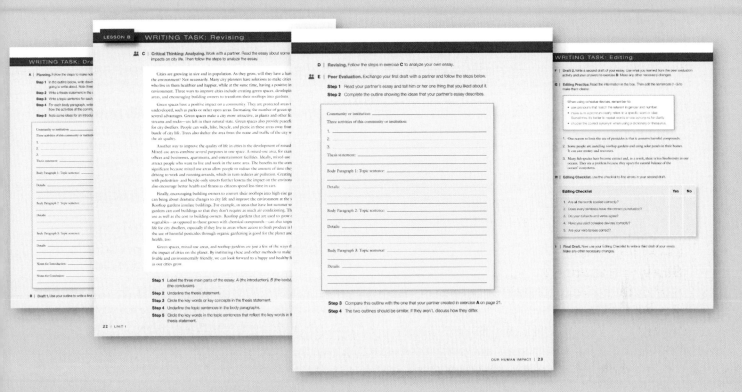

Assessment CD-ROM with ExamView®

containing a bank of ready-made questions for quick and effective assessment.

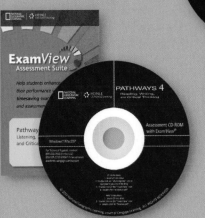

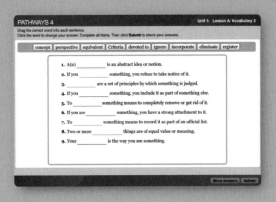

Online Workbook, powered by MyELT, with both teacher-led and self-study options. This contains the 10 National Geographic video clips, supported by interactive, automatically graded activities that practice the skills learned in the Student Books.

Classroom Presentation Tool CD-ROM

featuring audio and video clips, and interactive activities from the Student Book. These can be used with an interactive whiteboard or computer projector.

Credits

Text

6–12: Adapted from "The Age of Man," by Elizabeth Kolbert: NGM March 2011 **30-35** Adapted from "A Cry for the Tiger," by Caroline Alexander: NGM December 2011 **52-58** Adapted from the Introduction to "Simply Beautiful Photographs" pp. 25-31, by Annie Griffiths: National Geographic Books 2010 **76-82** Adapted from "Our Energy Challenge," by Bill McKibben: NGM Special Issue "Energy," March 2009 **100-105** Adapted from "Swarm Theory," by Peter Miller: NGM July 2007 **124-128** Adapted from "The Secret Language" by Daisy Zamora, reprinted with permission of the National Geographic Society from the book "How I Learned English." Edited by Tom Miller. Copyright ©2007 Tom Miller **146-152** Adapted from "The Shape of Africa," by Jared Diamond: NGM September 2005 **171-177** Adapted from "On Beyond 100," by Peter S. Hall: NGM May 2013 **194-199** Adapted from "Welcome Stranger," by Sebastian Junger: National Geographic Adventure magazine May 2006. Copyright © 2006 by Sebastian Junger. Reprinted by permission of the Stuart Krichevsky Literary Agency, Inc. **216-218** Adapted from "My Mars," by Ray Bradbury: NGM Special Issue "Space," October 2008 **194-199** Excerpts from "The Martian Chronicles," by Ray Bradbury. Reprinted by permission of Don Congdon Associates, Inc. Copyright © 1950, renewed 1977 by Ray Bradbury

NGM = National Geographic Magazine

Photos, Illustrations and Maps

IFC: Courtesy of Don Usner; Courtesy of Daisy Zamora; Evan Agostini/Getty Images; Alberto E. Rodriguez/WireImage/Getty Images; Linda Makarov/NGC; Courtesy of Stephen S. Hall; AP Photo/Peter Dejong; Jim Spellman/WireImage/Getty Images; Courtesy of Peter Miller on behalf of NGC; Ron Galella Collection/Getty Images **i:** Chris Gray/NGC **iii:** Paul Chesley/NGC; Steve Winter/NGC; Jef Meul/Minden Pictures; Michael Melford/NGC; David Alan Harvey/NGC; Justin Guariglia/NGC; Chris Johns/NGC; Fritz Hoffmann/NGC; Joel Sartore/NGC; NASA Images **iv:** James L. Stanfield/NGC; Raul Touzon/NGC; Andrew Henderson/NGC; Mauricio Handler/NGC **iv-v:** NASA Goddard Space Flight Center Image by Reto Stöckli (land surface, shallow water, clouds) **v:** Gianluca Colla/NGC; Steve Winter/NGC; Raymond Gehman/NGC; Chris Johns/NGC **vi:** Jim Richardson/NGC; Steve Winter/NGC; Sam Abell/NGC; Ben Hortan/NGC; Peter Essick/NGC **viii:** Tyrone Turner/NGC; Stephen Alvarez/NGC; Gianluca Colla/NGC; Frans Lanting/NGC; Twentieth Century-Fox Film Corporation/The Kobal Collectiom/Picture Desk **1:** Jim Richardson/NGC **2:** James L. Stanfield/NGC **2-3:** National Geographic Maps **3:** Chris Gray/NGC; Brian Gordon Green/NGC **4:** Joel Sartore/NGC **6:** Paul Chesley/NGC **9:** Michael Nichols/NGC **10:** Randy Olson/NGC, **12:** Jim Richardson/NGC **14:** Justin Guariglia/NGC; Paul Chesley/NGC; Michael Nichols/NGC; Brian Gordon Green/NGC **17:** James P. Blair/NGC **25:** Steve Winter/NGC **26:** Frans Lanting/NGC; IS/National Geographic Creative; Joel Sartore/NGC **27:** Jason Edwards/NGC; (all others) Joel Sartore/NGC **28:** Joel Sartore/NGC **30, 32:** Steve Winter/NGC **33:** Virginia W Mason/NGC **34, 35:** Steve Winter/NGC **39:** Michael Nichols/NGC **44:** Joel Sartore/NGC **47:** Jef Meul/Minden Pictures **48-49:** Taylor S. Kennedy/NGC **50:** Galerie Janette Ostier, Paris, France/The Bridgeman Art Library; INTERFOT/Alamy **52:** Raymond Gehman/NGC **54:** Sam Abell/NGC **55:** James L. Stanfield/NGC **56:** Martin Kers/Minden Pictures **57:** Annie Griffiths/NGC **58:** Rich Reid/NGC **62:** Phil Schermeister/NGC **66:** Richard Nowitz/NGC **71:** Tyrone Turner/NGC **72-73:** Sean McNaughton/NGC **76:** Andrew Henderson/NGC **78-79:** Michael Melford/NGC **80:** Joe McNally/NGC **81:** Ben Hortan/NGC **82:** National Geographic **87:** SeanPavonePhoto/Shutterstock.com **95:** Peter Essick/NGC **96-97:** David Alan Harvey/NGC **100:** Frans Lanting/NGC **102:** Mauricio Handler/NGC **103:** Mark Thiessen/NGC **104-105:** Dean Conger/NGC **110:** Joel Sartore/NGC **116:** Joel Sartore/NGC; David Liittschwager/NGC **119:** Justin Guariglia/NGC **120-121:** Frans Lanting/NGC **124:** Medford Taylor/NGC **126:** Tyrone Turner/NGC **127:** John G Ross/Photo Researchers/Getty Images **133:** Mike Theiss/NGC **141:** Lynn Johnson/NGC **142-143:** National Geographic Maps **144:** Andrew Aitchison/Alamy **146-147:** Art by Kees Veenenbos based on satellite image by Earth Observatory, NASA Goddard Space Flight Center **148:** Frans Lanting/NGC **149:** Chris Johns/NGC **150:** Frans Lanting/NGC **151:** Stephen Alvarez/NGC **156:** Chris Johns/NGC **165:** Gianluca Colla/NGC **166-167:** National Geographic Maps **171, 173:** Fritz Hoffmann/NGC **174:** NGM ART/National Geographic **175:** Gianluca Colla/NGC **176:** Oliver Uberti/NGC **177:** Fritz Hoffmann/NGC **181:** Gianluca Colla/NGC **189:** Aaron Huey/NGC **190-191:** Frans Lanting/NGC **194:** Joel Sartore/NGC **196:** James P. Blair/NGC **197:** Thomas J. Abercrombie/NGC **198:** Raul Touzon/NGC **203:** Reza/NGC **211:** Anthony Fiala/NGC **212-213:** Courtesy of Michael Whelan **214:** Twentieth Century-Fox Film Corporation/The Kobal Collection/Picture Desk **216:** NASA/NGC **218:** NASA/NGC **219:** NASA Images **220:** NASA/NGC **222:** Ludek Pesek/NGC **227:** NASA/NGC **234:** Charles Fries Prods/The Kobal Collection **243, 255:** Joel Sartore/NGC **256:** James L. Stanfield/NGC

IFC = Inside Front Cover   NGC = National Geographic Creative

Our Human Impact

ACADEMIC PATHWAYS

Lesson A: Understanding cohesion
Analyzing arguments

Lesson B: Reviewing essay writing
Writing a cause-effect essay

Think and Discuss

1. In what ways have humans changed the planet?

2. What are some of the positive and negative effects of the changes humans have made on the planet?

▲ Terraced rice farming has transformed the rural landscape in Yunnan Province, China.

Exploring the Theme

A. Look at the maps and answer the questions.

1. What four types of human impact does the main map show?

2. What are megacities? Find some examples.

3. Which regions experience the most deforestation, desertification, and pollution?

4. Look at the inset map on page 3. Which regions are most—and least—affected by human activity?

B. Read the information and discuss the questions.

1. What are some causes of air pollution, deforestation, and desertification?

2. How does the human impact in developed countries compare with the impact in less developed countries?

Deforestation

Loss of forest cover, such as in this part of Alberta, Canada, contributes to a buildup of carbon dioxide (a greenhouse gas) in the atmosphere. It also causes soil erosion and a loss of soil nutrients.

The Human Impact

Around the world, natural environments are under pressure from the release of air and water pollutants, and by the removal of vegetation to extract mineral resources or to create land for farming.

In more developed countries, industries create waste and pollution; farmers use fertilizers and pesticides that run off into water supplies; and motor vehicles release exhaust fumes into the air.

In less developed countries, forests are cut down for fuel or to clear land for farming; grasslands are turned into deserts as farmers and herders overuse the land; and expanding urban areas face problems of water quality and sanitation.

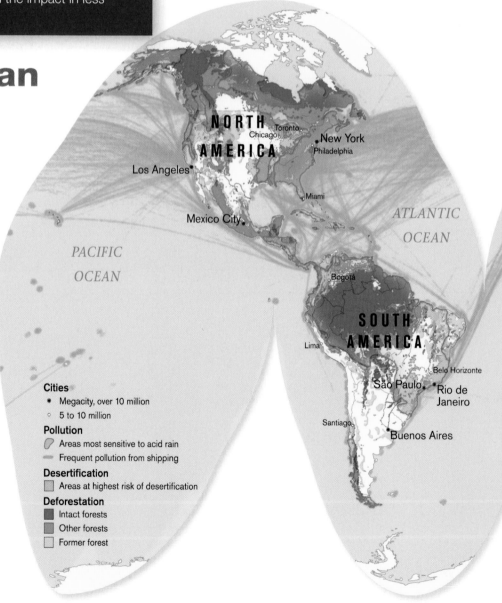

Cities
- ● Megacity, over 10 million
- ○ 5 to 10 million

Pollution
- Areas most sensitive to acid rain
- Frequent pollution from shipping

Desertification
- Areas at highest risk of desertification

Deforestation
- Intact forests
- Other forests
- Former forest

Desertification

In semiarid and arid areas, which receive limited rainfall, land that is overgrazed or overcultivated can become desertlike, such as in Namibia (above).

Pollution

Poor air quality is a serious environmental problem in many parts of the world. Smoke from industrial plants, such as this one in Arizona, USA, may contain particles that contribute to acid rain.

The map below uses population density, land use, transportation, and energy production and use, to identify areas of Earth where human impact is greatest.

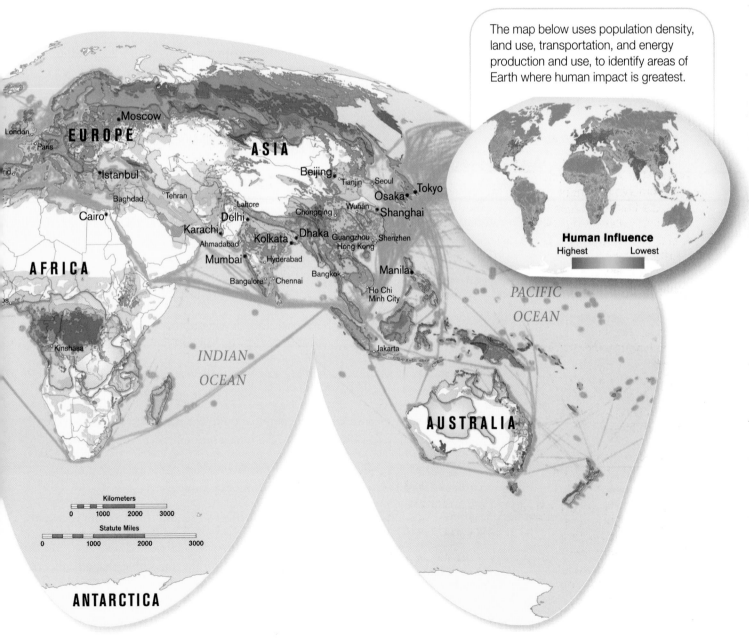

Human Influence
Highest — Lowest

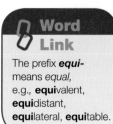

Word Link

The prefix *equi-* means *equal*, e.g., **equi**valent, **equi**distant, **equi**lateral, **equi**table.

A | Building Vocabulary. Read the following paragraph about an event in Qatar. Use the context to guess the meaning of the words in **blue**. Then write the words next to their definitions (1–6).

Diplomats and scientists from around the world met to discuss climate issues at the 2012 United Nations Climate Change **Conference** in Qatar. The conference **was devoted to** discussing a commitment to reducing global carbon emissions, which contribute to global warming. One **perspective** on global warming is that human activities are not the cause; however, most climate scientists do not agree. Carbon emissions have increased dramatically in the last several years, and most climate scientists believe we can no longer **ignore** the issue. While most experts agree that it is impossible to completely **eliminate** carbon emissions, they do believe that it is possible to cool down the planet. One goal that resulted from the conference is to keep any future global temperature rise within 2° Celsius—the **equivalent** of an increase of 3.6° Fahrenheit.

1. _____: to not pay attention to

2. _____: something that is equal to or corresponds with another in value

3. _____: focused exclusively on

4. _____: a meeting organized to examine a particular subject

5. _____: to remove completely

6. _____: a way of thinking about something

B | Building Vocabulary. Complete the sentences with the words from the box. Use a dictionary to help you.

compound	concept	criteria	incorporate	register	shifting

▲ An endangered golden-cheeked warbler

1. As a result of global warming, some bird species are moving to new places. For example, the North American warbler is _____ its habitat 65 miles to the north.

2. One of the _____ for naming a new animals species is that the name must be easy to remember.

3. Researchers have recently discovered that a combination of chemicals in a common weed killer, a _____ called POE-15, can have a serious effect on human health.

4. If you _____ an invention with the patent office, your idea will go into an official record, and it will be protected so that it cannot be copied.

5. A basic scientific _____ is cause and effect—the idea that an event is caused by or affected by another event.

6. To _____ something means to include it within something that already exists.

C | Using Vocabulary. Answer the questions. Share your ideas with a classmate.

1. What environmental issues do you think are too important to **ignore**? Why?

   _____

   _____

2. Can you name any of the chemical **compounds** in the products you use around the house? Do you think any of them might cause health or environmental problems?

   _____

   _____

3. What are some different **perspectives** on the causes of climate change?

   _____

   _____

D | Brainstorming. Discuss your answers to these questions in small groups: What are some ways that scientists make hypotheses about what Earth was like in the past? For instance, how do we know that certain plants or animals existed in the past? Where (or how) do we find evidence of them?

Example: *Scientists find bones of animals that no longer exist.*

E | Previewing and Predicting. Look at the photos and infographics on pages 6–12 and read the captions. Read the title and the first sentence of each paragraph. Circle your answers to the questions.

1. What area of science is this passage mainly about?

   a. biology   b. climatology   c. geology

2. What time period do you think *Anthropocene* describes?

   a. an ancient period   b. the current period   c. a future period

3. What do you think this reading is about? Circle your answer (a–c).

   It's an explanation of how _____ on the planet is changing the way people in the future might describe the current geological period.

   a. the effect of global warming

   b. the overall human impact

   c. the increasing population

THE HUMAN AGE

by Elizabeth Kolbert

> Human beings have altered the planet so much in just the past century or two that we now have a new name for a new epoch: the Anthropocene.

track 1-01

THE WORD *ANTHROPOCENE* was coined by Dutch chemist Paul Crutzen about a decade ago. One day Crutzen, who shared a Nobel Prize for discovering the effects of ozone-depleting **compounds**, was sitting at a scientific **conference**. The conference chairman kept referring to the Holocene, the epoch that began at the end of the last ice age, 11,500 years ago, and that—officially, at least—continues to this day.

"Let's stop it," Crutzen recalls blurting out. "We are no longer in the Holocene. We are in the Anthropocene." It was quiet in the room for a while. When the group took a coffee break, the Anthropocene was the main topic of conversation. Someone suggested that Crutzen copyright the word.

Way back in the 1870s, an Italian geologist named Antonio Stoppani proposed that people had introduced a new era, which he labeled the Anthropozoic. Stoppani's proposal was **ignored**; other scientists found it unscientific. The Anthropocene, by contrast, struck a chord. Human impacts on the world have become a lot more obvious since Stoppani's day, in part because the size of the population has roughly quadrupled,[1] to nearly seven billion. "The pattern of human population growth in the 20th century was more bacterial than primate," biologist E. O. Wilson has written. Wilson calculates that human biomass[2] is already a hundred times larger than that of any other large animal species that has ever walked the Earth.

In 2002, when Crutzen wrote up the Anthropocene idea in the journal *Nature*, the **concept** was immediately picked up by researchers working in a wide range of disciplines. Soon it began to appear regularly in the scientific press. "Global Analysis of River Systems: From Earth System Controls to Anthropocene Syndromes" ran the title of one 2003 paper. "Soils and Sediments in the Anthropocene" was the headline of another, published in 2004.

[1] If something **quadruples**, it increases by a factor of four.
[2] **Biomass** refers to the total amount of living matter in an area.

◄ **Western Minnesota:** Vast wheat fields and long train lines have created a distinctive human landscape in the Midwestern United States.

At first, most of the scientists using the new geologic term were not geologists. Jan Zalasiewicz, a British geologist, found the discussions intriguing. "I noticed that Crutzen's term was appearing in the serious literature, without quotation marks and without a sense of irony," he says. In 2007, Zalasiewicz was serving as chairman of the Geological Society of London's Stratigraphy[3] Commission. At a meeting, he decided to ask his fellow stratigraphers what they thought of the Anthropocene. Twenty-one of 22 thought the concept had merit.

The group agreed to look at it as a formal problem in geology. Would the Anthropocene satisfy the **criteria** used for naming a new epoch? In geology, epochs are relatively short time spans, though they can extend for tens of millions of years. (Periods, such as the Ordovician and the Cretaceous, last much longer, and eras, like the Mesozoic, longer still.) The boundaries between epochs are defined by changes preserved in sedimentary rocks[4]—the emergence of one type of commonly fossilized organism, say, or the disappearance of another.

The rock record of the present doesn't exist yet, of course. So the question was: When it does, will human impacts show up as "stratigraphically significant"? The answer, Zalasiewicz's group decided, is yes—though not necessarily for the reasons you would expect.

[3] **Stratigraphy** is a branch of geology concerned with the study of rock layers.
[4] **Sedimentary rocks** are formed from sediment—solid material that settles at the bottom of a liquid, especially earth and pieces of rock that have been carried along and then left somewhere by water, ice, or wind.

Earth's Geological Timeline

start of the Anthropocene?

Era	Period		Epoch	Millions of Years
Cenozoic	Quaternary		Holocene	
			Pleistocene	
	Neogene		Pliocene	1.5
			Miocene	2.3
	Paleogene		Oligocene	
			Eocene	
			Paleocene	65
Mesozoic	Cretaceous			
	Jurassic			
	Triassic			250
Paleozoic	Permian			
	Carboniferous	Pennsylvanian		
		Mississippian		
	Devonian			
	Silurian			
	Ordovician			
	Cambrian			540
Precambrian	Proterozoic			2500
	Archean			3800
	Hadean			4600

▲ **Humboldt County, California:** The effects of timber logging are clearly visible from the air above Maple Creek, near Redwood National Park.

PROBABLY THE MOST OBVIOUS way humans are altering the planet is by building cities, which are essentially vast stretches of man-made materials—steel, glass, concrete, and brick. But it turns out most cities are not good candidates for long-term preservation for the simple reason that they're built on land, and on land the forces of erosion tend to win out over those of sedimentation. From a geologic **perspective**, the most plainly visible human effects on the landscape today "may in some ways be the most transient,[5]" Zalasiewicz has observed.

Humans have also transformed the world through farming; something like 38 percent of the planet's ice-free land is now **devoted to** agriculture. Here again, some of the effects that seem most significant today will leave behind only subtle traces at best.

Fertilizer factories, for example, now take more nitrogen from the air—converting it to a biologically usable form—than all the plants and microbes on land; the runoff from fertilized fields is triggering life-throttling blooms of algae[6] at river mouths all over the world. But this global perturbation[7] of the nitrogen cycle will be hard to detect because synthesized nitrogen is just like its natural **equivalent**. Future geologists are more likely to grasp the scale of 21st-century industrial agriculture from the pollen[8] record—from the monochrome[9] stretches of corn, wheat, and soy pollen that will have replaced the varied record left behind by rain forests or prairies.

[5] **Transient** describes a situation that lasts only a short time or is constantly changing.

[6] **Algae** are organisms with no stems or leaves that grow in water or on damp surfaces.

[7] A **perturbation** is a small change in something, especially an unusual change.

[8] **Pollen** is a fine powder produced by flowers. It fertilizes other flowers of the same species so that they produce seeds.

[9] If something is **monochrome**, it is all one color.

Why Is Our Impact Growing?

Is population growth the root cause? Or is it affluence, which leads to greater consumption of energy and other resources? Or technology, which offers new tools for exploiting and consuming? The IPAT formula is a way of thinking about the issue: It says the three factors compound. Since 1900, world GDP (a measure of A) and the number of patent applications (a measure of T) have grown even faster than population (P).

$$I = P \times A \times T$$

I		**P**		**A**		**T**
Human Impact		**Population**		**Affluence**		**Technology**

Affluence
World GDP
(Gross Domestic
Product)
$55 trillion

2011

Population
Worldwide
7 billion

$5.3 trillion

$2 trillion

2.5 billion

1.8 billion

1950

1900

412,000

141,000

Technology
Patent
applications
1.9 million

> **" Do we decide the Anthropocene's here, or do we wait 20 years and things will be even worse? "**

THE LEVELING OF THE WORLD'S FORESTS will send at least two coded signals to future stratigraphers, though deciphering the first may be tricky. Massive amounts of soil eroding off denuded[10] land are increasing sedimentation[11] in some parts of the world—but at the same time, the dams we've built on most of the world's major rivers are holding back sediment that would otherwise be washed to sea. The second signal of deforestation should come through clearer. Loss of forest habitat is a major cause of extinctions, which are now happening at a rate hundreds or even thousands of times higher than during most of the past half billion years. If current trends continue, the rate may soon be tens of thousands of times higher.

Probably the most significant change, from a geologic perspective, is one that's invisible to us—the change in the composition of the atmosphere. Carbon dioxide emissions are colorless, odorless, and, in an immediate sense, harmless. But their warming effects could easily push global temperatures to levels that have not been seen for millions of years. Some plants and animals are already **shifting** their ranges toward the Poles, and those shifts will leave traces in the fossil record. Some species will not survive the warming at all. Meanwhile, rising temperatures could eventually raise sea levels 20 feet or more.

Long after our cars, cities, and factories have turned to dust, the consequences of burning billions of tons' worth of coal and oil are likely to be clearly discernible. As carbon dioxide warms the planet, it also seeps into the oceans and acidifies them. Sometime this century, they may become acidified to the point that corals can no longer construct reefs, which would **register** in the geologic record as a "reef gap." Reef gaps have marked each of the past five major mass extinctions. The most recent one, which is believed to have been caused by the impact of an asteroid, took place 65 million years ago, at the end of the Cretaceous period; it **eliminated** not just the dinosaurs but also the plesiosaurs, pterosaurs, and ammonites.[12] The scale of what's happening now to the oceans is, by many accounts, unmatched since then. To future geologists, Zalasiewicz says, our impact may look as sudden and profound as that of an asteroid.

---

[10] If a place is **denuded**, all the plants in the area have been destroyed.
[11] **Sedimentation** is the process by which solid material, especially earth and pieces of rock, settles at the bottom of a liquid.
[12] **Plesiosaurs**, **pterosaurs**, and **ammonites** are extinct, prehistoric organisms.

IF WE HAVE INDEED entered a new epoch, then when exactly did it begin? When did human impacts rise to the level of geologic significance?

William Ruddiman, a paleoclimatologist at the University of Virginia, has proposed that the invention of agriculture some 8,000 years ago, and the deforestation that resulted, led to an increase in atmospheric CO_2 just large enough to stave off what otherwise would have been the start of a new ice age. In his view, humans have been the dominant force on the planet practically since the start of the Holocene. Crutzen has suggested that the Anthropocene began in the late 18th century, when, ice cores show, carbon dioxide levels began what has since proved to be an uninterrupted rise. Other scientists put the beginning of the new epoch in the middle of the 20th century, when the rates of both population growth and consumption accelerated rapidly.

Zalasiewicz now heads a working group of the International Commission on Stratigraphy (ICS) that is tasked with officially determining whether the Anthropocene deserves to be **incorporated** into the geologic timescale. A final decision will require votes by both the ICS and its parent organization, the International Union of Geological Sciences. The process is likely to take years. As it drags on, the decision may well become easier. Some scientists argue that we've not yet reached the start of the Anthropocene—not because we haven't had a dramatic impact on the planet, but because the next several decades are likely to prove even more stratigraphically significant than the past few centuries. "Do we decide the Anthropocene's here, or do we wait 20 years and things will be even worse?" says Mark Williams, a geologist and colleague of Zalasiewicz's at the University of Leicester in England.

Crutzen, who started the debate, thinks its real value won't lie in revisions to geology textbooks. His purpose is broader: He wants to focus our attention on the consequences of our collective action—and on how we might still avert the worst. "What I hope," he says, "is that the term *Anthropocene* will be a warning to the world."

▼ **Trotternish, Isle of Skye:** Millions of years of history are recorded in the rocks of Scotland. Are we creating a new chapter in Earth's geological history?

A | Identifying Main Ideas. Write answers to the questions.

1. What is the purpose of Kolbert's article? Complete the main idea.

   Kolbert's purpose is to present the idea of a new _____ and to show how our human impact will be noted in the future.

2. What does "Anthropocene" mean? Explain it in your own words.

   _____

   _____

3. The reading passage has three main parts. Where could you place each of these section heads? Write paragraph letters: **A**, **H**, and **N**.

Section Head	Before Paragraph . . .
How We Are Changing the Planet	_____
Tracing the Origins of the Anthropocene	_____
A New Perspective on Earth's History	_____

4. What four main areas does Kolbert examine for signs of human impact?

   cities, _____

B | Identifying Key Details. Write answers to the questions.

1. When was the idea of a new era first proposed? What was it called?

   _____

2. What do cities basically consist of, according to Kolbert? Why might cities not be visible in the future?

   _____

   _____

3. How do fertilizers and industrial farming affect the environment?

   _____

   _____

4. What are two effects of cutting down forests?

   _____

   _____

5. How does climate change affect plants and animals? How is it affecting the oceans?

   _____

   _____

👥 **C** | **Critical Thinking: Evaluating.** Use your answers to exercise **B** to complete the chart summarizing the human impact. Then discuss this question in a small group: Of the four kinds of human impact, which do you think will leave the most obvious record in the future? Why?

	The Human Effect	Will It Leave a Trace? Why, or Why Not?
Cities	by building _____ structures	No—structures built on land; _____ may make them disappear
Farming	by using fertilizers	_____—but only from the _____ record of the shift from a variety of plants to a few types
Forests	by _____	Maybe—sedimentation and _____ may be noticed
Atmosphere	by _____ the atmosphere	Most likely—shifts in habitat range will leave traces in _____; _____ of the world's oceans and corals will cause _____ _____

👥 **D** | **Understanding Infographics.** Look at the infographic on page 10 and answer the questions. Then discuss your answers with a partner.

1. What is the main purpose of the infographic? Circle the best answer.

   a. to show the importance of changes in human technology since 1900

   b. to show how different factors have contributed to our human impact

   c. to show how population growth has risen faster than affluence

2. Look at the "I=PAT" formula. What does it mean? Explain it in your own words.

   _____

   _____

3. Describe how the following factors have increased since 1900.

   population: _____

   GDP (affluence): _____

   technology: _____

CT Focus: Analyzing arguments

An argument usually presents a debatable issue and includes evidence that supports the issue. When you read a passage that presents an argument, first identify the issue—the writer's argument. Then analyze the writer's evidence. Is it fully developed? Is it accurate? Is it detailed? Is it current? How do you know?

E | **Critical Thinking: Analyzing Evidence.** In the reading on pages 6–12, what evidence does the writer present in support of either side of the main issue? Take notes in the chart. Then discuss answers to the questions below with a partner.

Issue: Our impact on the planet is so great that we are now living in a new epoch.	
Arguments For	**Arguments Against**

1. Are the arguments on both sides equally balanced, or is there more evidence for one side than the other?

2. Are we at the start of a new epoch? Should we name the current period "Anthropocene"? Why, or why not?

F | **Identifying Meaning from Context.** Find and underline the following words and expressions in the reading passage. Use context to guess their meanings. Then match the sentence parts.

1. _____ Paragraph A: If a word is **coined by** someone,

2. _____ Paragraph C: If an idea **struck a chord**,

3. _____ Paragraph D: If a concept is **picked up**,

4. _____ Paragraph J: If something is **life-throttling**,

5. _____ Paragraph M: If a consequence is **discernible**,

6. _____ Paragraph O: If you **stave off** an event,

7. _____ Paragraph P: When something **drags on**,

a. it moves slowly.

b. you can detect it.

c. other people thought it sounded logical.

d. you prevent it from happening.

e. people decide to adopt it.

f. it was invented by that person.

g. it causes things to die.

Reading Skill: Understanding Cohesion

Cohesion is the way that ideas are linked in a text. Writers use certain techniques (sometimes called "cohesive devices") to refer to ideas mentioned elsewhere in the passage. Some of these techniques include pronouns (*one[s], another, the other*), demonstratives (*this, that, these, those*), and synonyms.

Look at these examples from "The Human Age."

> In 2002, when Crutzen wrote up <u>the Anthropocene idea</u> in the journal Nature, <u>the concept</u> was immediately picked up by researchers working in a wide range of disciplines.

The writer uses a synonym, *the concept*, to refer to *the idea* in the first part of the sentence.

> Wilson calculates that human <u>biomass</u> is already a hundred times larger than <u>that</u> of any other large animal species that has ever walked the Earth.

In this example, the writer uses *that* to refer to *biomass*.

Note: The referent—the word or idea that is referred to—is not always close to the cohesive device. It may be in a different part of the sentence, or in a different sentence or section of the text.

A | Analyzing. Circle the word or idea that each underlined word in these extracts refers to.

1. Paragraph D: "Global Analysis of River Systems: From Earth System Controls to Anthropocene Syndromes" ran the title of one 2003 paper. "Soils and Sediments in the Anthropocene" was the headline of <u>another</u>, published in 2004.

   a. title   b. paper   c. river system

2. Paragraph H: But it turns out most cities are not good candidates for long-term preservation for the simple reason that they're built on land, and on land the forces of erosion tend to win out over <u>those</u> of sedimentation.

   a. forces   b. cities   c. candidates

B | Analyzing. Find the following excerpts in "The Human Age." Write the words or ideas that each underlined words or phrases refer to.

1. Paragraph E: At first, most of the scientists using <u>the new geologic term</u> were not geologists.

   _____

2. Paragraph F: The boundaries between epochs are defined by changes preserved in sedimentary rocks—the emergence of one type of commonly fossilized organism, say, or the disappearance of <u>another</u>. _____

3. Paragraph L: Probably the most significant change, from a geologic perspective, is <u>one</u> that's invisible to us—the change in the composition of the atmosphere. _____

4. Paragraph M: The most recent <u>one</u>, which is believed to have been caused by the impact of an asteroid, took place 65 million years ago, at the end of the Cretaceous period.

   _____

Man-Made Earthquakes

Before Viewing

A | **Using a Dictionary.** Here are some words you will hear in the video. Match each one with the correct definition. Use a dictionary to help you.

| excavation | extract | induced | perturb | stress (v.) |

1. _____ disturb greatly

2. _____ the act of digging in the earth

3. _____ put pressure on

4. _____ caused; triggered

5. _____ take out; remove

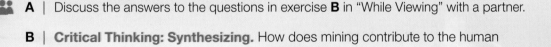

B | **Thinking Ahead.** Discuss these questions with a partner: What are some examples of materials that are mined? What are some possible positive and negative effects of mining?

_____

_____

_____

While Viewing

Read the questions (1–5). Think about the answers as you view the video.

1. Where did the earthquake described in the video occur?
2. What were the effects of this earthquake?
3. What was a possible cause of the earthquake?
4. What are "pre-existing conditions"? How do earthquakes affect them?
5. What percentage of earthquakes around the world may be caused by mining?

After Viewing

A | Discuss the answers to the questions in exercise **B** in "While Viewing" with a partner.

B | **Critical Thinking: Synthesizing.** How does mining contribute to the human impact on the planet?

▼ Gold miners at Serra Pelada Mine, Brazil

GOAL: Writing about the Human Impact on the Planet

In this lesson, you are going to plan, write, revise, and edit an essay on the following topic:
Describe how the activities of a community or an institution are impacting the planet.

A | Brainstorming. Choose a community or an institution that you want to write about (for example, your city or your school). Then think about how its activities are impacting the planet. Write as many activities and impacts (or effects) in the chart as you can. Share your ideas with a partner.

Activities	Impacts (Effects)
the school mails brochures to prospective students	use of ink and paper leads to deforestation and pollution

B | Vocabulary for Writing. The following words and expressions can be useful when writing about the human impact on the planet. Find these words and expressions—or forms of them—in the reading passage on pages 6–12. Use context to guess their meanings. Then complete each definition.

> **deplete** (paragraph A)   **transform** (paragraph I)
> **the emergence** (paragraph F)   **traces** (paragraph L)
> **preserve** (paragraph H)   **the dominant force** (paragraph O)

1. If something leaves _____, it leaves evidence that it was there or it existed.

2. To _____ something is to reduce it.

3. To _____ something is to save or protect it.

4. To _____ something is to change it in a significant way.

5. If something is _____, it is the most important or powerful effect on a thing.

6. _____ of something is its coming into being.

Free Writing. Write for five minutes. Write about one human activity that is having an impact on the planet. Use some of the words and expressions from exercise **B**.

C | Read the information in the box. Then use the cues to complete the second sentence in each pair (1–5) below. Use reference words, synonyms, or word forms for the underlined words in the first sentence.

Language for Writing: Using Cohesive Devices

Writers use cohesive devices to emphasize key concepts they have already mentioned and to avoid repetition. Cohesive devices include reference words such as *it, these, those,* and *that*. They also include synonyms and word forms.

Reference Words and Synonyms:

In 2002, when Crutzen wrote up the Anthropocene idea in the journal *Nature*, **the concept** was immediately picked up by researchers working in a wide range of disciplines. Soon **it** began to appear regularly in the scientific press.

The writer uses *the concept* and *it* to refer to *the Anthropocene idea*.

Word Forms:

Way back in the 1870s, an Italian geologist named Antonio Stoppani proposed that people had introduced a new era, which he labeled the Anthropozoic. Stoppani's **proposal** was ignored; other scientists found it unscientific.

The writer uses *proposal* to refer to what Stoppani *proposed*.

1. Cities are filled with structures made of glass, steel, and concrete. Many people might think that _____ are indestructible materials. (reference word)

2. This era has been called Anthropozoic. Today, geologists are using *Anthropocene* to refer to this _____. (synonym)

3. Humans have destroyed forests, built over animal habitats, and heated up the atmosphere with CO$_2$ emissions. Of all these _____, the changes in the atmosphere may leave the most lasting traces. (synonym)

4. By creating pedestrian-only streets in city centers, planners are reducing the amount of time people spend in cars. This _____ of car use will have a positive impact on the environment. (word form)

5. Chemicals used in pesticides may harm people and animals. These _____ compounds can have a negative impact on the soil and water as well. (word form)

D | Write additional sentences that refer back to ideas in six of your original Free Writing sentences. Use reference words, synonyms, and word forms in the new sentences.

Writing Skill: Reviewing Essay Writing

An essay is a short piece of writing that includes an **introduction**, a **body**, and a **conclusion**. The introduction presents general information on the topic and usually includes a **thesis statement**. The thesis statement presents the main idea of the entire essay. The body paragraphs support the thesis with facts, details, explanations, and other information. **Key words** or ideas in the thesis are reflected in the topic sentences of the body paragraphs. **Transitions** between paragraphs help the reader follow the essay. The conclusion restates the thesis and leaves the reader with some final thought on the topic.

You usually write an essay in response to an **essay prompt**. The prompt might be a statement (*Describe / Explain . . .*), or it might be a question (*Why . . . ? To what extent . . . ? How . . . ?*). When you respond to a prompt, think about your position on the topic (which will become your thesis statement) and ways to support or explain your position (which may become the topic sentences of your body paragraphs). Use the key words or synonyms of the key words in the prompt in your thesis statement and in your topic sentences.

E | Critical Thinking: Evaluating. Read the following essay prompt. Choose the best thesis statement for it. Why is it the best? Discuss your answer with a partner.

What are some ways that people can help heal the planet through their food choices?

a. People can make much better food choices.

b. People can help heal the planet by making environmentally friendly food choices.

c. People can help heal the planet by driving less and using fewer resources.

d. It's important that we start caring about the future of the planet right now.

F | Critical Thinking: Evaluating. Think about ways to support or explain the thesis statement. Assume you are going to write three body paragraphs. Choose the three best supporting ideas from the list below.

Make food choices that _____.

☐ a. are cheap   ☐ b. promote health   ☐ c. don't contribute to pollution

☐ d. preserve endangered species   ☐ e. use fewer resources such as water

G | Applying. Complete topic sentences for three body paragraphs based on the ideas you chose in exercise **F**.

One way that we can help heal the planet is _____.

Another way we can _____

_____.

Finally, _____

_____.

H | Discussion. Discuss the following essay prompt. Think of a good thesis statement and at least three possible ideas to support it. Share your ideas with a partner.

Describe new policies that would improve the quality of life at your college or school.

A | **Planning.** Follow the steps to make notes for your essay.

Step 1 In the outline below, write down the name of the community or institution you are going to write about. Note three of its activities that impact the planet.

Step 2 Write a thesis statement in the outline.

Step 3 Write a topic sentence for each of your body paragraphs.

Step 4 For each body paragraph, write two or three examples, details, or facts that explain how the activities of the community or institution affect the planet.

Step 5 Note some ideas for an introduction and a conclusion for your essay.

Community or institution: _____

Three activities of this community or institution:

1. _____

2. _____

3. _____

Thesis statement: _____

_____

Body Paragraph 1: Topic sentence: _____

_____

Details: _____

_____

_____

Body Paragraph 2: Topic sentence: _____

_____

Details: _____

_____

_____

Body Paragraph 3: Topic sentence: _____

_____

Details: _____

_____

_____

Notes for Introduction: _____

_____

Notes for Conclusion: _____

_____

B | **Draft 1.** Use your outline to write a first draft of your essay.

👥 **C** | **Critical Thinking: Analyzing.** Work with a partner. Read the essay about some positive impacts on city life. Then follow the steps to analyze the essay.

Cities are growing in size and in population. As they grow, will they have a harmful impact on the environment? Not necessarily. Many city planners have solutions to make cities and the people who live in them healthier and happier, while at the same time, having a positive impact on the environment. Three ways to improve cities include creating green spaces, developing mixed-use areas, and encouraging building owners to transform their rooftops into gardens.

Green spaces have a positive impact on a community. They are protected areas that remain undeveloped, such as parks or other open areas. Increasing the number of green spaces in a city has several advantages. Green spaces make a city more attractive, as plants and other features—such as streams and rocks—are left in their natural state. Green spaces also provide peaceful recreation areas for city dwellers. People can walk, hike, bicycle, and picnic in these areas away from the hustle and bustle of city life. Trees also shelter the area from the noise and traffic of the city while improving the air quality.

Another way to improve the quality of life in cities is the development of mixed-use areas. Mixed-use areas combine several purposes in one space. A mixed-use area, for example, may contain offices and businesses, apartments, and entertainment facilities. Ideally, mixed-use developments attract people who want to live and work in the same area. The benefits to the community are significant because mixed-use areas allow people to reduce the amount of time they spend in cars driving to work and running errands, which in turn reduces air pollution. Creating mixed-use areas with pedestrian- and bicycle-only streets further lessens the impact on the environment, and it can also encourage better health and fitness as citizens spend less time in cars.

Finally, encouraging building owners to convert their rooftops into high-rise gardens and farms can bring about dramatic changes to city life and improve the environment at the same time. Rooftop gardens insulate buildings. For example, in areas that have hot summer weather, rooftop gardens can cool buildings so that they don't require as much air conditioning. This reduces energy use as well as the cost to building owners. Rooftop gardens that are used to grow organic fruits and vegetables—as opposed to those grown with chemical compounds—can also improve the quality of life for city dwellers, especially if they live in areas where access to fresh produce is limited. Limiting the use of harmful pesticides through organic gardening is good for the planet and for human health, too.

Green spaces, mixed-use areas, and rooftop gardens are just a few of the ways that we can lessen the impact of cities on the planet. By instituting these and other methods to make cities more livable and environmentally friendly, we can look forward to a happy and healthy future as our cities grow.

Step 1 Label the three main parts of the essay: *A* (the introduction), *B* (the body), and *C* (the conclusion).

Step 2 Underline the thesis statement.

Step 3 Circle the key words or key concepts in the thesis statement.

Step 4 Underline the topic sentences in the body paragraphs.

Step 5 Circle the key words in the topic sentences that reflect the key words in the thesis statement.

D | Revising. Follow the steps in exercise **C** to analyze your own essay.

E | Peer Evaluation. Exchange your first draft with a partner and follow the steps below.

Step 1 Read your partner's essay and tell him or her one thing that you liked about it.

Step 2 Complete the outline showing the ideas that your partner's essay describes.

Community or institution: _____

Three activities of this community or institution:

1. _____

2. _____

3. _____

Thesis statement: _____

_____

Body Paragraph 1: Topic sentence: _____

_____

Details: _____

_____

_____

Body Paragraph 2: Topic sentence: _____

_____

Details: _____

_____

_____

Body Paragraph 3: Topic sentence: _____

_____

Details: _____

_____

_____

Step 3 Compare this outline with the one that your partner created in exercise **A** on page 21.

Step 4 The two outlines should be similar. If they aren't, discuss how they differ.

F | **Draft 2.** Write a second draft of your essay. Use what you learned from the peer evaluation activity and your answers to exercise **D**. Make any other necessary changes.

G | **Editing Practice.** Read the information in the box. Then edit the sentences (1–3) to make them clearer.

When using cohesive devices, remember to:

- use pronouns that match the referent in gender and number.
- make sure a pronoun clearly refers to a specific word or idea. Sometimes it's better to repeat words or use synonyms for clarity.
- choose the correct synonym when using a dictionary or thesaurus.

---

1. One reason to limit the use of pesticides is that it contains harmful compounds.

2. Some people are installing rooftop gardens and using solar panels in their homes. It can save money and resources.

3. Many fish species have become extinct and, as a result, there is less biodiversity in our oceans. They are a problem because they upset the natural balance of the oceans' ecosystems.

H | **Editing Checklist.** Use the checklist to find errors in your second draft.

Editing Checklist	Yes	No
1. Are all the words spelled correctly?		
2. Does every sentence have correct punctuation?		
3. Do your subjects and verbs agree?		
4. Have you used cohesive devices correctly?		
5. Are your verb tenses correct?		

I | **Final Draft.** Now use your Editing Checklist to write a third draft of your essay. Make any other necessary changes.

Conservation and Protection

DILARANG MELINTAS
DO NOT CROSS

DILARANG MEL
DO NOT CROSS

Think and Discuss

1. What endangered species are you aware of?
2. What are some reasons these animals are endangered?

▲ A child holds a photo of Sheila, a Sumatran tiger killed in her cage by poachers.

25

Read the information and discuss the questions.

1. Which of the big cats on these pages are most in danger?

2. Why do you think conservationists believe it is important to protect these animals?

3. What do you think George B. Schaller means when he talks about "the ultimate test"?

Big Cats in Crisis

These eight top predators are all in danger of disappearing. Human population growth in the areas where they live leads to habitat loss, illegal poaching for skins and other body parts, and killing by angry ranchers when the cats eat their livestock. But according to conservationists, we can save the big cats if we make a genuine effort. Biologist George B. Schaller writes, "The great cats represent the ultimate test of our willingness to share this planet with other species."

1. Puma

Sometimes called cougar, mountain lion, or panther, the puma's habitat spreads from Canada to the tip of Chile. Its population in the U.S. Midwest is growing, but experts believe its overall population is declining.

Estimated wild population: 30,000 (U.S. count only)

Population in zoos: 397

Status: Least concern

2. Lion

The lion once roamed all of Africa and into Asia. Tanzania now has the biggest population.

Estimated wild population: 20,000 to 30,000

Population in zoos: 1,888

Status: Vulnerable

3. Leopard

The leopard can be found from Africa to Southeast Asia; most live in sub-Saharan Africa.

Estimated wild population: No reliable data

Population in zoos: 853

Status: Near threatened

4. Snow Leopard

The snow leopard is known as the "ghost of the mountains" because it is so hard to find. Its home is in the Himalayas and surrounding ranges of Central Asia.

Estimated wild population: 4,000 to 6,500

Population in zoos: 414

Status: Endangered

5. Jaguar

This is the third largest big cat after tigers and lions. It is the most powerful predator in Central and South America.

Estimated wild population: At least 10,000

Population in zoos: 365

Status: Near threatened

8. Tiger

This is the biggest cat, with some males weighing over 600 pounds (9,270 kilograms). Three tiger subspecies have gone extinct since the 1930s; five or six other subspecies survive in Asia.

Estimated wild population: Fewer than 4,000

Population in zoos: 1,660

Status: Endangered

6. Clouded Leopard

This is the smallest of the big cats. It hunts in trees as well as on the ground in forests across Southeast Asia.

Estimated wild population: 10,000

Population in zoos: 222

Status: Vulnerable

7. Cheetah

The world's fastest mammal is found mainly in east and southwest Africa; approximately 70 to 110 live in Iran.

Estimated wild population: 7,000 to 10,000

Population in zoos: 1,015

Status: Vulnerable

A | Building Vocabulary. Read the following paragraph about species extinction. Use the context to guess the meanings of the words in **blue**. Use the correct word to complete each sentence (1–6).

All over the world, species are dying out. Species extinction is not a **hypothetical** problem; it's very real. Despite decades of awareness of species endangerment, the problem has not gone away, and experts **project** that it will continue to get worse if we don't make some major changes. Some conservationists and wildlife **authorities** argue that it is time to **assess** our strategies for wildlife protection again. They **acknowledge** that many of our past attempts to protect endangered animals have been ineffective. They believe that wildlife protection must become a global **priority** if we are to save wild endangered animals from complete extinction.

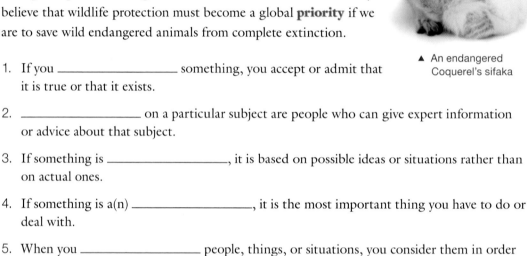

▲ An endangered Coquerel's sifaka

1. If you _____ something, you accept or admit that it is true or that it exists.

2. _____ on a particular subject are people who can give expert information or advice about that subject.

3. If something is _____, it is based on possible ideas or situations rather than on actual ones.

4. If something is a(n) _____, it is the most important thing you have to do or deal with.

5. When you _____ people, things, or situations, you consider them in order to make a judgment about them.

6. If you _____ that something will happen, you predict or expect it.

B | Building Vocabulary. Complete the definitions with the words from the box. Use a dictionary to help you.

| apparently | induce | infinite | intrinsic | maximum | resolve |

1. You use the word "_____" to describe an amount that is the largest possible.

2. If you describe something as _____, you mean that it has no limit.

3. _____ is determination to do what you have decided to do.

4. If something has _____ value or interest, it is valuable or interesting because of its basic nature or character, not because of its connection with other things.

5. You use the word "_____" to indicate that the information you are giving is something that you have heard, but you are not certain it is true.

6. If you _____ a state or condition, you cause it to occur.

C | **Using Vocabulary.** Answer the questions (1–4). Share your ideas with a partner.

1. Do you know any people who are **authorities** on a particular subject?

   _____

   _____

2. What are your top three personal **priorities**? Describe them.

   _____

   _____

3. What do you **project** will be your top three personal priorities in ten years?

   _____

   _____

4. When was the last time you **resolved** to do something difficult? What was it, and were you successful?

   _____

   _____

D | **Brainstorming.** Discuss your answers to these questions in a small group.

1. What are some reasons that certain animals are endangered?

   _____

   _____

2. What do you think people can do to help endangered animals?

   _____

   _____

E | **Predicting.** Skim the reading passage and look at the photos on pages 30–35. What topics do you think the author will discuss? List your ideas. Check your predictions after you've read the article.

   _____

   _____

A Cry for the Tiger

by Caroline Alexander

▲ A lone tiger hunts in the forests of northern Sumatra, Indonesia.

> We have the means to save
> the mightiest cat on Earth.
> But do we have the will?

track 1-02

DAWN, AND MIST HOLDS THE FOREST.
Only a short stretch of red dirt track can be seen.
Suddenly—emerging from the red-gold haze of dust
and misted light—a tigress ambles into view. First, she
stops to rub her right-side whiskers against a roadside
tree. Then she crosses the road and rubs her left-side
whiskers. Then she turns to regard us with a look of
infinite and bored indifference.

Consider the tiger, how she is formed. With
claws up to four inches long and retractable,[1] like
a domestic cat's, and teeth that shatter bone. While
able to achieve bursts above 35 miles an hour, the
tiger is built for strength, not sustained speed. Short,
powerful legs propel its trademark[2] lethal lunge and
fabled[3] leaps. Recently, a tiger was captured on video
jumping—flying—from flat ground to 13 feet in the
air to attack a ranger riding an elephant. The eye of
the tiger is backlit by a membrane[4] that reflects light
through the retina,[5] the secret of the big cat's famous
night vision and glowing night eyes. The roar of the
tiger—Aaaaauuuunnnn!—can carry more than a mile.

For weeks, I had been traveling through some
of the best tiger habitats in Asia, from remote
forests to tropical woodlands and, on a previous
trip, to mangrove swamps—but never before had I
seen a tiger. Partly this was because of the animal's
legendarily secretive nature. The tiger is powerful
enough to kill and drag prey five times its weight,
yet it can move through high grass, forest, and even
water in unnerving silence. The common refrain[6] of
those who have witnessed—or survived—an attack is
that the tiger "came from nowhere."

But the other reason for the dearth of sightings
is that the ideal tiger landscapes have very few tigers.
The tiger has been a threatened species for most of
my lifetime, and its rareness has come to be regarded
matter-of-factly, as an **intrinsic**, defining attribute,
like its dramatic coloring. The complacent[7] view that
the tiger will continue to be "rare" or "threatened"
into the foreseeable future is no longer tenable.[8]
In the early 21st century, tigers in the wild face
the black abyss[9] of annihilation. "This is about
making decisions as if we're in an emergency room,"
says Tom Kaplan, co-founder of Panthera, an
organization dedicated to big cats. "This is it."

The tiger's enemies are well known: loss
of habitat exacerbated by exploding human
populations, poverty—which **induces** poaching[10]
of prey animals—and, looming over all, the
dark threat of the black market for tiger parts.
Less **acknowledged** are botched conservation
strategies that for decades have failed the tiger.
The tiger population, dispersed among Asia's 13
tiger countries, is estimated at fewer than 4,000
animals, though many conservationists believe there
are hundreds less than that. To put this number
in perspective: Global alarm for the species was
first sounded in 1969, and early in the 1980s it
was estimated that some 8,000 tigers remained in
the wild. So decades of concern for tigers—not to
mention millions of dollars donated by well-meaning
individuals—has failed to prevent the demise of
perhaps half of the already imperiled population.

---

[1] If something is **retractable**, it can be moved in and out.

[2] If you say something is the **trademark** of something, you mean
that it is characteristic of it.

[3] If you describe something as **fabled**, you mean it is well known
because there are a lot of stories told about it.

[4] A **membrane** is a thin piece of skin that connects or covers parts of
a person's or an animal's body.

[5] The **retina** is the area at the back of the eye.

[6] A **refrain** is a comment or saying that people often repeat.

[7] A **complacent** person feels he or she does not have to do anything
about a situation.

[8] If you say that an argument, a point of view, or a situation is **tenable**,
it is reasonable and can be defended against criticism.

[9] An **abyss** is a deep and seemingly bottomless pit or chasm.

[10] **Poaching** is the illegal catching or killing of animals.

MY DETERMINATION TO SEE a wild tiger in my lifetime brought me to Ranthambore Tiger Reserve, one of 40 in India. India is home to some 50 percent of the world's wild tigers. The 2010 census reported a **maximum** estimate of 1,909 in the country—up 20 percent from the previous estimate. While this is welcome news, most authorities regard the new figure as reflecting better census methods rather than growth of the tiger population: Tiger counts, in India or elsewhere, are still at best only estimates. A modest 41 of these tigers were living in Ranthambore.

Reserves such as Ranthambore exist as islands of fragile habitat in a vast sea of humanity, yet tigers can range over a hundred miles, seeking prey, mates, and territory. An unwelcome revelation of the new census is that nearly a third of India's tigers live outside tiger reserves, a situation that is dangerous for both humans and animals. Prey and tigers can only disperse if there are recognized corridors[11] of land between protected areas to allow unmolested[12] passage. No less critical, such passages serve as genetic corridors, essential to the long-term survival of the species.

[11] **Corridors** are strips of land that connect one place to another.

[12] If someone does something **unmolested**, he or she does it without being stopped or interfered with.

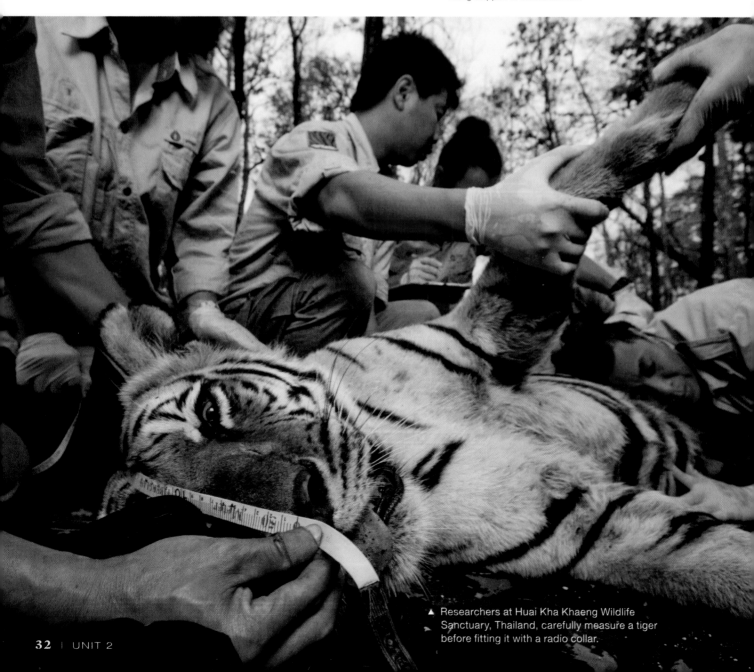

▲ Researchers at Huai Kha Khaeng Wildlife Sanctuary, Thailand, carefully measure a tiger before fitting it with a radio collar.

Last Stronghólds

An estimated 100,000 tigers roamed Asia a hundred years ago. Fewer than 4,000 may remain in the wild today. Most tigers survive only in protected areas.

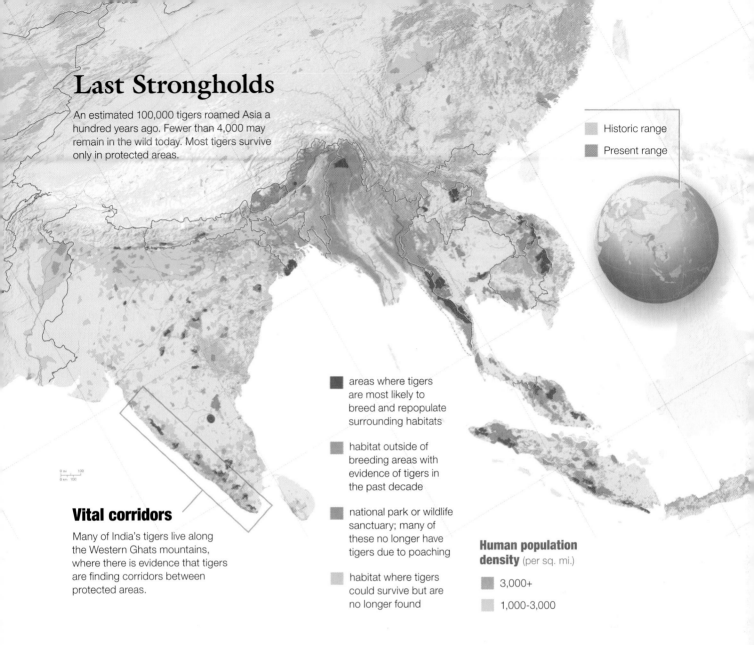

Historic range

Present range

areas where tigers are most likely to breed and repopulate surrounding habitats

habitat outside of breeding areas with evidence of tigers in the past decade

national park or wildlife sanctuary; many of these no longer have tigers due to poaching

habitat where tigers could survive but are no longer found

Vital corridors

Many of India's tigers live along the Western Ghats mountains, where there is evidence that tigers are finding corridors between protected areas.

Human population density (per sq. mi.)

3,000+

1,000-3,000

IT IS A HEADY[13] EXPERIENCE to see an idealistic map of Asia's tiger landscapes linked by arteries of these not-yet-existent corridors. A spiderweb of green tendrils weaves among core populations to form a network that encompasses breathtaking extremes of habitat—Himalayan foothills, jungle, swamp, forest, grasslands—that pay tribute[14] to the tiger's adaptability. Close scrutiny breaks the spell. The places that have actual tigers—here-and-now, flesh-and-blood tigers—as opposed to **hypothetical** tigers, are represented by a scattering of mustard-colored blobs. The master plan represents a visionary undertaking, but is it feasible? Over the next decade, infrastructure projects—the kind of development that often destroys habitat—are **projected** to average some $750 billion a year in Asia.

"I've never met a head of state who says, 'Look, we're a poor country. If it comes between tigers and people, you just have to write off tigers,'" said Alan Rabinowitz, a renowned **authority** on tigers and the CEO of Panthera. "The governments don't want to lose their most majestic animal. They consider it part of what makes their country what it is, part of the cultural heritage. They won't sacrifice a lot to save it, but if they can see a way to save it, they will usually do it."

[13] A **heady** experience strongly affects your senses, for example, by making you feel excited.

[14] If you **pay tribute** to something, you show how good it is, or give it public recognition.

Seeing a way has proved difficult amid the plethora of tiger strategies, programs, and initiatives jostling for attention—and funding. The U.S. National Fish and Wildlife Foundation's Save the Tiger Fund (which has now partnered with Panthera), Global Tiger Patrol, Saving Wild Tigers, All for Tigers!, World Wildlife Fund (WWF), Wildlife Conservation Society (WCS), Panthera, International Year of the Tiger Foundation, the National Geographic Society's Big Cats Initiative—the list is impressive. "Five to six million dollars is spent a year for tigers, from all philanthropic organizations," said Mahendra Shrestha, former director of the Save the Tiger Fund, which gave grants totaling more than $17 million between 1995 and 2009. "In many instances, the NGOs [non-governmental organizations] and tiger-range governments just fight each other."

Long-term conservation must focus on all aspects of a tiger landscape: core breeding populations, sanctuaries, wildlife corridors, and the surrounding human communities. In an ideal world, all would be funded; as it is, different agencies adopt different strategies for different components. With time running out, tough **priorities** must be set. "Since the 1990s, there has been what I would sum up as mission drift," said Ullas Karanth of the WCS, who is one of the world's most respected tiger biologists. The drift toward tiger conservation activities like eco-development and social programs, which possibly have greater fund-raising appeal than antipoaching patrols, siphons[15] funds and energy from the single most vital task: safeguarding core breeding populations of tigers. "If these are lost," Karanth said, "you will have tiger landscapes with no tigers."

Decades of experience and failures have yielded a conservation strategy that, according to Rabinowitz, "allows any site or landscape to increase its tigers if followed correctly." Central to this protocol are relentless, systematic, boots-on-the-ground patrolling and monitoring of both tiger and prey in those sites **assessed** as harboring realistically defensible core tiger populations. Under the protocol, a population of a mere half dozen breeding females can rebound.[16]

"There is 1.1 million square kilometers of tiger habitat remaining," said Eric Dinerstein, chief scientist and vice president of conservation science of the WWF. "Assuming two tigers for every 100 square kilometers, that's a potential 22,000 tigers."

[15] If you **siphon** money or resources away from something, you take it away to use it for a different, less worthy purpose.

[16] If something **rebounds** after some difficulty, it successfully goes back to a previous level.

> " If the core breeding grounds are lost, you will have tiger landscapes with no tigers. "

◄ A Bengal tiger in the Sundarbans, India, pauses in a river to listen to another tiger's roar.

▲ Tiger cubs at a water hole in Bandhavgarh National Park, India

For now, the nonnegotiable task is to save the few tigers that actually exist. And the story of the tiger's fate is relentlessly swift-moving. The Year of the Tiger, the celebration of which, in 2010, was the number-one objective of a lauded tiger workshop in Kathmandu, has come and gone with no discernible benefit to the world's wild tigers. In November 2010, the 13 tiger countries attending the St. Petersburg Global Tiger Summit in Russia pledged to "strive to double the number of wild tigers across their range by 2022." In March 2010, a mother and two cubs were poisoned in Huai Kha Khaeng, the first poaching casualties in four years. The deaths prompted the Thai government to offer a $3,000 bounty for capture of the poachers. In the same month, two young tigers were poisoned in

Ranthambore, **apparently** by villagers who had lost goats to tiger attacks, while two new cubs were later born.

Most authorities agree that the fight to save the tiger can be won—but that it must be waged with unremitting[17] professional focus that adheres to a proven strategy. It will require the human species to display not merely **resolve** but outright zealotry.[18]

"I want it in my will," Fateh Singh Rathore—Ranthambore's Assistant Field Director—told me, his eyes burning bright behind his spectacles. "When I die, you spread my ashes on these grounds so the tiger can walk upon my ashes."

[17] Something that is **unremitting** continues without pausing or giving up.
[18] If someone shows **zealotry**, he or she displays very extreme views and behavior, especially in following a particular religious or political belief.

A | Identifying Main Ideas. Which paragraph describes each of the following items?

1. the intrinsic beauty of the tiger
   a. Paragraph A   b. Paragraph B   c. Paragraph C
2. reasons why tigers are in danger
   a. Paragraph C   b. Paragraph D   c. Paragraph E
3. a plan for future tiger habitats
   a. Paragraph F   b. Paragraph G   c. Paragraph H
4. what needs to be done to protect tigers
   a. Paragraph I   b. Paragraph J   c. Paragraph K

B | Scanning for Key Details. Match each question with the correct answer. Three items are extra.

1. _____ What year did the world first realize that tigers were endangered?
2. _____ How many tigers were estimated to be alive in the early 1980s?
3. _____ What portion of the world's tigers lives in India?
4. _____ How many tigers are in Ranthambore?
5. _____ Approximately how many tigers in India live outside of tiger reserves?
6. _____ How many square kilometers of tiger habitat are left in the world?
7. _____ How many Asian countries have natural tiger habitats?
8. _____ What year was the Year of the Tiger?
9. _____ By what year do the tiger countries promise to double the number of wild tigers?

a. 1.1 million
b. 41
c. the 1990s
d. 4,000
e. 1969
f. 1/3
g. 2010
h. 2022
i. 8,000
j. 20%
k. 50%
l. 13

C | Identifying Reasons and Solutions. Complete the chart with information from the reading.

Problem: Tigers are endangered.	
Possible Reasons	**Possible Solutions**
Past efforts were not effective	
Growth of human populations	

CT Focus: Analyzing Text Organization

Writers **organize their texts** in specific ways in order to reveal certain information at specific times. Identifying and understanding the organizational structure of a text can help with reading comprehension. The organizational structure can reveal a writer's purpose and point of view. The reader can also anticipate what kind of information might be coming next.

D | **Critical Thinking: Analyzing Organization.** How does the writer organize the article? Number the ideas in the order that they appear (1–5). Note paragraph letters for each section.

_____ a. provides some reasons for why tigers have become rare _____

_____ b. outlines a variety of global initiatives to save the tiger _____

_____ c. describes the power and mystery of tigers _____

_____ d. explains in detail how one country is trying to protect tiger habitats _____

_____ e. emphasizes the urgency of saving the last remaining tigers _____

E | **Critical Thinking: Evaluating.** Answer the questions with a partner.

1. Why do you think the writer organized the article in this way?

2. Do you think the opening of the article is effective? Why, or why not?

3. How else could the writer have organized the article?

F | **Identifying Meaning from Context.** Find and underline the following words and phrases in the reading passage. Use context to help you identify the meaning of each word or phrase. Then match each word or phrase with its definition.

1. _____ Paragraph D: **dearth**

2. _____ Paragraph D: **defining attribute**

3. _____ Paragraph D: **annihilation**

4. _____ Paragraph E: **botched**

5. _____ Paragraph G: **unwelcome revelation**

6. _____ Paragraph J: **plethora**

7. _____ Paragraph L: **protocol**

a. unpleasant and surprising discovery

b. a characteristic that is essential to a person or thing's identity

c. procedure; set of rules

d. total defeat or destruction

e. severe shortage

f. failed

g. a large amount of something

G | **Critical Thinking: Personalizing.** Write an answer to this question and share your answer in a small group.

Different causes attract different people. Why do you think certain people are interested in helping big cats or other endangered animals?

Reading Skill: Understanding Appositives

An appositive is a noun or a noun phrase that explains, defines, or gives more information about another noun or noun phrase that is close to it. Writers use commas, dashes, or colons to separate appositives from the nouns that they describe. For example, the underlined phrases in the sentences below are appositives. The double-underlined words are the nouns that they describe.

"I've never met a head of state who says, 'Look, we're a poor country. If it comes between tigers and people, you just have to write off tigers,'" said <u>Alan Rabinowitz</u>, <u>a renowned authority on tigers and the CEO of Panthera.</u>

A spiderweb of green tendrils weaves tantalizingly among core populations to form a network that encompasses breathtaking <u>extremes of habitat</u>—<u>Himalayan foothills, jungle, swamp, forest, grasslands</u>—that pay tribute to the tiger's adaptability.

Long-term conservation must focus on all aspects of <u>a tiger landscape</u>: <u>core breeding populations, sanctuaries, wildlife corridors, and the surrounding human communities.</u>

A | **Understanding Appositives.** In each of these sentences from the passage, underline the appositive and circle the noun or noun phrase that it refers to. One sentence has two noun phrase appositives that refer to two different nouns.

1. My determination to see a wild tiger in my lifetime brought me to Ranthambore Tiger Reserve, one of 40 in India.

2. "This is about making decisions as if we're in an emergency room," says Tom Kaplan, co-founder of Panthera, an organization dedicated to big cats.

3. The places that have actual tigers—here-and-now, flesh-and-blood tigers—as opposed to hypothetical tigers, are represented by a scattering of mustard-colored blobs.

4. Over the next decade, infrastructure projects—the kind of development that often destroys habitat—are projected to average some $750 billion a year in Asia.

5. "Five to six million dollars is spent a year for tigers, from all philanthropic organizations," said Mahendra Shrestha, former director of the Save the Tiger Fund. . .

6. "There is 1.1 million square kilometers of tiger habitat remaining," said Eric Dinerstein, chief scientist and vice president of conservation science of the WWF.

B | **Applying.** Scan for and underline other examples of appositives in the reading passage in Unit 1 (pages 6–12). Share your answers with a partner.

Tigers in the Snow

Before Viewing

A | Using a Dictionary. Here are some words and phrases you will hear in the video. Match each one with the correct definition. Use your dictionary to help you.

> **dominant   food chain   stronghold**

1. _____ a place of survival or refuge
2. _____ more powerful, successful, influential, or noticeable than others
3. _____ the process by which one living thing is eaten by another, which is then eaten by another, and so on

 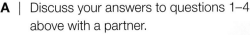 **B | Thinking Ahead.** List possible threats to tigers living in the Russian far-east.

_____

_____

_____

While Viewing

A | Watch the video about Siberian tigers. As you watch, check your answers to exercise **B** above. Note any additional threats mentioned in the video.

B | Read the questions (1–4). Think about the answers as you view the video.

1. How is a Siberian tiger different from other tigers?
2. How big does a male Siberian tiger's territory have to be? A female Siberian tiger's territory?
3. According to the video, what are the two main threats to Siberian tigers?
4. How has the tiger's decline changed since the mid-90s?

After Viewing

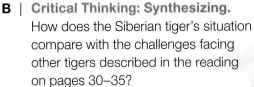 **A |** Discuss your answers to questions 1–4 above with a partner.

B | Critical Thinking: Synthesizing. How does the Siberian tiger's situation compare with the challenges facing other tigers described in the reading on pages 30–35?

A Siberian tiger at the Minnesota ▶ Zoological Garden. There are estimated to be twice as many Siberian tigers in captivity as in the wild.

GOAL: Writing about a Problem and a Possible Solution

In this lesson, you are going to plan, write, revise, and edit an essay on the following topic: *Describe an animal, a building, or a natural place that people are working to protect. Explain why it should be protected.*

A | Brainstorming. Make a list of animals, buildings, or natural places that people are trying to protect. Research online for more ideas.

_____

_____

_____

B | Vocabulary for Writing. The words below can be useful when writing about problems and solutions. Find the words in the reading passage on pages 30–35. Use context to guess their meanings. Then use the words to complete each definition.

> **exacerbates** (paragraph E)   **strategy** (paragraph E)   **sacrifice** (paragraph I)
> **initiative** (paragraph J)   **funding** (paragraph J)   **program** (paragraph J)
> **grant** (paragraph J)   **relentless** (paragraph L)   **objective** (paragraph N)

1. A(n) _____ is a type of _____ that a government or an organization provides for a particular purpose.

2. A(n) _____ is an organized service that is usually intended to meet a social need.

3. Your _____ is what you're trying to achieve.

4. If something _____ a problem or bad situation, it makes it worse.

5. A(n) _____ is an important new act or statement that is intended to solve a problem.

6. A(n) _____ is a general plan or set of plans intended to achieve something, especially over a long period.

7. Someone who is _____ is determined to do something and refuses to give up, even if what that person is doing is difficult or unpleasant.

8. If you _____ something that is valuable or important, you give it up, usually to obtain something else for yourself or for other people.

Free Writing. Write for five minutes. Choose three of the ideas that you listed in exercise **A**. Write down any details that you know about them. Use some of the words and expressions from exercise **B**.

C | Read the information in the box. Then use appositives to combine the sentence pairs (1–5).

Language for Writing: Using Appositives

As you saw in the Reading Skill (page 38), writers use appositives to give more information about a noun. Appositives help writers avoid redundancy and short, choppy sentences. You can separate appositives with commas, dashes, or colons.

With an appositive:

"I've never met a head of state who says, 'Look, we're a poor country. If it comes between tigers and people, you just have to write off tigers,'" said Alan Rabinowitz, <u>a renowned authority on tigers and the CEO of Panthera</u>.

Without an appositive:

"I've never met a head of state who says, 'Look, we're a poor country. If it comes between tigers and people, you just have to write off tigers,'" said Alan Rabinowitz. Rabinowitz is a renowned authority on tigers and the CEO of Panthera.

1. The Bengal tiger is one of India's most popular attractions. The Bengal tiger is India's national animal.

   _____

   _____

2. In addition to tigers, other animals live in Ranthambore. Monkeys, deer, wild boars, owls, and parakeets live in Ranthambore.

   _____

   _____

3. Ranthambore is home to 41 tigers. Ranthambore is a former private hunting estate.

   _____

   _____

4. Fateh Singh Rathore used to work at Ranthambore when it was a hunting estate. Fateh Singh Rathore is the assistant field director of the reserve.

   _____

   _____

5. Zaw Win Khaing once saw a tiger in 2002. Zaw Win Khaing is the head ranger of a tiger reserve in Myanmar.

   _____

   _____

Writing Skill: Reviewing the Thesis Statement

Individual paragraphs have main ideas. Similarly, essays have main ideas. A **thesis statement** is a statement that expresses the main idea of an entire essay. A good thesis statement has the following characteristics:

- It presents your position or opinion on the topic.
- It includes the reasons for your opinion or position on the topic.
- It expresses only the ideas that you can easily explain in your body paragraphs.
- It includes key words that connect with the topic sentences of the body paragraphs.

D | Critical Thinking: Evaluating. Read the following pairs of thesis statements. Check (✓) the statement in each pair that you think is better. Then share your answers with a partner.

1. a. _____ Palisades Park should be protected for three main reasons: It is the only park in the city, it is a gathering place for families, and it is a safe place for children to play after school.

    b. _____ Palisades Park is a beautiful place for parents to spend time with their children and for people in the community to gather for events.

2. a. _____ The Mitchell Library, our city's first public building, is both a wonderful resource for the community and a piece of the city's history, so we should do everything we can to protect it.

    b. _____ In my opinion, I don't think Mitchell Library should be torn down; I think it should be protected by the citizens of the community.

E | Critical Thinking: Evaluating. Read the question below about tiger conservation. Write your opinion and two reasons. Then use your opinion and your reasons to write a thesis statement.

Should governments spend more money to protect tigers?

My opinion: _____

Reason 1: _____

Reason 2: _____

Thesis statement: _____

_____

_____

A | Planning. Follow the steps to make notes for your essay.

Step 1 Choose one idea to write about from your brainstorming list on page 40.

Step 2 Complete the outline below with notes about the idea. Go online to do some research if you need more information.

Introduction

Information about the animal/plant/building/place: _____

_____

_____

How is it valuable? _____

Why is it in danger? _____

Thesis statement: We need to protect _____

because _____ and _____.

Body Paragraph 1

Topic sentence: (Reason 1) _____

_____

Supporting detail: _____

Supporting detail: _____

Body Paragraph 2

Topic sentence: (Reason 2) _____

_____

Supporting detail: _____

Supporting detail: _____

Conclusion

What can be done to protect it? _____

_____

_____

B | Draft 1. Use your outline to write a first draft of your essay.

WRITING TASK: Revising

C | Critical Thinking: Analyzing. Work with a partner. Read the essay about protecting a natural place. Then follow the steps to analyze it.

The rain forest island of Borneo, the world's third largest island, is about the size of the state of Texas in the United States. The island is one of the most biodiverse places in the world. It is home to endangered animals such as the Sumatran tiger, the Sumatran rhinoceros, the pygmy elephant, and the Bornean orangutan. Sadly, this island's diverse and beautiful rain forest is in danger. In the past 20 years, 80 percent of the rain forest has been destroyed because of illegal logging, forest fires, and development. At the same time, people are capturing and selling some of the wildlife, particularly the orangutans. We need to protect Borneo because it is home to so many different species, and because the rain forest helps reverse damage from climate change.

It's important to protect Borneo so that we can save all the different forms of life that live on the island. Thousands of species of plants, animals, and insects live there. Many, like the pygmy elephant, cannot be found anyplace else on Earth. In addition, scientists continue to find new species of plants and animals. Some of these might provide medicines for diseases, or teach us more about biology.

We also need to protect Borneo—home of one of the world's remaining rain forests—in order to protect the globe from climate change. Carbon dioxide, a greenhouse gas, is heating up the Earth's atmosphere and causing a number of problems such as extreme weather and melting polar ice. Rain forests absorb carbon dioxide and create more oxygen. They also help produce rain all around the world. If we lose rain forests, we will lose one of our best weapons against global warming.

So, what can be done to protect Borneo? Both international and local communities are involved in saving the island. An organization called WWF, formerly the World Wildlife Fund, is working to create safety corridors and protect the 220,000-square-kilometer (85,000-square-mile) area from destruction. The organization is raising funds to help make this happen. The Borneo Project—an international organization—provides support to local communities. These communities protect the rain forests of Borneo in various ways: They stop loggers from cutting down trees, they educate the local community about the need to save the rain forest, and they block developers from building on the land. With a combination of international and local efforts, Borneo may be saved from destruction.

▲ **Endangered:** an eared frog from Borneo

Step 1 Underline the thesis statement.

Step 2 Circle the key words in the thesis statement.

Step 3 Underline the topic sentences of the body paragraphs. Does the order of the body paragraphs reflect the order of the ideas in the thesis?

Step 4 Circle the key words in the topic sentences. Do they reflect the key words in the thesis statement?

Step 5 What details in the body paragraphs does the writer use to develop the key concepts in each of the topic sentences?

D | Revising. Now follow steps 1–5 in exercise **C** to analyze your own essay.

E | Peer Evaluation. Exchange your first draft with a partner and follow the steps below.

Step 1 Read your partner's essay and tell him or her one thing that you liked about it.

Step 2 Complete the outline showing the ideas that your partner's essay describes.

Introduction

Information about the animal/plant/building/place: _____

_____

_____

How is it valuable? _____

Why is it in danger? _____

Thesis statement: We need to protect _____

because _____ and _____.

Body Paragraph 1

Topic sentence: (Reason 1) _____

_____

Supporting detail: _____

Supporting detail: _____

Body Paragraph 2

Topic sentence: (Reason 2) _____

_____

Supporting detail: _____

Supporting detail: _____

Conclusion

What can be done to protect it? _____

_____

_____

Step 3 Compare this outline with the one that your partner created on page 43.

Step 4 The two outlines should be similar. If they aren't, discuss how they differ.

F | **Draft 2.** Write a second draft of your essay. Use what you learned from the peer evaluation activity and your answers to exercise **D**. Make any other necessary changes.

G | **Editing Practice.** Read the information in the box. Then find and correct one mistake with appositives in each of the sentences (1–5).

> In sentences with appositives, remember that an appositive must:
> - be a noun or a noun phrase.
> - come right after a noun or noun phrase.
> - be separated by commas, dashes, or colons.

1. Tigers, they are an endangered species, live throughout Asia.

2. Ranthambore, a tiger reserve is in India.

3. Tiger conservationists—people who protect tigers, are looking for new solutions.

4. Corridors, are paths for safe travel, may help tigers survive in wild areas.

5. There are fewer than 4,000 tigers. The biggest cat in the world.

H | **Editing Checklist.** Use the checklist to find errors in your second draft.

Editing Checklist	Yes	No
1. Are all the words spelled correctly?		
2. Does every sentence have correct punctuation?		
3. Do your subjects and verbs agree?		
4. Have you used appositives correctly?		
5. Are your verb tenses correct?		

I | **Final Draft.** Now use your Editing Checklist to write a third draft of your essay. Make any other necessary changes.

Beautiful

Think and Discuss

1. What do you think makes certain things—for example,
   landscapes, buildings, or images—beautiful?

2. What is the most beautiful thing you have ever seen?

▲ Water drops, with flowers
reflected, provide nourishment

Exploring the Theme

Read the information and discuss the questions.

1. What is *aesthetics*?
2. According to the text, what factors affect aesthetic principles?
3. Is the image on these pages beautiful, in your opinion? If so, what makes it beautiful?

Aesthetics

Aesthetics is a branch of philosophy concerned with the study of beauty. Aesthetic principles provide a set of criteria for creating and evaluating artistic objects such as sculptures and paintings, as well as music, film, and other art forms.

Aesthetic principles have existed almost as long as people have been producing art. Aesthetics were especially important to the ancient Greeks, whose principles have had a great influence on Western art. The Greeks believed that beautiful objects were intrinsically beautiful; that is, their beauty did not depend on people's interpretation of them. Concepts such as proportion, symmetry, and order made objects beautiful.

Today, most people would agree that aesthetic principles are culturally influenced. Ideas on how the human form is represented, for example, vary widely. In traditional African art, sculpture is often abstract and stylized rather than realistically representing particular individuals. Aesthetic principles may also vary over time. In the past, for example, an important value in European art was that it should be didactic. In other words, it needed to have a moral or an educational function. The idea of art for its own sake came into prominence in the nineteenth century.

The landscape, architecture, paintings, and sculptures of the Peterhof Palace in Russia represent classical European views of aesthetics.

A | Building Vocabulary. Read the following text about 19th-century art. Use the context to guess the meanings of the words in **blue**. Then write each word next to its definition (1–7).

The time and place in which a work of art is created often influence its aesthetic value. Therefore, understanding the historical and social **context** of a work of art can help you to appreciate it better and give you **insight** into its significance. For example, many works of European and American art during the mid- to late 19th century have Asian—or specifically Japanese—influences.

Artists such as Vincent van Gogh and James McNeill Whistler incorporated into their own work the subjects, colors, and arrangement of objects of Japanese prints. They were **exposed to** Japanese art partly because Japan opened up to the West in the mid-1800s. As a result, European exhibitions started showing art objects from Japan. Artists who were looking for new styles were especially influenced by Japanese woodblock prints, which **violated** the rules of traditional Western art. To Western eyes, objects in Japanese woodblock prints look flat instead of three-dimensional. Scenes do not have perspective, as in Western paintings. There were other **crucial** elements that pointed to the differences in Western and Asian **notions** of beauty. For example, the arrangement of objects in Japanese prints is often irregular and asymmetrical, and the focal point—the central object in a print—is often off center, not in the middle as in a Western painting. Some artists were so inspired by these new ideas that they even moved to Japan during the late 19th century in order to **pursue** their interest in Asian art.

1. _____: to follow

2. _____: brought into contact with

3. _____: extremely important

4. _____: the general situation that an idea or an event relates to

5. _____: an accurate and deep understanding of something

6. _____: broke or failed to comply with

7. _____: ideas or beliefs about something

Left: *Sudden Shower Over Ohashi Bridge,* by Hiroshige

Right: *The Bridge in the Rain,* by Vincent van Gogh

B | Building Vocabulary. Complete the definitions with the words and phrases from the box. Use a dictionary to help you.

| confer | depression | ethics | in the abstract | proportions |

Word Partners

Use **proportion** with nouns and adjectives: *(n.)* proportion **of the population, sense of** proportion, *(adj.)* **large** proportion, **significant** proportion, **greater** proportion, **higher** proportion, **in direct** proportion to (something).

1. _____ is a mental state in which you are sad and feel that you cannot enjoy anything.

2. If you refer to the _____ of something, you are referring to its size or its relationship to other objects in terms of size and shape.

3. When you talk about something _____, you talk about it in a general or idealistic way.

4. _____ are ideas or moral beliefs that influence the behavior, attitudes, or philosophy of a group of people.

5. If you _____ something, such as an honor or a particular meaning, on someone or something, you give or award that honor or meaning.

C | Using Vocabulary. Answer the questions. Share your ideas with a partner.

1. What kinds of art were you **exposed** to at school?

2. What are some famous works of art in your country? In what historical **contexts** were they made?

3. Think of a famous work of art that most people consider great. In your opinion, what is a **crucial** aspect of its greatness?

D | Brainstorming. Discuss your answers to this question in a small group.

Think of some everyday objects, such as pieces of furniture or vegetables. Can they be beautiful? What makes them beautiful?

E | Predicting. Look at the photos on pages 52–58 and read the first sentence of each paragraph. Answer the question below. Then check your ideas as you read the passage.

What aspects of photography does the reading passage discuss?

_____

_____

_____

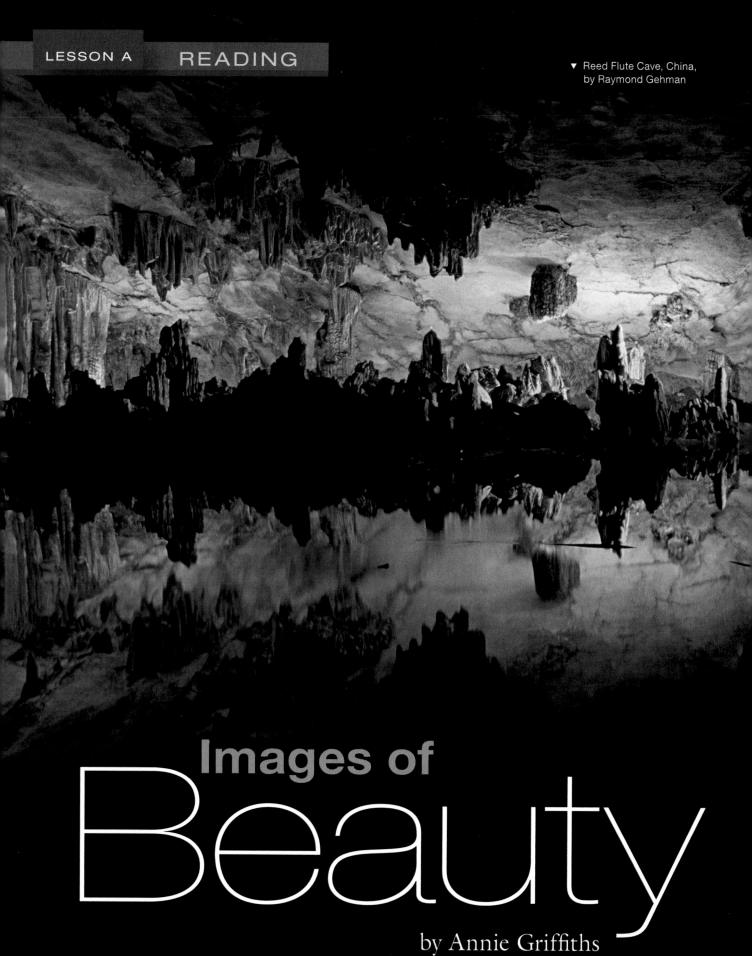

▼ Reed Flute Cave, China,
by Raymond Gehman

Images of
Beauty

by Annie Griffiths

> Some photographs rise above the others. These are photos that catch a moment of emotion or light that make them ignite a deeper response in the viewer.

track **1-03**

A PHOTOGRAPHY HAS OPENED OUR EYES to a multitude of beauties, things we literally could not have seen before the advent of the frozen image. It has greatly expanded our **notion** of what is beautiful, what is aesthetically pleasing. Items formerly considered trivial, and not worth an artist's paint, have been revealed and honored by a photograph: things as pedestrian as a fence post, a chair, a vegetable. And as technology has developed, photographers have explored completely new points of view: those of the microscope, the eagle, the cosmos.

B What is it that delights the human eye and allows us to proclaim that a photograph is beautiful? Photography depends on the trinity of light, composition, and moment. Light literally makes the recording of an image possible, but in the right hands, light in a photograph can make the image soar. The same is true with composition. What the photographer chooses to keep in or out of the frame is all that we will ever see—but that combination is vital. And the moment that the shutter is pressed, when an instant is frozen in time, endows the whole image with[1]

meaning. When the three—light, composition, and moment—are in concert, there is visual magic.

C Let us begin with light. Light literally reveals the subject. Without light, there is nothing: no sight, no color, no form. How light is **pursued** and captured is the photographer's constant challenge and constant joy. We watch it dance across a landscape or a face, and we prepare for the moment when it illuminates or softens or ignites the subject before us. Light is rarely interesting when it is flawless. Photographers may be the only people at the beach or on the mountaintop praying for clouds, because nothing condemns a photograph more than a blazingly bright sky. Light is usually best when it is fleeting or dappled,[2] razor sharp or threatening, or atmospheric. On a physiological level, we are all solar powered. Scientific studies have proved that our moods are profoundly affected by the amount of light we are **exposed to**.

[1] If you **endow** something **with** a particular feature or quality, you provide it with that feature or quality.
[2] **Dappled** light is a combination of dark and light patches on the object or person that is being illuminated.

Lack of sun has been linked to loss of energy and even **depression.** Light in a photograph sets an emotional expectation. It can be soft or harsh, broad or delicate, but the mood that light sets is a preface to the whole image. Consider the light in a stunning scene by Sam Abell (below). It is the quality of light through morning fog that blesses this image and turns a forest into a field of light, shadow, and color, where every tree takes on a personality.

Composition represents the structural choices the photographer makes within the photographic frame. Everything in the photo can either contribute or distract. Ironically, the definition of what makes a picture aesthetically pleasing often comes down to mathematics: the geometric **proportions** of objects and their placements within the frame. When we look at a beautiful photograph with an objective eye, we can often find serpentine[3] lines, figure eights, and triangular arrangements formed by the objects within the frame. The balance, or mathematical proportion, of the objects makes up the picture's composition: a key element in any beautiful image. Look closely at photographer James Stanfield's charming composition of a child jumping for joy in a doorway at the Louvre (right). It is the moment that draws us in, but that moment is set in a striking composition of the doorway and the architecture beyond. The geometric composition of the photograph makes the child look small, and even more appealing.

The third **crucial** element in a photograph is the moment when the shutter is pressed. The moment captured in a beautiful image is the storytelling part of the photograph. Whether a small gesture or a grand climax, it is the moment within a picture that draws us in and makes us care. It may be the photographer's most important choice. If a special moment is caught, it endows the whole image with meaning. Often, waiting for that moment involves excruciating patience, as the photographer anticipates that something miraculous is about to happen. At other times, it's an almost electric reaction that seems to bypass the thought process entirely and fire straight to instinct. Capturing that perfect moment may be a photographer's biggest challenge because most important moments are fleeting. Hands touch. The ball drops. A smile flashes. Miss the moment and it is gone forever.

Light, composition, and moment are the basic elements in any beautiful photograph. But there are three other elements that draw the viewer in and encourage an emotional response. These are palette, time, and wonder.

[3] Something that is **serpentine** is curving and winding in shape, like a snake.

▲ Morning fog at Kelly's Ford, Virginia, USA, by Sam Abell

Girl at the Louvre, Paris, ▶
by James Stanfield

Palette refers to the selection of colors in a photograph that create a visual **context**. Colors can range from neon to a simple gradation of grays in a black-and-white photograph. Even **in the abstract**, colors can make us feel elated or sad. The chosen palette sets up the mood of the whole image. It can invite or repel, soothe or agitate. We feel calm in a palette of pastels. Icy blues can make us shiver. Oranges and reds tend to energize. For example, Martin Kers's photograph below has a soothing palette of yellows and greens that almost glows. It beckons us to walk down a path in the Netherlands. It's a simple composition made memorable by its palette.

Other images stand out because of the freezing or blurring of time. There are the lovely images of raindrops falling, lightning flashing, and athletes frozen in midair. There are also time exposures[4] that allow us to see a choreography of movement within the still frame. The laundry flutters, the traffic merges, the water flows. In a photograph of a bird in flight, the high-speed exposure allows us to see things that our eyes literally cannot see: every feather supporting the bird's flight, the arc of the wings, the light in the bird's eye. High-speed photography has been a gift to both art and science.

[4] A **time exposure** is a photograph that results when the camera's shutter is left open for a long time.

▲ Tree-lined road covered with yellow flowers, Knardijk, Netherlands, by Martin Kers

▲ Time exposure of cars speeding past a cowboy on horseback, Badlands, USA, by Annie Griffiths

Wonder refers to the measure of human response when the photograph reveals something extraordinary—something never seen before, or seen in a fresh, new way. Wonder is about **insight** and curiosity. It is an expression of the child inside every one of us. Some photographers, following their childlike sense of wonder, have literally given their lives in pursuit of images so wonderful that they must be seen.

Light, composition, and moment come together in a photograph to bring us the ultimate reality: a view of the world unknown before the invention of the camera. Before photography, the basic artistic rules of painting were rarely **violated**. Images were made to please, not to capture reality. But as photography evolved, painterly[5] rules were often rejected in the pursuit of fresh vision. Photographers became interested in the real world, warts and all, and it was the accidental detail that was celebrated. Photography invited the world to see with new eyes—to see photographically—and all of the arts benefited from this new point of view. Painters, sculptors, designers, weavers, and dancers all expanded their vision of beauty by embracing the photographer's love of reality. And when the photographer is creative with the basic elements in a photograph, the resulting image has greater appeal. A surprising truth about photography is that each element is most effective not when it captures perfection but rather when it reveals the imperfect. Photographs are most eloquent when they impart a new way of seeing. What is more wonderful than the imperfect moment, when a simple scene turns sublime[6] because a cat entered the room, the mirror caught a reflection, or a shaft of light came through the window? And real beauty depends upon how the image moves us: A photograph can make us care, understand, react, emote,[7] and empathize with the wider world by humanizing and honoring the unknown. Photographs have been a crucial element in saving whales, demystifying cultures, and bringing the wide world closer.

[5] **Painterly** means relating to or characteristic of painting or painters.
[6] If you describe something as **sublime**, you mean that it has a wonderful quality that affects you deeply.
[7] To **emote** is to express emotion in an intense way.

With these basic aesthetic tools, photographers have evolved from scientists longing to "fix" an image—any image—to artistic visionaries. Along the way, the still image has evolved from being merely a document to being a stunning documentary of the 19th and 20th centuries. Photographs have created a new **ethic** of seeing. They have greatly expanded our notion of what is beautiful. It is to photography's credit that it has found beauty in the most humble places, and that it has ushered in a new democracy of vision. People from all walks of life are able to feast their eyes on subjects remote and grand. They are able to hold them in their hands. Perhaps most important, all people can see themselves and their private worlds in beautiful ways because, in the words of Susan Sontag, "to photograph is to **confer** importance." Photographs have given us visual proof that the world is grander than we imagined, that there is beauty, often overlooked, in nearly everything.

K

◀ Hugging, twisted carrots in Oak View, California, by Rich Reid

A | **Identifying Main Ideas.** Answer the questions about the main ideas in the passage on pages 52–58.

1. What are the three main elements that make a photograph beautiful? _____

   _____

2. What additional elements make a photograph beautiful? _____

   _____

3. The passage is divided into two main parts. Which paragraph begins the first part? _____

   Which paragraph begins the second part? _____

B | **Identifying Key Details.** Write answers to the questions (1–6).

1. How has photography changed our notion of beauty? _____

   _____

2. Write a definition for each of the main elements you listed in Exercise A question 1.

   _____

   _____

   _____

3. What is the effect of color in a photograph, according to Griffiths? _____

   _____

4. What does the element of time help us to see in a photograph? _____

   _____

5. What is wonder as it applies to a photograph, according to Griffiths? Explain it in your

   own words. _____

   _____

6. How has photography affected other art forms? _____

   _____

   _____

C | Critical Thinking: Applying Ideas. Find the following three quotes in paragraph J of the reading passage. Then discuss with a partner your answers to the questions.

1. "Before photography, the basic artistic rules of painting were rarely violated. Images were made to please, not to capture reality." What are some famous paintings that are examples of this idea?

2. "A surprising truth about photography is that each element is most effective not when it captures perfection but rather when it reveals the imperfect." Do you agree? Can you think of any examples?

3. "A photograph can make us care, understand, react, emote, and empathize with the wider world by humanizing and honoring the unknown. Photographs have been a crucial element in saving whales, demystifying cultures, and bringing the wide world closer." Do you agree? Can you think of any specific examples? Can you find any photographs in this book that have these purposes?

D | Identifying Meaning from Context. Find the following words and phrases in **bold** in the reading passage. Use context to complete each definition. Then check your answers in a dictionary.

1. Paragraph A: If something is **pedestrian**, it's ordinary / extraordinary.

2. Paragraph B: A **trinity** is a group of _____ things.

3. Paragraph B: You use **in concert** to say things work _____.

4. Paragraph D: If an idea **comes down to** something in particular, it means it is equal / unequal to it.

5. Paragraph E: If a moment is **fleeting**, it goes by very _____.

6. Paragraph I: If a photograph shows images of real life, **warts and all**, then it is showing us just the positive / both the positive and the negative aspects of reality.

7. Paragraph J: If something has **ushered in** a thing, such as a new era or way of thinking, it has _____ it into being.

8. Paragraph J: **People from all walks of life** are people who come from _____ backgrounds.

 E | Critical Thinking: Reflecting. Discuss with a partner your answers to these questions.

What was your opinion of photography before you read "Images of Beauty"? Did your opinion change after reading the passage? Explain your answer.

Reading Skill: Using a Concept Map to Identify Supporting Details

A **concept map** is a type of graphic organizer. It helps you see how main ideas and details in a reading passage relate to each other. Taking notes in a concept map can help you understand and remember information so you can use it later in a discussion, a writing assignment, or a test.

When you take notes in any kind of graphic organizer, be as brief as possible. Use abbreviations and leave out unimportant or repeated information.

A | **Using a Concept Map.** Complete the concept map using information from paragraphs B–E of "Images of Beauty."

The Elements of a Beautiful Photograph

light
↓
reveals subject; makes
everything else visible:
e.g., color, form
↓
Abell photo: light gives
personality to trees

B | **Applying.** Now continue the concept map above with key information about the three additional elements from paragraphs F–I.

Oregon Coast

Oregon, USA

Before Viewing

A | Using a Dictionary. Here are some words you will hear in the video. Match each one with the correct definition. Use a dictionary to help you.

| counterculture | humbling | theatrical | treacherous | wavelength |

1. _____ very dangerous and unpredictable
2. _____ making you feel that you aren't as important as you thought you were
3. _____ exaggerated; creating an effect
4. _____ a particular way of thinking
5. _____ values or attitudes in opposition to the social norm

B | Thinking Ahead. Think about the times you have been at a beach or coastline. Discuss these questions with a partner: How did the experience make you feel? How would you describe the area?

While Viewing

Read the questions (1–4). Think about the answers as you view the video.

1. Who was Ken Kesey (1935–2001)? What was his profession?
2. How does Kesey describe the effect that the Oregon coast has on him? What does it make him think about?
3. Why might Kesey describe being on the Oregon coast as a "humbling" experience?
4. Based on the scenes in the video, how would you describe the Oregon coast?

After Viewing

A | Discuss the answers to the questions in "While Viewing" with a partner.

B | Critical Thinking: Synthesizing. Think about the aesthetic criteria for a good photograph that you read about in "Images of Beauty." What aspects of the Oregon coast might a photographer try to capture to create an image that conforms to these criteria?

A scenic view of Pacific waves rolling up to the Oregon coast at Samuel H. Boardman State Park.

GOAL: Writing about a Visual Art Form

In this lesson, you are going to plan, write, revise, and edit an essay on the following topic:
Choose an example of a visual art form (e.g., a painting, a photograph, a piece of sculpture, a building) and evaluate it using aesthetic criteria.

A | **Brainstorming.** Choose three works of visual arts that you think are great. Use details to describe each one. Then think of criteria you can use to evaluate it. Explain how each one follows your criteria.

Title of work			
Details			
Criteria			

B | **Vocabulary for Writing.** The words and phrases below can be useful when writing about visual art forms. Find the words in the reading passage on pages 52–58. Use context to guess their meanings. Then complete each definition with one of the words.

> **aesthetically pleasing** (paragraph A) **illuminate** (paragraph C) **atmospheric** (paragraph C)
> **geometric** (paragraph D) **within the frame** (paragraph D) **pastels** (paragraph G)
> **gradation** (paragraph G)

1. If a scene is _____, it has a particular quality that is interesting or exciting and makes you feel a particular emotion.

2. If a work of art is _____, it is beautiful.

3. In a photograph, things that are _____ are the things that the photographer has chosen to include in the image.

4. To _____ something means to shine light on it.

5. A _____ is a small change in something, such as a slight change from one color to another.

6. If something is _____, it illustrates mathematical principles such as lines, angles, shapes, and curves.

7. _____ are pale colors.

Free Writing. Write for five minutes. Write a description of one of the works of visual art you discussed in exercise **A**. Try to use some of the words and phrases in exercise **B**.

C | Read the information in the box. Then read the pairs of sentences below (1–4). The second sentence in each pair provides extra information. Join the sentences using a nonrestrictive adjective clause for the extra information.

Language for Writing: Using Nonrestrictive Adjective Clauses

Writers use adjective clauses to give more information about nouns. An adjective clause has a subject and a verb.

> *Palette refers to the selection of colors in a photograph __that__ create a visual context.*
>
> *Susan Sontag was a writer __who__ was interested in photography.*

Restrictive adjective clauses give essential information about a noun, as in the examples above. Nonrestrictive adjective clauses give nonessential information, as in the following examples.

> *Our concept of beauty has been influenced by photography, __which__ is a relatively recent art form.*
>
> *Annie Griffiths, __who__ is a professional photographer, is the executive director of an organization that empowers women in developing countries.*
>
> *Annie Leibovitz, __whose__ photographs have been published in several magazines, is famous for her use of light and color.*

Nonrestrictive adjective clauses are a good way to add details to your writing. They help vary your sentence types and make your sentences more interesting.

Note: Remember to use commas in nonrestrictive adjective clauses. Use one comma before a nonrestrictive adjective clause that appears at the end of a sentence. Use commas before and after a nonrestrictive adjective clause when it appears in the middle of a sentence. Use *which* (not *that*) for objects in nonrestrictive adjective clauses.

See page 249 for more information.

1. Vivian Maier was an amateur photographer. Her work was discovered after her death.

   _____

2. Ansel Adams was an American photographer. He was most known for his images of the Californian wilderness.

   _____

3. The house known as Fallingwater was designed as a country retreat. It was built for a wealthy family who owned a department store in Pittsburgh, USA.

   _____

4. Vincent van Gogh was influenced by Japanese art. He made a copy of Hiroshige's print *Sudden Storm Over Ohashi Bridge*.

   _____

D | Add more information to your Free Writing sentences using nonrestrictive relative clauses.

Writing Skill: Supporting a Thesis

As you saw in Unit 2, a thesis statement expresses the main idea of an entire essay. Each body paragraph in an essay then provides details for and explanation of the main idea. To effectively support a thesis statement, make sure you do the following:

- Order your body paragraphs according to the order of the key concepts in your thesis statement.
- Restate the key concepts of the thesis statement in the topic sentence of each body paragraph.
- Develop the key concepts in the body paragraphs.
- In the body paragraphs, provide adequate details, facts, and examples that develop each key concept in your thesis statement.

E | **Critical Thinking: Analyzing.** Read this excerpt from an introduction to an essay on Frank Lloyd Wright's Fallingwater. Underline the key concepts in the thesis statement and then answer the questions (1–3).

The term *organic architecture*, which was coined by the American architect Frank Lloyd Wright, applies to structures that create a sense of harmony with the natural world. Fallingwater, the western Pennsylvania house designed by Wright, is a perfect example of the organic approach to architecture due to the way the house is integrated into its natural surroundings and because of the materials used in its construction.

Thesis statement

1. How many body paragraphs will the essay have? _____

2. What ideas will appear in the topic sentences of the body paragraphs?

   _____

   _____

   _____

3. Number your answers to question 2 above to show the order in which the body paragraphs will appear.

F | **Supporting a Thesis.** Read the topic sentences below for the essay about Fallingwater. Underline the key words. Notice how the writer restates key concepts from the thesis statement.

Body paragraph 1:

Topic sentence: The way Fallingwater is assimilated into its natural environment is an example of organic architecture.

Body paragraph 2:

Topic sentence: The organic approach is also shown in the natural materials Wright used to build Fallingwater.

G | **Applying.** Now read some notes for the essay. Which body paragraph from exercise **F** does each note best support? Match a paragraph (1–2) with each note.

Notes:

_____ a. exterior color matches color of leaves on surrounding plants

_____ b. natural spring drips water into house

_____ c. built from stones found in local area

_____ d. living room fireplace incorporates boulders from a nearby building site

_____ e. house is built around a tree and a waterfall

_____ f. simple walls made of large pieces of glass with no frames

Fallingwater, designed ▶ by Frank Lloyd Wright

A | Planning. Follow the steps to make notes for your essay.

Step 1 Choose a work of art and write the title and the name of the artist in the outline below. (The artist could be a painter, a photographer, a sculptor, or an architect.)

Step 2 Choose three criteria to use to evaluate your work of art.

Step 3 Complete the thesis statement in the outline.

Step 4 Write a topic sentence for each paragraph. Remember to connect these to the the key concepts in your thesis statement.

Step 5 For each paragraph, write two or three examples or details for each criterion.

Step 6 Note some ideas for an introduction and a conclusion for your essay. Your introduction should include a brief description of the work.

Title of work: _____ Artist: _____

What three criteria does it exemplify? _____ ,

_____ , _____

Thesis statement: _____

1st body paragraph: How is this work of art an example of the first criterion?

Topic sentence: _____

_____

Details: _____

_____

2nd body paragraph: How is this work of art an example of the second criterion?

Topic sentence: _____

_____

Details: _____

_____

3rd body paragraph: How is this work of art an example of the third criterion?

Topic sentence: _____

_____

Details: _____

_____

Ideas for introduction and conclusion: _____

_____

B | Draft 1. Use your outline to write a first draft.

C | **Critical Thinking: Analyzing.** Work with a partner. Read the following essay, which discusses a building in terms of how well it exemplifies certain criteria. Then follow the steps to analyze the essay.

What makes a work of architecture great? Most people would say that aesthetics are most important. For example, many people agree that the Eiffel Tower in Paris and the Blue Mosque in Istanbul are beautiful structures. It is true that aesthetics are important; however, according to the Roman architect Marcus Vitruvius Pollio, there are two additional principles that we should consider when judging a structure. They are durability—how strong and long-lasting a structure is designed to be—and function—how well the structure serves its intended purpose. The new Rossville Library is a good example of Vitruvius's principles because it is durable, functional, and aesthetically pleasing.

The Rossville Library, which is built entirely of granite—a hard and very tough stone—is an example of durability. Granite is likely to remain strong and unaffected by environmental pollution. For example, it is resistant to acid rain. Granite structures are stable and resistant to vibrations, so the Rossville Library will likely be able to withstand an earthquake. The Rossville Library is also durable in terms of sustainability, because it uses solar energy for heating, and a rooftop garden provides insulation that keeps the building cool in hot weather.

Designed to provide free access for members of the community to a variety of print and digital information, the Rossville Library is also an example of Vitruvius's principle of functionality. The Rossville Library conveys a feeling of openness and accessibility. For example, it has large double doors that are at street level; there are no stairs at the entrance. Furthermore, the entire library is on one level, and it has an open design—there are no interior walls or dividers. In addition, large windows let in plenty of natural light, so it's easy to see and get to each department within the library.

Finally, the Rossville Library is beautiful. Aesthetically pleasing details make it attractive, both inside and out. The large windows are framed in copper. The copper color offers an interesting contrast to the light gray color of the granite structure, and the contrast will remain as the copper ages. Growth from the rooftop garden, which cascades down the sides of the building, adds to the aesthetics of the building. It softens the lines of the structure and helps it to blend into its natural surroundings.

Durability, functionality, and beauty make the Rossville Library a great structure. Architects and designers who follow Vitruvius's principles help to make urban environments more pleasant places to live. Structures that exemplify these criteria provide peace of mind as well as beauty for the people who use them.

Step 1 Underline the thesis statement.

Step 2 Circle the key words in the thesis statement.

Step 3 Underline the topic sentences of the body paragraphs. Does the order of the body paragraphs reflect the order of the ideas in the thesis? Yes / No

Step 4 Circle the key words in the topic sentences. Do they reflect the key concepts in the thesis statement? Yes / No

Step 5 What details in the body paragraphs does the writer use to develop the key concepts in each of the topic sentences?

D | Revising. Follow steps 1–5 in exercise **C** to analyze your own essay.

E | Peer Evaluation. Exchange your first draft with a partner and follow the steps below.

Step 1 Read your partner's essay and tell him or her one thing that you liked about it.

Step 2 Complete the outline showing the ideas that your partner's essay describes.

Title of work: _____ Artist: _____

What three criteria does it exemplify? _____ ,

_____ , _____

Thesis statement: _____

1st body paragraph: How is this work of art an example of the first criterion?

Topic sentence: _____

_____

Details: _____

_____

2nd body paragraph: How is this work of art an example of the second criterion?

Topic sentence: _____

_____

Details: _____

_____

3rd body paragraph: How is this work of art an example of the third criterion?

Topic sentence: _____

_____

Details: _____

_____

Ideas for introduction and conclusion: _____

_____

Step 3 Compare this outline with the one that your partner created in exercise **A** on page 67.

Step 4 The two outlines should be similar. If they aren't, discuss how they differ.

WRITING TASK: Editing

F | Draft 2. Write a second draft of your essay. Use what you learned from the peer evaluation activity and your answers to exercise **D**. Make any other necessary changes.

G | Editing Practice. Read the information in the box. Then find and correct one mistake with nonrestrictive adjective clauses in each of the sentences (1–4).

> When using nonrestrictive adjective clauses, remember to:
> - use one comma before a nonrestrictive adjective clause that appears at the end of a sentence. Use two commas, one before and one after, when the nonrestrictive adjective clause appears in the middle of a sentence.
> - use *which* (not *that*) for objects in nonrestrictive adjective clauses.

1. This image is an excellent example of composition which is the way objects are arranged in a photograph.

2. That photograph, that I like best of all, is Berenice Abbott's *Pennsylvania Station*.

3. Another important element is light, that illuminates the objects in a photograph.

4. Moment which captures time in a photograph helps to tell the image's story.

H | Editing Checklist. Use the checklist to find errors in your second draft.

Editing Checklist	Yes	No
1. Are all the words spelled correctly?		
2. Does every sentence have correct punctuation?		
3. Do your subjects and verbs agree?		
4. Have you used nonrestrictive adjective clauses correctly?		
5. Are your verb tenses correct?		

I | Final Draft. Now use your Editing Checklist to write a third draft of your essay. Make any other necessary changes.

Powering Our Planet

ACADEMIC PATHWAYS

Lesson A: Recognizing a writer's tone
         Interpreting figurative language
Lesson B: Avoiding plagiarism
         Writing a summary essay

Think and Discuss

1. What kinds of everyday things do you use energy for?
2. Do you know where most of the energy used in your country comes from?

▲ High-occupancy vehicle (HOV) lanes, such as these near Washington, D.C., are meant to reduce traffic congestion and pollution. The lanes are reserved for cars that contain a driver and at least one passenger.

71

Exploring the Theme

Study the information on these pages and discuss the questions.

1. What do these charts show?

2. What are some reasons for the changes over the 30-year period? Which region shows the biggest change over 30 years?

3. Which region has the biggest difference between production and use? What might account for this?

ENERGY PRODUCED AND USED
MILLIONS OF METRIC TONS OF CRUDE OIL EQUIVALENT

- PACIFIC
- EUROPE
- U.S.S.R.
- ASIA
- MIDDLE EAST
- SOUTH AMERICA
- NORTH AMERICA
- AFRICA

Note: Total energy production comprises all energy produced from raw sources, including fossil fuels and renewable sources.
Total energy use comprises all forms of energy produced in each country, imported, or taken from or added to reserves, and fuel used in international shipping.

TOTAL ENERGY PRODUCTION
WORLD 6,628

1976

TOTAL ENERGY USE
WORLD 6,533

PACIFIC 81

PACIFIC 72

EUROPE 774

EUROPE 1,506

U.S.S.R. 1,173

U.S.S.R. 998

ASIA 978

ASIA 1,278

75 AUSTRALIA 62

120 POLAND 109
126 U.K. 206
41 FRANCE 178
174 GERMANY

341

106 INDONESIA 44
33
170

512

KUWAIT 7 JAPAN 326
115 IRAQ 7 INDIA 186
124 U.A.E. 3
97 CHINA 505

444 SAUDI ARABIA 12

314 IRAN

INTERNATIONAL SHIPPING 106

32

143 VENEZUELA 26 BRAZIL 96
54
68 MEXICO 64 CANADA 172
182
1,418 UNITED STATES 1,771

MIDDLE EAST 1,159

MIDDLE EAST 81

SOUTH AMERICA 276

SOUTH AMERICA 209

NORTH AMERICA 1,695

NORTH AMERICA 2,048

102 LIBYA 4
60 ALGERIA 7
144 NIGERIA 44
49 SOUTH AFRICA 56

AFRICA 492

AFRICA 234

World Energy Flow

From 1976 to 2006, the production and use of energy increased significantly worldwide. The main reasons for this were industrialization and population growth. However, while industry and population changed, sources and types of energy remained largely the same. This pattern will likely continue for a couple of decades. Experts predict that we will continue to use massive amounts of fossil fuels and that global warming will increase due to rising CO_2 levels.

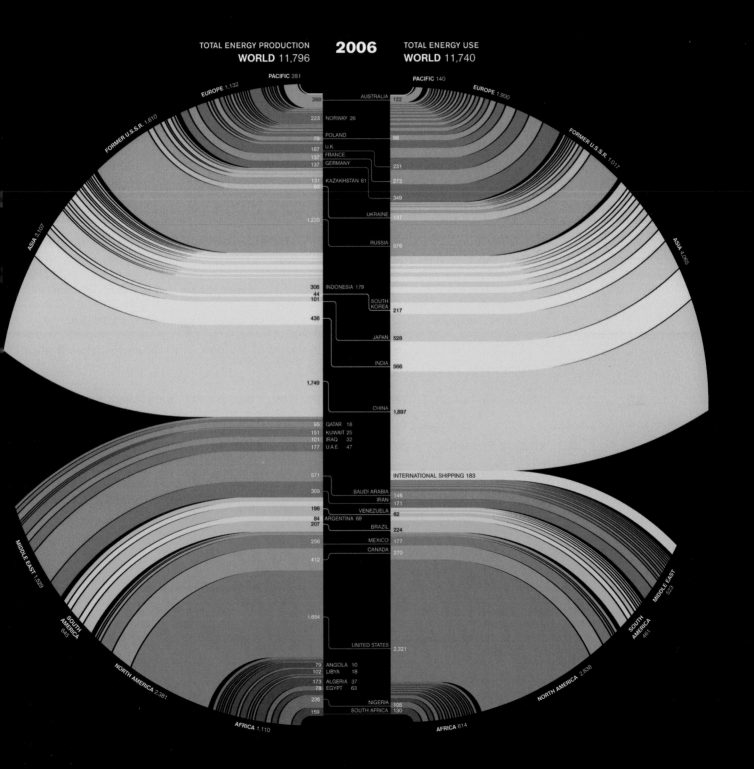

TOTAL ENERGY PRODUCTION
WORLD 11,796

2006

TOTAL ENERGY USE
WORLD 11,740

PACIFIC 281   PACIFIC 140

EUROPE 1,132   EUROPE 1,900

FORMER U.S.S.R. 1,610   FORMER U.S.S.R. 1,017

ASIA 3,107   ASIA 4,065

268	AUSTRALIA	122
223	NORWAY 26	
78	POLAND	98
187	U.K.	
137	FRANCE	231
137	GERMANY	
131	KAZAKHSTAN 61	273
83		349
1,220	UKRAINE	137
	RUSSIA	676
308	INDONESIA 179	
44		
101	SOUTH KOREA	217
436	JAPAN	528
	INDIA	566
1,749		
	CHINA	1,897
95	QATAR 18	
151	KUWAIT 25	
101	IRAQ 32	
177	U.A.E. 47	

INTERNATIONAL SHIPPING 183

571		
309	SAUDI ARABIA	146
	IRAN	171
196	VENEZUELA	62
84	ARGENTINA 69	
207	BRAZIL	224
256	MEXICO	177
	CANADA	270
412		
1,654	UNITED STATES	2,321

MIDDLE EAST 1,529   MIDDLE EAST 523

SOUTH AMERICA 645   SOUTH AMERICA 461

NORTH AMERICA 2,381   NORTH AMERICA 2,838

79	ANGOLA 10	
102	LIBYA 18	
173	ALGERIA 37	
78	EGYPT 63	
235	NIGERIA	105
159	SOUTH AFRICA	130

AFRICA 1,110   AFRICA 614

A | **Building Vocabulary.** Read the following paragraphs. Use the context to guess the meanings of the words in **blue**. Then write the correct word to complete each definition (1–7).

Is global warming a real threat? Over the past few decades, our use of energy has gone up. **Correspondingly,** our effects on the planet have risen, too. Many scientists have **confirmed** that our use of fossil fuels has warmed Earth's atmosphere to dangerous levels. We have to find effective ways to **offset** our use of fossil fuels. We've tried different **substitutes,** including **nuclear** energy. However, our best chance at protecting the planet requires the use of renewable energy such as wind, solar, or water power.

A second reason to look for a new, renewable source of energy is that we are running out of fossil fuels. The **prospect** of a future without oil is scary. For many people on the planet, it will mean a very different way of life, particularly in terms of what and how much we consume. In fact, we may have to **redefine** what it means to live a good life.

Word Partners

Use **prospect** with *of* + noun or gerund: *(n.)* prospect **of peace,** prospect **of war,** prospect **of a future;** *(gerund)* prospect **of having** (something), prospect **of being** (something)

1. If one thing is _____ by another, the effect of the first thing is reduced by the second.

2. If you _____ something, you cause people to consider it in a new way.

3. You use "_____" when describing a situation that is closely connected with or similar to a situation you have just mentioned.

4. If someone has _____ a belief, they have shown that it is definitely true.

5. If there is a(n) _____ of something happening, it is likely to happen.

6. _____ means relating to the nuclei of atoms, or to the energy released when these nuclei are split or combined.

7. _____ are things that you have or use instead of something else.

B | **Building Vocabulary.** Complete the definitions with the items from the box. Use a dictionary to help you.

Word Partners

Use **on behalf** with: *(possessive adj.)* on **his** behalf, on **your** behalf, on **my** behalf; *of + (n.)* on behalf **of my team,** on behalf **of the company**

automatically	economist	on someone's behalf
revolution	sums up	

1. If something _____ a situation, it describes it in a concise way.

2. If you do something _____, you do it without thinking.

3. A(n) _____ in a particular area of human activity is an important change in that area.

4. If you do something _____, you do it for that person as his or her representative.

5. A(n) _____ is someone who studies, teaches, or writes about money, industry, and commerce in society.

C | Using Vocabulary. Write answers to the questions (1–4). Share your ideas with a partner.

1. When you read a story or some information on a social networking site and you are not sure if it's true, how do you **confirm** it?

_____

_____

2. Globally, humans produce billions of tons of garbage every year. What are some ways you can **offset** your own production of garbage?

_____

_____

3. Some people don't eat meat because they believe that meat production is bad for the environment. What are some things that people eat as **substitutes** for meat?

_____

_____

4. The information **revolution** started with the first computer chip, and it has had a huge impact on our lives. What are some ways the information revolution is good—and bad— for the environment?

_____

_____

D | Predicting. Read the first paragraph and the last line of the reading passage on pages 76–82. What do you think the writer's purpose is? Circle your answer. Check your idea as you read the rest of the passage.

a. to recount a personal experience   b. to persuade   c. to inform

Our Energy Challenge

by Bill McKibben

> We are stuck right now—stuck between a played-out rock and a hot place. And it's an open question whether or not we can work our way free.

track 1-04

A ENERGY, OF COURSE, is not just another part of our economy. For all intents and purposes,[1] it *is* our economy. The great **economist** John Maynard Keynes once reckoned that the standard of living for most humans had at most doubled in all the millennia since history dawned—until the turn of the 18th century, when we learned how to use coal to run engines. Then, suddenly, it's as if each of us had rubbed a bottle and come away with our own genie,[2] ready to do work **on** our **behalf** for a very reasonable price. All of a sudden, living standards in the energy-using West were doubling every few decades. (There's a reason, after all, that "industrialized world" and "developed world" are very nearly synonyms.)

B In essence, we were no longer stuck with the interest we could earn off the sunlight falling on the planet—no longer stuck with the energy we could harness to feed our own muscles and those of our draft animals, with the wind that filled the sails of our ships when the sun warmed some spot and created a difference in pressure. All of a sudden, we could draw on the capital[3] in the bank—those millions of years of deposits of ferns and plankton and dinosaurs that time had compressed into coal and gas and oil. We were, almost literally, like the lucky heirs of someone long dead and very rich whose will was finally deciphered.[4] And we spent without thinking twice. That spending made us who we are. Every one of our **revolutions** (the industrial, the chemical, the electronic, even the information) at its base owes its strength to this newfound blood now coursing through the veins of our economy. Most of all, perhaps, the consumer revolution.

C All this was, seemingly, fine. Plan A for the human race was that we'd all get rich eventually, that everyone would harness the same energy slaves that have served the West so well. Sure, there'd be some trouble along the way: Early generations of coal-fired power plants would produce great clouds of smog in Beijing just as they once had in Great Britain; vast fleets of cars would pollute China's skies as once they had California's. But quite quickly, as more energy produced more riches, those places, too, would have the cash to install scrubbers on their smokestacks and catalytic converters on their exhaust pipes, and before long the air would clear.

---

[1] You say **for all intents and purposes** to suggest that a situation is not exactly as you describe it, but that the effect is the same.

[2] In stories, a **genie** is a spirit that appears and disappears by magic and obeys the person who controls it.

[3] **Capital** is a large sum of money that you use to start a business, or that you invest in order to make more money.

[4] If you **decipher** a piece of writing or a message, you figure out what it says, even though it is very difficult to read or understand.

◀ Wind turbines provide energy for the residents of Samsø Island in Denmark, the world's leading producer of wind-generated energy.

Everything seemed to be working as planned: The boom years of the 1990s saw our mass prosperity, and, of course, our massive energy use, starting to spread to Asia. But there were two little problems, new wrinkles that we hadn't considered before—and that we really didn't want to consider, even as they became more obvious. Twenty years ago, if people thought of global warming at all, it was as an unlikely and distant threat. Five years ago, most people hadn't heard of peak oil.[5] Now they are the twin jaws of a closing vise,[6] limiting our options at a time when options are what we desperately need. Examined carefully, they may tell us what the future looks like—a future where we are running out of some of the energy we need and can't use the rest for fear of wrecking the atmosphere. A future that, all of a sudden, looks nothing like what we've long assumed.

Let's do a little math to see why. The Energy Information Administration, an arm of the U.S. government, forecast last year that, all things being equal, world energy consumption would increase 50 percent by 2030. That's a good round number, **summing up** the desire of people across the world for refrigerators, televisions, ice cubes, hamburgers, motorbikes, and maybe even a little air conditioning in the tropics.

[5] **Peak oil** is the point at which the earth's supply of oil begins to decline.
[6] A **vise** is a tool with a pair of parts that hold an object tightly while you do work on it.

At Nevada Solar One, one of the world's largest solar power plants, 182,000 mirrors turn throughout the day to catch the sun's energy. The concentrated heat generates enough electricity to power 14,000 homes. Many more solar plants are in development as nations seek clean, renewable solutions to the world's energy crisis.

But it's not at all clear where that energy can come from, because we happen to be alive at the moment when the oil is starting to run out. In November 2008, the International Energy Agency estimated that production from the world's mature oil fields was declining 6.7 percent a year, a rate that is expected to get even worse over time. **Offsetting** this decline will require finding a new Kuwait's worth of output every year, or somehow squeezing that much more from existing fields. Many observers think we've already passed the peak of oil production. An optimist in this world is someone who thinks it might still be a matter of years. But there's little question where the future lies, which is why the cost of a barrel of oil recently spiked to $147. It took the **prospect** of a Great Recession to bring it back down to $40. Curbing[7] high gas prices with recurrent economic slumps is probably not the smartest of remedies.

What are the options? There are the other fossil fuels. But natural gas will last us only so long. The obvious **substitute** is coal, of which we have quite a bit—except that coal brings us squarely to the other horn of this dilemma. It's the dirtiest of our fuels: Burn it and you **automatically** release lots and lots of carbon dioxide into the atmosphere, and that carbon dioxide is the culprit behind global warming. Which, like peak oil, is happening rather faster than we might like.

In the summer of 2007, for instance, the Arctic melted. By the end of the summer, there was 22 percent less sea ice than ever observed before. A comparable melt the following summer briefly opened the Northwest and Northeast Passages simultaneously, very likely offering human beings their first chance to circumnavigate[8] the Arctic on open water. This melt was 30 years ahead of the computer forecasts about global warming. It **confirmed** that we were warming the planet. There was no other explanation on offer. Worse, it was one of a number of feedback loops that would amplify that warming: Instead of the nice, white sheet of ice covering the Arctic, a mirror that reflected 80 percent of incoming solar radiation back out to space, we all at once had big pools of blue water, which absorb 80 percent of those rays of the sun. We'd kicked off the warming, but now nature was taking over and doing the

[7] If you **curb** something, you control it and keep it within limits.
[8] If you **circumnavigate** something, you sail all the way around it.

job on her own. And that wasn't the only such feedback. As permafrost thawed in northern tundra, for instance, carbon dioxide and methane, another greenhouse gas, began to seep out into the atmosphere. The warmer seasons we were producing led to the spread of various pests that killed tens of millions of acres of trees across the North American West—and the fires all that dead wood fueled added new clouds of carbon to the atmosphere. We weren't producing it directly, but it all led back to us. Our cars and factories had clearly triggered a worldwide reaction, which in retrospect shouldn't surprise us. After all, we were taking millions of years' worth of stored carbon—all those old ferns and plankton—and pouring it into the atmosphere in the course of a few generations. Why wouldn't it cause problems?

Even now, only two decades after the public first heard of global warming, we're clearly on the edge of one tipping point[9] after another. The data predict rapid increases in drought (because warm air holds more water vapor than cold) and **correspondingly** rapid rises in deluge and flood (because what goes up must come down), shocking expansion in the range of disease-bearing mosquitoes, and equally shocking shrinkage in the size of the ice fields that water the cities of the Andes and the Asian subcontinent. Perhaps most ominously, new research on the great ice fields in Greenland and the west Antarctic is threatening to make us **redefine** the phrase "glacial pace."[10] Undermined[11] by the warming seas, the ice sheets were suddenly surging toward the ocean. One study published last fall said that a sea-level rise of six and a half feet this century was within the realm of possibility. That's a civilization-shaking number. It turns much of the world's most fertile land into the equivalent of Myanmar's Irrawaddy Delta, where paddies were recently flooded with seawater by Typhoon Nargis. It puts the human enterprise in doubt in ways we've never considered before—or rather, only once before, at the height of our **nuclear** terrors.

[9] A **tipping point** is a stage in a process when a big change takes place.
[10] The phrase **"glacial pace"** means moving very slowly, like a glacier.
[11] If you **undermine** something such as a feeling or a system, you make it less strong or less secure than it was before, often by a gradual process or by repeated efforts.

◄ An office building in Manhattan, New York, consumes energy into the night.

One of America's foremost climatologists, NASA scientist James Hansen, has given us a number to define the new boundary condition for life as we know it. He and his team studied the historical relation between atmospheric carbon and phenomena like sea-level rise (for all of human history until the industrial revolution, the air held no more than 275 parts per million CO_2) and then examined the latest real-time data from planet Earth. Their conclusion? "If humanity wishes to preserve a planet similar to that on which civilization developed and to which life on Earth is adapted . . . CO_2 will need to be reduced from its current 385 ppm [parts per million] to at most 350 ppm." We're too high now, in other words—that's why the Arctic is melting. Global warming is not a problem for the future; it's a crisis for this moment.

Instantly, 350 became the planet's most important number, the 98.6[12] of an entire globe. And scrambling back to it will require change on a scale hard to imagine. Essentially, says Hansen, we'd need to stop burning coal anywhere on the planet by 2030—and sooner in the developed world. (We could, alternatively, trap the carbon dioxide coming from power-plant smokestacks and store it underground somewhere, but that technology has been slow to develop.)

[12] **98.6** is the average human body temperature in degrees Fahrenheit.

Closing down the fossil-fuel economy would mean a loss of vast sums of money already sunk into old technology that still has decades of useful life; we'd need to stop bailing out brokerage houses and start bailing out coal-fired boilers. And unless you have a plan for convincing Americans, and the rest of the world, that they don't want refrigerators after all, it would mean we'd need to find other sources for all that energy.

That's the task of our generation.

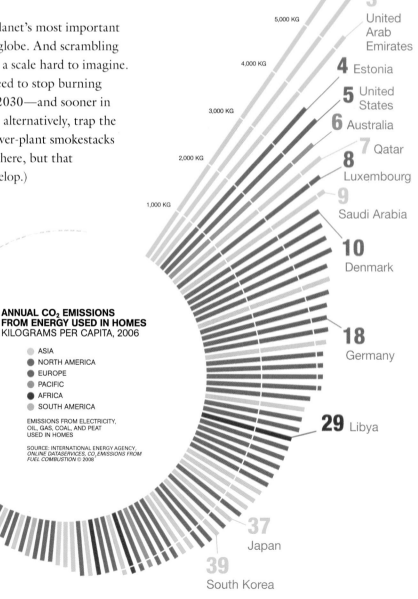

ANNUAL CO₂ EMISSIONS
FROM ENERGY USED IN HOMES
KILOGRAMS PER CAPITA, 2006

- ASIA
- NORTH AMERICA
- EUROPE
- PACIFIC
- AFRICA
- SOUTH AMERICA

EMISSIONS FROM ELECTRICITY,
OIL, GAS, COAL, AND PEAT
USED IN HOMES

SOURCE: INTERNATIONAL ENERGY AGENCY,
ONLINE DATASERVICES, CO₂ EMISSIONS FROM
FUEL COMBUSTION © 2008

A | Identifying Main Ideas. Write the correct paragraph letter (A, D, G, H, J) next to each main idea from the reading (1–5).

1. _____ We started global warming, but nature is increasing the problem.

2. _____ We thought everything was fine, but we realized that we're running out of oil and Earth is getting warmer.

3. _____ Energy is a very important part of our economy.

4. _____ We have to reduce our atmospheric CO_2 to a certain number.

5. _____ Other fuel options are not ideal.

B | Identifying Key Details. Write answers to the questions.

1. Why did living standards begin to double every few decades after the start of the 18th century?

_____

2. According to the Energy Information Administration, how much will energy use go up by 2030? _____

3. What is the effect of peak oil on oil prices?

_____

4. Why will global warming cause drought?

_____

5. Why might we need to redefine "glacial pace"?

_____

6. How will rising sea levels affect farmland?

_____

7. According to NASA scientist James Hansen, what is a safe amount of CO_2 to have in the atmosphere? _____

8. What do we need to do to reduce CO_2 in the atmosphere to this amount?

_____

_____

C | Interpreting Charts. Look at the chart on page 82. Discuss answers to the questions (1–3) with a partner.

1. What does this chart show?

2. Look at the top three countries. Why do you think they are ranked so high?

3. Is any of the information surprising? In what way?

👥 **D** | **Understanding a Process.** Work with a partner. Find these events in paragraph H. Put each event from the box in the correct place in the chart.

a. the fires created more carbon
b. the dead trees caused a lot of fires
c. the Arctic melted a second time
d. ocean passages opened
e. there was 22 percent less sea ice
f. carbon dioxide and methane were released
g. the Arctic melted
h. there were more pests
i. trees died
j. permafrost thawed in the subarctic tundra
k. more water absorbed more heat from the sun

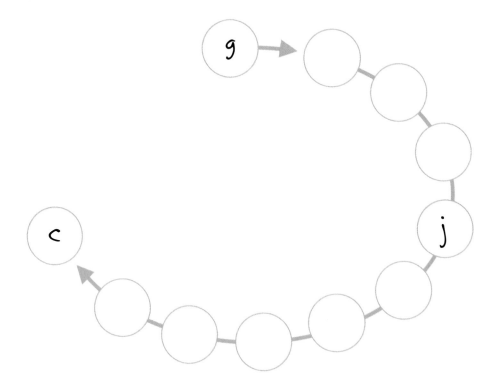

E | **Identifying Meaning from Context.** Find and underline the following words and phrases in the reading passage on pages 76–82. Use context to help you match each word or phrase with its meaning.

1. _____ Paragraph B: **in essence**
2. _____ Paragraph E: **all things being equal**
3. _____ Paragraph F: **happen to be**
4. _____ Paragraph H: **on offer**
5. _____ Paragraph H: **feedback loops**
6. _____ Paragraph H: **taking over**

a. if everything else is the same; if everything goes as expected
b. to be (in a situation) by chance
c. processes of cause and effect in which each effect causes another effect
d. basically
e. getting control of something
f. available

F | **Critical Thinking: Interpreting Figurative Language.** Read each sentence or phrase from the reading. Circle the best interpretation for each one.

1. (Paragraph B) All of a sudden, we could draw on the capital in the bank—those millions of years of deposits of ferns and plankton and dinosaurs that time had compressed into coal and gas and oil.

   a. The writer is comparing fossil fuels to money in a bank.

   b. The writer is comparing plants and dinosaurs to coal, gas, and oil.

2. (Paragraph B) We were, almost literally, like the lucky heirs of someone long dead and very rich whose will was finally deciphered.

   a. The writer is comparing fossil fuels with an inheritance from a relative who died long ago.

   b. The writer is comparing a rich relative with countries that consume the most energy.

3. (Paragraph B) Every one of our revolutions (the industrial, the chemical, the electronic, even the information) at its base owes its strength to this newfound blood now coursing through the veins of our economy.

   a. The writer is comparing revolutions in history with changes that lead to a strong economy.

   b. The writer is comparing the effect of fossil fuels on the economy with the effect of blood on a body.

4. (Paragraph D) Twenty years ago, if people thought of global warming at all, it was as an unlikely and distant threat. Five years ago, most people hadn't heard of peak oil. Now they are the twin jaws of a closing vise.

   a. The writer is comparing the effects of global warming and peak oil with the effects of being squeezed in a vise.

   b. The writer is comparing our consumption of fossil fuels, such as oil, with an animal using its jaws to tear apart food.

5. (Paragraph K) Instantly, 350 became the planet's most important number, the 98.6 of an entire globe.

   a. The writer is comparing 350 ppm of CO_2 in Earth's atmosphere with a high fever or an illness in a human being.

   b. The writer is comparing the goal of 350 ppm of CO_2 in Earth's atmosphere with the healthy temperature of a human being.

G | **Critical Thinking: Evaluating Reasons.** What are some reasons for using figurative language? How might it be more effective than literal language? Discuss your ideas with a partner.

Reading Skill: Recognizing a Writer's Tone

In written compositions, a writer's **tone** is his or her attitude toward a topic. A writer's tone can be objective or subjective.

Objective writing is neutral and formal, and provides facts and explanations. The tone is unbiased—the writer does not reveal any positive or negative feelings about a topic.

Subjective writing, which can be formal or informal, is commonly found in personal essays. The writer may include facts and explanations; however, the writer also provides his or her feelings, judgments, or opinions about those facts.

Recognizing the tone of a passage will help you understand how to interpret the information. Look carefully at the language the writer uses, and ask yourself these questions.

Does the writer . . .

- address the reader directly or use personal pronouns (*we, you, I*)?
- use strong, emotive, or figurative language (e.g., *unbelievable, a waste of time*)?
- use language that assumes the reader's agreement (e.g., *of course, clearly, obviously*)?
- use irony or sarcasm (saying or writing the opposite of what he or she means)?
- make any judgments, for example, saying something is good or bad?
- indicate his or her feeling or opinion about the topic, for example, optimism or pessimism?

If the answer is *yes* to any of these questions, the author's tone is probably subjective.

Look at the example of subjective tone from the reading. Here the author is making a judgment and being pessimistic.

*Curbing high gas prices with recurrent economic slumps is **probably not the smartest of remedies**.*

 A | **Identifying Tone.** The excerpts below are from the reading on pages 76–82. With a partner, discusswhat makes each one subjective. Use the information above as a guide.

1. Energy, of course, is not just another part of our economy.

2. But there were two little problems, new wrinkles that we hadn't considered before—and that we really didn't want to consider, even as they became more obvious

3. But there's little question where the future lies, which is why the cost of a barrel of oil spiked to $147 last year.

4. After all, we were taking millions of years' worth of stored carbon—all those old ferns and plankton—and pouring it into the atmosphere in the course of a few generations. Why wouldn't it cause problems?

5. One study published last fall said that a sea-level rise of six and a half feet this century was within the realm of possibility. That's a civilization-shaking number.

6. It puts the human enterprise in doubt in ways we've never considered before—or rather, only once before, at the height of our nuclear terrors.

7. Global warming is not a problem for the future; it's a crisis for this moment.

VIEWING

One Bryant Park, ▶
New York City.

POWERING CITIES

Before Viewing

A | **Using a Dictionary.** Here are some words and phrases you will hear in the video. Match each one with the correct definition. Use your dictionary to help you.

| make a dent | circulate | filter out | particulate | ventilation |

1. _____ a very small mass of solid or liquid matter (usually a pollutant)
2. _____ to move easily and freely through or around a place
3. _____ movement of air into and out of a building
4. _____ have a major effect (on something)
5. _____ clean something by passing it through a device

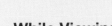 **B** | **Thinking Ahead.** In the U.S., buildings account for 40% of energy consumption. Why do you think buildings consume a lot of energy? How might large office buildings reduce their energy consumption? List ideas with a partner.

While Viewing

A | Watch the video about a green building. As you watch, check your answers to exercise **B**, above. Circle any ideas that are mentioned in the video.

B | Read questions 1–3. Think about the answers as you view the video.

1. How does the building's ventilation system affect the surrounding area?
2. What are two benefits of the building's rainwater collection system?
3. What is special about the building's windows?

After Viewing

A | Discuss answers to the questions 1–3 above with a partner.

B | **Critical Thinking: Synthesizing.** Do you think green buildings such as the one in the video will have much impact on the problems outlined on pages 76–82? Why, or why not?

GOAL: Writing a Summary Essay

In this lesson, you are going to plan, write, revise, and edit an essay on the following topic: *Write a summary of "Our Energy Challenge."*

A | Read the information in the box. Then choose the best synonym for each underlined word (1–3).

Language for Writing: Avoiding Plagiarism

When you write a summary, it's important to paraphrase; that is, to use your own words. One method is to use synonyms for words that are in the original text.

For example, look at this sentence from "Our Energy Challenge." Notice that some of the words can be replaced with synonyms.

The ~~boom~~ years of the 1990s saw our ~~mass prosperity,~~ and of course our ~~massive~~ energy use, ~~starting to spread to~~ Asia.

(handwritten annotations: growth / extreme wealth / vast / beginning to reach)

If you don't know a synonym for a word, you can use a thesaurus. However, it's important to make sure that the synonym that you choose matches the word in the context of your sentence. For example, *rise*, *increase*, and *explosion* are all synonyms for *boom*, but only *growth* works in the context of the sentence above.

Synonyms are useful for paraphrasing, but you may also need to change sentence structure and use different parts of speech. For example:

In the growth years of the 1990s, Asia began to experience the extreme wealth and vast energy use that we had been experiencing.

---

1. Twenty years ago, if people thought of global warming at all, it was as an unlikely and <u>distant</u> threat.

   a. distracted   b. far-off   c. unfriendly

2. Curbing high gas prices with <u>recurrent</u> economic slumps is probably not the smartest of remedies.

   a. frequent   b. chronic   c. repeated

3. It puts the human enterprise in doubt in ways we've never <u>considered</u> before—or rather, only once before, at the height of our nuclear terrors.

   a. judged   b. believed   c. contemplated

B | **Applying.** Find a synonym for one other word in each of the sentences in exercise **A**. Then rewrite each sentence, changing the sentence structure and using different parts of speech when possible.

Writing Skill: Writing a Summary

A summary is shorter than the original passage. When you write a summary, you report—in your own words—only the most important information from a passage in the same order that it is given in the original. Follow these steps to summarize successfully.

1. Read the passage once. As you read, underline the important facts. Then, without looking at it, write notes about the passage.
2. Reread the passage, comparing your notes against it to check your understanding. Correct any incorrect notes.
3. Use your notes to write a summary. Remember that the introductory statement in a summary is not quite the same as the thesis statement in a regular essay. The introductory statement is more like a restatement of the original author's main idea.
4. Compare your summary with the original. Make sure that your summary expresses the same meaning as the original.
5. Check your sentence structures and word choices. If your summary is very similar to the original, change your sentence structures and replace some content words (e.g., key nouns or noun phrases) with synonyms.

C | **Critical Thinking: Evaluating.** Read the summaries of paragraph **A** of "Our Energy Challenge." Answer the questions about the summaries below. With a partner, decide which summary is more successful. Why do you think so?

a   In "Our Energy Challenge," author Bill McKibben explains that the use of coal-powered engines had an enormous impact on Western economies. According to economist John Maynard Keynes, between the beginning of history until the start of the 18th century, living standards had merely doubled. After humans started using coal-powered engines at the turn of the 18th century, Western living standards began doubling every 30 or 40 years.

b   In "Our Energy Challenge," author Bill McKibben argues that energy is our economy. He explains that the economist John Maynard Keynes said that the human standard of living had doubled since the beginning of time until the 18th century. At that time, it began doubling every few decades. Why? Because we began using coal-powered engines at that time.

	Summary a	Summary b
1. Does the summary express the same meaning as the original?		
2. Is the language different from the language in the original?		
3. Are the structures different from the structures in the original?		
4. Is the summary shorter than the original?		

D | **Brainstorming.** Without looking back at the reading on pages 76–82, write down the main ideas and details that you can remember. Share your ideas with a partner.

Author's main idea	
How and when we started using fossil fuels	
Effect of fossil fuels on living standards	
Effects of fossil fuels on Earth	
What we have to do now	

E | **Taking Notes.** Now reread the article on pages 76–82. Compare the information with your notes from exercise **D** to check your understanding. Make any necessary corrections or additions.

F | **Vocabulary for Writing.** The words below can be useful when writing a summary. You can use these verbs to introduce an author's idea. Some are used to introduce an objective fact, while others introduce the author's opinion. Put each word into the correct category. Use a dictionary to help you.

analyzes	argues	believes	calls for	claims
demands	discusses	disputes	examines	explains
explores	focuses on	mentions	provides	questions
recommends	reports	requests	suggests	urges

Subjective	Objective

A | **Planning.** Follow the steps to make notes for your summary.

Step 1   Complete the introductory statement in the outline.

Step 2   Answer the questions to write a topic sentence for each of your body paragraphs.

Step 3   For each body paragraph, write two or three examples or details that support your topic sentence.

Step 4   As a conclusion, write down Bill McKibben's ideas for what he believes we need to do now.

Introductory statement:

In "Our Energy Challenge," author Bill McKibben _____

_____

1st body paragraph: How and when did we start using fossil fuels?

Topic sentence: _____

_____

Explanation and examples: _____

_____

_____

2nd body paragraph: What is the relationship between energy and our economy?

Topic sentence: _____

_____

Explanation and examples: _____

_____

_____

3rd body paragraph: How do fossil fuels affect Earth?

Topic sentence: _____

_____

Explanation and examples: _____

_____

_____

Concluding paragraph: What do we have to do now?

_____

_____

_____

B | **Draft 1.** Use your outline to write a first draft of your summary.

C | **Critical Thinking: Analyzing.** Read an essay that summarizes the article "A Cry for the Tiger" from Unit 2. Then follow the steps to analyze it. Discuss your answers with a partner.

In the article "A Cry for the Tiger," author Caroline Alexander argues that the beautiful and regal tiger is worth protecting, and that we need to find effective ways to keep it from disappearing.

According to Alexander, the tiger faces several threats. First, tigers are losing habitat because of quickly growing human populations. Second, this rapid population growth leads to poaching. Third, tiger parts are valuable in the black market. Finally, one of the least-discussed threats is the fact that strategies to protect tigers have been ineffective. In fact, experts estimated that there were about 8,000 tigers in the wild in the early 1980s. Now, decades later, there are fewer than 4,000.

Alexander explains that India is home to about 50 percent of the wild tiger population, and about one-third of these tigers live outside tiger reserves. In order for these tigers to survive in the wild, we need to ensure there are protected corridors of land between the safe areas. This way, the tigers outside of reserves can move freely without being killed by humans. Also, these corridors will allow tigers to mate and reproduce with tigers that live in different areas, resulting in greater genetic diversity. These corridors are necessary, but Alexander wonders if they are possible. Future infrastructure projects may make the creation of the corridors very difficult.

Alexander reports that the countries that have wild tigers want to protect the animals, but it's difficult to find an effective solution. Right now, there are many tiger-conservation programs, and a lot of money is spent on tiger protection. However, each program focuses on a different strategies. Alexander argues that we need to spend our money and energy on four specific issues in order to protect tigers in the long run: core breeding populations, tiger reserves, wildlife corridors, and safety from poaching and killing. She believes that we have to prioritize these four issues, especially the protection of a core breeding population, and not spend money on things like eco-development and social programs.

Is it possible not only to protect the remaining tigers but also to increase the wild tiger population? According to Alexander, most authorities believe that it is possible. But it won't be an easy fight. The author calls on tiger conservationists to work extremely hard and to remain determined in order to save the tiger from extinction.

Step 1 Underline the introductory statement. Does it correctly restate the original author's main idea?

Step 2 Does the order of the body paragraphs reflect the order of ideas in the original passage?

Step 3 Circle the details in each body paragraph. Do they reflect the important details in the original?

Step 4 Does the conclusion reflect the final ideas in the original?

D | Revising. Follow steps 1–4 in exercise **C** to analyze your summary of "Our Energy Challenge."

E | Peer Evaluation. Exchange your first draft with a partner and follow the steps below.

Step 1 Read your partner's essay and tell him or her one thing that you liked about it.

Step 2 Complete the outline showing the ideas that your partner's essay describes.

Introductory statement:

In "Our Energy Challenge," author Bill McKibben _____

_____

1st body paragraph: How and when did we start using fossil fuels?

Topic sentence: _____

_____

Explanation and examples: _____

_____

_____

2nd body paragraph: What is the relationship between energy and our economy?

Topic sentence: _____

_____

Explanation and examples: _____

_____

_____

3rd body paragraph: How do fossil fuels affect Earth?

Topic sentence: _____

_____

Explanation and examples: _____

_____

_____

Concluding paragraph: What do we have to do now?

_____

_____

_____

Step 3 Compare this outline with the one that your partner created in exercise **A** on page 91.

Step 4 The two outlines should be similar. If they aren't, discuss how they differ.

F | **Draft 2.** Write a second draft of your summary. Use what you learned from the peer evaluation activity and your answers to exercise **D**. Make any other necessary changes.

G | **Editing Practice.** Read the information in the box. Then find and correct one mistake with underlined synonyms in each of the paraphrases (1–3).

> When you use synonyms, remember to make sure your synonym:
> - has the same meaning as the original word.
> - fits in the context of the sentence. For example,
>
>   <u>energy</u> source: power ✓   vitality ✗   liveliness ✗

1. Original: The Energy Information Administration, an arm of the U.S. government, forecast last year that, <u>all things being equal</u>, <u>world</u> energy <u>consumption</u> would increase 50 percent by 2030.

   Paraphrase: According to the Energy Information Administration, if <u>everything goes as expected</u>, <u>global</u> energy <u>feeding</u> would go up 50 percent by 2030.

2. Original: But it's not at all <u>clear</u> where that energy can <u>come from</u> because we happen to be alive <u>at the moment</u> when the oil is <u>starting</u> to <u>run out</u>.

   Paraphrase: However, it's not <u>apparent</u> where we can <u>get</u> that energy, because <u>right now</u>, oil is <u>beginning</u> to <u>escape</u>.

3. Original: In November 2008, the International Energy Agency <u>estimated</u> that <u>production</u> from <u>the world's</u> oil fields was <u>declining</u> 6.7 percent a year.

   Paraphrase: In November 2008, the International Energy Agency <u>projected</u> an annual 6.7 percent <u>refusal</u> in oil production from <u>global</u> oil fields.

H | **Editing Checklist.** Use the checklist to find errors in your second draft.

Editing Checklist	Yes	No
1. Are all the words spelled correctly?		
2. Does every sentence have correct punctuation?		
3. Do your subjects and verbs agree?		
4. Have you used synonyms correctly?		
5. Are your verb tenses correct?		

I | **Final Draft.** Now use your Editing Checklist to write a third draft of your essay. Make any other necessary changes.

Working Together

Think and Discuss

1. In what situations do people work together in large groups to make decisions or solve problems?

2. What are some advantages of working together in large groups? What are some of the disadvantages?

▲ Stock exchanges, such as this one in Chicago, use the decision-making power of crowds to decide market prices.

Exploring the Theme

Read the information and discuss the questions.

1. How is the photo an example of collaboration?

2. In what ways did primitive people collaborate?

3. What are some modern examples of collaboration? What purposes do they serve?

People collaborate when they work together to accomplish a task. Collaboration among early humans helped to ensure their survival. For example, they used teamwork in order to find food and raise children. In the modern world, collaboration is a key feature in organizational settings such as businesses. Most organizational behavior experts agree that collaboration increases productivity. When people work together, they can use each other's knowledge to advance new ideas.

In recent years, collaboration has been greatly enhanced by the development of the Internet. In the past, people had to be in the same place in order to work together. Today, online collaboration allows people to accomplish a range of tasks collectively at any time and from any location. Crowdsourcing, which uses a network of a large number of people to help solve a problem, is increasing our scientific knowledge. Data collected from a crowdsourcing website called Cerberus, for example, is helping astronomers analyze satellite images of Mars.

What makes humans want to collaborate? James K. Rilling, an anthropologist at Emory University, looked at brain activity while participants were engaged in cooperative activities. His study showed that the desire to cooperate with others may be innate in humans. Researchers are also looking into ways to enhance human collaboration. Studies of the ways in which animal and insect groups—such as ants—collaborate may help us figure out ways to work together even more efficiently.

col | lab | o | ra | tion *noun*

Collaboration is the act of working together on a joint project.

◄ Collaboration among construction workers in El Kef, Tunisia, enables them to carry supplies to the top of a building site.

A | Building Vocabulary. Read the following paragraph. Use the context to guess the meaning of the words in **blue**. Then write each word next to its definition (1–7).

Insects may help us improve the way we deal with dangerous situations. Scientists around the world are studying insect behavior to create tiny robots that have many of the same **capabilities** as insects. Insects, for example, can fly in and land **precisely** on a tiny surface, and then flap their wings to fly off with amazing speed. One application for these tiny insectlike machines is in **defense**—robots will be able to scout battlefields and record images as they hover over dangerous areas. Engineers are also building ornithopters—aircraft that get all of their thrust and most of their lift from flapping wings. The flight mechanism of an ornithopter is essentially a **simulation** of the way that an insect flaps its wings to take off and fly. These **emergent** technologies offer several advantages. One benefit is that operators can **manipulate** the devices from a distance. As a result, they can stay out of harm's way while they perform dangerous missions in **unpredictable** environments, such as war zones.

1. _____: action taken to protect against attack; also, the organization of a country's armies and weapons

2. _____: to control, manage, or use carefully

3. _____: model; imitation of behaviors or processes

4. _____: skills or qualities

5. _____: not able to be known in advance

6. _____: coming into existence

7. _____: accurately and exactly

B | Building Vocabulary. Complete the definitions with the words from the box. Use a dictionary to help you.

complementary	coordinate	decentralized	declare	relevant

1. If people _____ something, they formally announce it.

2. Something that is _____ to a situation is important or significant.

3. To _____ with others is to work together efficiently.

4. A _____ system is one in which power is not in one place or individual, but spread out.

5. _____ things are different from each other, but they make a good combination.

C | **Using Vocabulary.** Write answers to the questions (1–3). Share your ideas with a partner.

1. What are some **capabilities** of groups versus individuals?

   _____

   _____

2. Think of a group that you belong to. Are the skills of the group members **complementary**? Give examples.

   _____

   _____

3. What are some **emergent** technologies today? How might they be useful?

   _____

   _____

Word Usage

Complementary describes things that go together well or that make something good even better: "The members of the team have **complementary** skills." *Complimentary* refers to a polite remark that you make to or about someone: "The manager's remarks about the team's work were very **complimentary**."

D | **Brainstorming.** Discuss your answers to these questions in a small group.

1. What are some examples of group behavior among animals? Think about insects, fish, and herd animals (such as buffalo).

   _____

   _____

2. For what kinds of jobs is collaboration very important?

   _____

   _____

E | **Predicting.** Look at the photos and captions on pages 100–105. Read paragraphs A and W. Then discuss your answers to the questions below with a partner. Check your predictions as you read the rest of the passage.

1. What animals might the passage discuss?

   _____

   _____

2. What aspects of their behavior might the passage discuss?

   _____

   _____

3. What human activities or inventions might the passage discuss?

   _____

   _____

4. What do you think is the main purpose of the article?

   _____

   _____

The Smart Swarm

by Peter Miller

> The study of swarms is providing insights that can help humans manage complex systems, from online search engines to military robots.

track 1-05

HOW DO THE SIMPLE ACTIONS of individuals add up to the complex behavior of a group? How do hundreds of honeybees make a critical decision about their hive if many of them disagree? What enables a school of herring to **coordinate** its movements so **precisely** it can change direction in a flash, like a single, silvery organism? The answer has to do with a remarkable phenomenon I call *smart swarm*.

A smart swarm is a group of individuals who respond to one another and to their environment in ways that give them the power, as a group, to cope with uncertainty, complexity, and change. Take birds, for example. There's a small park near the White House in Washington, D.C., where I like to watch flocks of pigeons swirl over the traffic and trees. Sooner or later, the birds come to rest on ledges of buildings surrounding the park. Then something disrupts them, and they're off again in synchronized flight.

The birds don't have a leader. No pigeon is telling the others what to do. Instead, they're each paying close attention to the pigeons next to them, each bird following simple rules as they wheel across the sky. These rules add up to a kind of swarm intelligence—one that has to do with precisely coordinating movement.

Craig Reynolds, a computer graphics researcher, was curious about what these rules might be. So, in 1986, he created a deceptively simple steering program called boids. In this simulation, generic birdlike objects, or boids, were each given three instructions: (1) avoid crowding nearby boids, (2) fly in the average direction of nearby boids, and (3) stay close to nearby boids. The result, when set in motion on a computer screen, was a convincing **simulation** of flocking,[1] including lifelike and **unpredictable** movements.

At the time, Reynolds was looking for ways to depict animals realistically in TV shows and films. (*Batman Returns* in 1992 was the first movie to use his approach, portraying a swarm of bats and an army of penguins.) Today he works at Sony doing research for games, such as an algorithm[2] that simulates in real time as many as 15,000 interacting birds, fish, or people.

By demonstrating the power of self-organizing models to mimic swarm behavior, Reynolds was also blazing the trail for robotics engineers. A team of robots that could coordinate its actions like a flock of birds could offer significant advantages over a solitary robot. Spread out over a large area, a group could function as a powerful mobile sensor net, gathering information about what's out there. If the group encountered something unexpected, it could adjust and respond quickly, even if the robots in the group weren't very sophisticated, just as ants are able to come up with various options by trial and error. If one member of the group were to break down, others could take its place. And, most important, control of the group could be **decentralized**, not dependent on a leader.

[1] When animals **flock**, they congregate and do things as a large group.
[2] An **algorithm** is a series of mathematical steps, especially in a computer program, that will give you the answer to a problem.

◄ Monarch butterflies in flight in Michoacan, Mexico

66 It's much harder for a predator to avoid being spotted by a thousand fish. 99

▲ Safety in numbers: A school of sardines acts as a single entity to defend against attack by an Atlantic sailfish.

"In biology, if you look at groups with large numbers, there are very few examples where you have a central agent," says Vijay Kumar, a professor of mechanical engineering at the University of Pennsylvania. "Everything is very distributed: They don't all talk to each other. They act on local information. And they're all anonymous. I don't care who moves the chair, as long as somebody moves the chair. To go from one robot to multiple robots, you need all three of those ideas."

Within five years, Kumar hopes to put a networked team of robotic vehicles in the field. One purpose might be as first responders. "Let's say there's a 911 call," he says. "The fire alarm goes off. You don't want humans to respond. You want machines to respond, to tell you what's happening. Before you send firemen into a burning building, why not send in a group of robots?"

Taking this idea one step further, computer scientist Marco Dorigo's group in Brussels is leading a European effort to create a "swarmanoid," a group of cooperating robots with **complementary** abilities: "foot-bots" to transport things on the ground, "hand-bots" to climb walls and **manipulate** objects, and "eye-bots" to fly around, providing information to the other units.

The military is eager to acquire similar **capabilities**. On January 20, 2004, researchers released a swarm of 66 pint-size robots into an empty office building at Fort A. P. Hill, a training center near Fredericksburg, Virginia. The mission: Find targets hidden in the building.

Zipping down the main hallway, the foot-long (30 cm) red robots pivoted this way and that on their three wheels, resembling nothing so much as large insects. Eight sonars[3] on each unit helped them avoid collisions with walls and other robots. As they spread out, entering one room after another, each robot searched for objects of interest with a small, Web-style camera. When one robot encountered another, it used wireless network gear to exchange information. ("Hey, I've already explored that part of the building. Look somewhere else.")

[3] **Sonar** is equipment that can detect the position of objects using sound waves.

In the back of one room, a robot spotted something suspicious: a pink ball in an open closet (the swarm had been trained to look for anything pink). The robot froze, sending an image to its human supervisor. Soon several more robots arrived to form a perimeter around the pink intruder. Within half an hour, all six of the hidden objects had been found. The research team conducting the experiment **declared** the run a success. Then they started a new test.

The demonstration was part of the Centibots project, an investigation to see if as many as a hundred robots could collaborate on a mission. If they could, teams of robots might someday be sent into a hostile village to flush out terrorists or locate prisoners; into an earthquake-damaged building to find victims; onto chemical-spill sites to examine hazardous waste; or along borders to watch for intruders. Military agencies such as DARPA (Defense Advanced Research Projects Agency)

have funded a number of robotics programs using collaborative flocks of helicopters and fixed-wing aircraft, schools of torpedo-shaped underwater gliders, and herds of unmanned ground vehicles. But, at the time, this was the largest swarm of robots ever tested.

"When we started Centibots, we were all thinking, this is a crazy idea, it's impossible to do," says Régis Vincent, a researcher at SRI International in Menlo Park, California. "Now we're looking to see if we can do it with a thousand robots."

In nature, of course, animals travel in even larger numbers. That's because, as members of a big group, whether it's a flock, school, or herd, individuals increase their chances of detecting predators, finding food, locating a mate, or following a migration route. For these animals, coordinating their movements with one another can be a matter of life or death.

▲ Swarm-bots work together using swarm theory.

"It's much harder for a predator to avoid being spotted by a thousand fish than it is to avoid being spotted by one," says Daniel Grünbaum, a biologist at **P** the University of Washington. "News that a predator is approaching spreads quickly through a school because fish sense from their neighbors that something's going on."

When a predator strikes a school of fish, the group is capable of scattering in patterns that make it almost impossible to track any individual. It might explode **Q** in a flash, create a kind of moving bubble around the predator, or fracture into multiple blobs,[4] before coming back together and swimming away.

That's the wonderful appeal of swarm intelligence. Whether we're talking about ants, bees, pigeons, or caribou, the ingredients of smart group behavior— **R** decentralized control, response to local cues, simple rules of thumb—add up to a shrewd strategy to cope with complexity.

"We don't even know yet what else we can do with this," says Eric Bonabeau, a complexity theorist **S** and the chief scientist at Icosystem Corporation in Cambridge, Massachusetts. "We're not used to solving decentralized problems in a decentralized way.

We can't control an **emergent** phenomenon like traffic by putting stop signs and lights everywhere. But the idea of shaping traffic as a self-organizing system, that's very exciting."

Social and political groups have already adopted crude swarm tactics. During mass protests eight years ago in Seattle, anti-globalization activists used mobile **T** communications devices to spread news quickly about police movements, turning an otherwise unruly crowd into a "smart mob" that was able to disperse and re-form like a school of fish.

The biggest changes may be on the Internet. Consider the way Google uses group smarts to find what you're looking for. When you type in a search query, Google surveys billions of Web pages on its index servers[5] to identify the most **relevant** ones. It **U** then ranks them by the number of pages that link to them, counting links as votes (the most popular sites get weighted votes since they're more likely to be reliable). The pages that receive the most votes are listed first in the search results. In this way, Google says, it "uses the collective intelligence of the Web to determine a page's importance."

[4] A **blob** is an indistinct or a shapeless form or object.
[5] A **server** is a part of a computer network that does a particular task such as maintaining an index of files.

▼ Living in a herd enables reindeer to survive the cold winter in Oymyakon, Siberia.

Wikipedia, a free collaborative encyclopedia, has also proved to be a big success, with millions of articles in more than 200 languages about everything under the sun, each of which can be contributed by anyone or edited by anyone. "It's now possible for huge numbers of people to think together in ways we never imagined a few decades ago," says Thomas Malone of MIT's new Center for Collective Intelligence. "No single person knows everything that's needed to deal with problems we face as a society, such as health care or climate change, but collectively we know far more than we've been able to tap so far."

Such thoughts underline an important truth about collective intelligence: Crowds tend to be wise only if individual members act responsibly and make their own decisions. A group won't be smart if its members imitate one another, slavishly follow fads, or wait for someone to tell them what to do. When a group is being intelligent, whether it's made up of ants or attorneys, it relies on its members to do their own part. For those of us who sometimes wonder if it's really worth recycling that extra bottle to lighten our impact on the planet, the bottom line is that our actions matter, even if we don't see how.

Wisdom of the Herd

Group behavior can be vital for herd animals to avoid predators. Karsten Heuer, a wildlife biologist, and his wife, Leanne Allison, were studying a large caribou herd in Canada. When they spotted a wolf creeping toward the caribou, they noted that the herd responded with a classic swarm **defense**.

"The nearest caribou [to the wolf] turned and ran, and that response moved like a wave through the entire herd until they were all running," Heuer said. Each animal turned and ran as the wolf approached it. In the end, the herd escaped over the ridge, and the wolf was left panting and gulping snow.

The herd's evasive maneuvers displayed not panic, but precision. Every caribou knew when it was time to run and in which direction to go, even if it didn't know exactly why. No leader was responsible for coordinating the rest of the herd. Instead, each animal was following simple rules evolved over thousands of years of wolf attacks.

A | **Identifying Main Ideas.** Answer the questions about the main ideas in the reading passage on pages 100–105. Write the paragraph letter(s) in which you find the answers.

1. What is a "smart swarm"? Explain it in your own words.

_____

_____ Paragraph _____

2. How does being part of a large group help animals?

_____

_____ Paragraph _____

3. What are the three key aspects of swarm intelligence?

_____

_____ Paragraph _____

4. How are search engines and online encyclopedias examples of collaboration?

_____

_____ Paragraph _____

B | **Identifying Purpose.** Write the correct paragraph letter(s) (B–C, D-N, O–Q, R, T–V, W) next to each purpose (1–6).

1. _____ to give examples of human activities and organizations that use swarm intelligence

2. _____ to summarize the three key ingredients of swarm intelligence

3. _____ to connect the topic with our everyday decisions and actions

4. _____ to show the purpose of swarm behavior for animals

5. _____ to give an example of swarm intelligence that most people are familiar with

6. _____ to describe technology applications that mimic swam behavior

C | **Identifying Meaning from Context.** Find and underline the following expressions in the reading passage on pages 100–105. Use context to match each expression with its meaning.

1. _____ **add up to** (Paragraph A)
2. _____ **set in motion** (Paragraph D)
3. _____ **blazing the trail** (Paragraph F)
4. _____ **by trial and error** (Paragraph F)
5. _____ **flush out** (Paragraph M)
6. _____ **a matter of life or death** (Paragraph O)
7. _____ **the bottom line** (Paragraph W)

a. to force people or animals to leave a place where they are hiding
b. the essential idea
c. to start; to initiate an action
d. to equal
e. something that is extremely important
f. doing something for the first time as an example for others
g. in a manner that requires experimentation

D | Summarizing Key Details. Complete the concept map with information from paragraphs B–N of "The Smart Swarms."

Swarm Intelligence

Example in the Animal World

- Flocks of _____ are an example of swarm intelligence.
- Characteristics: There's no _____.
  They watch and follow _____.

Human Applications

Entertainment

- Boids use bird rules to create computer graphics for entertainment.
- Rules: (1) avoid crowding, (2) _____,
  (3) _____

Robot Teams

- **Advantages:** Robot teams respond more effectively than individual robots. If one breaks down, another can _____.
- **Rules:** Everything is distributed; they use _____; they're anonymous.
- **Examples:** _____ for moving things; _____ to climb walls and manipulate things; _____ to fly around and collect _____.
- **Military uses:** Centibots could locate terrorists or _____; help people in disasters, such as _____; find and analyze dangerous _____ after chemical spill.

CT Focus: Evaluating Sources

Writers often quote experts—people who work in areas that are relevant to the topic—to support their main ideas. When you read a quote, ask yourself: What are the credentials of the person being quoted? What is his or her background or affiliation? How is his or her experience or expertise relevant to the topic? Then ask yourself how the quotes support the writer's main ideas.

E | Critical Thinking: Evaluating Sources. Find the following quotes in "The Smart Swarm." Note the paragraph where you find each one.

1. _____ "In biology, . . . you need all three of those ideas."

2. _____ "It's much harder for a predator . . . to avoid being spotted by one. . . .
   News that a predator is approaching spreads quickly . . . that something's going on."

3. _____ "It's now possible . . . in ways we never imagined a few decades ago. . . .
   No single person . . . we know far more than we've been able to tap so far."

Now discuss answers to questions 1–2 with a partner.

1. What are the credentials of the people being quoted? How is their experience or expertise relevant to the topic?

2. What main ideas do the quotes support? Match each quote (1–3) with one of the following ideas.

   a. _____ Swarm behavior is a survival strategy.

   b. _____ Modern technology has facilitated swarm intelligence among humans.

   c. _____ Decentralization is a key aspect of swarm intelligence.

F | Critical Thinking: Analyzing Information. In a small group, discuss your answers to the following questions about paragraph W.

1. What is the role of the individual in a group situation? What example of individual behavior does the author give? Give your own examples of this idea.

2. What does the author mean when he says, "The bottom line is that our actions matter, even if we don't see how"? What are some additional examples of this idea?

Reading Skill: Identifying Subjects in Complex Sentences

It's important for overall reading comprehension to be able to identify the subjects of sentences. However, it's sometimes difficult to locate the subject in complex sentences. One type of complex sentence has a main clause and a dependent clause.

main clause   dependent clause

A team of robots that could coordinate its actions like a flock of birds could offer significant advantages over a solitary robot.

The subject of the sentence is in the main clause. In this case, the subject is "A team of robots."

Another type of complex sentence has a main (independent) clause and a participial phrase or a prepositional phrase.

participial phrase   main clause

Spread out over a large area, a group could function as a powerful mobile sensor net.

prepositional phrase   main clause

In the back of one room, a robot spotted something suspicious.

A | Identifying Subjects in Complex Sentences. Underline the main clauses in these sentences from the reading passage, and circle the subjects.

1. Taking this idea one step further, Marco Dorigo's group in Brussels is leading a European effort to create a "swarmanoid," a group of cooperating robots with complementary abilities.

2. The result, when set in motion on a computer screen, was a convincing simulation of flocking, including lifelike and unpredictable movements.

3. [A] smart swarm is a group of individuals who respond to one another and to their environment in ways that give them the power, as a group, to cope with uncertainty, complexity, and change.

4. In this simulation, generic birdlike objects, or boids, were each given three instructions.

5. News that a predator is approaching spreads quickly through a school because fish sense from their neighbors that something's going on.

6. Whether we're talking about ants, bees, pigeons, or caribou, the ingredients of smart group behavior—decentralized control, response to local cues, simple rules of thumb—add up to a shrewd strategy to cope with complexity.

B | Applying. Scan paragraphs K, M, T, U, and W to find more examples of complex sentences. When you find them, underline the subjects.

Before Viewing

A | Using a Dictionary. Here are some words and expressions you will hear in the video. Match each one with the correct definition. Use a dictionary to help you.

churned	a menace	plagued by	tilled the soil	vanished

1. _____ disappeared
2. _____ prepared land for growing plants
3. _____ something that is likely to cause harm
4. _____ affected by unpleasant things
5. _____ moved around violently

B | Thinking Ahead. What insects can cause serious problems for humans? What kinds of problems do they cause? With a partner, note your ideas below.

_____

_____

While Viewing

Read questions (1–5). Think about the answers as you view the video.

1. What mystery is researcher Jeff Lockwood trying to solve?
2. In what parts of the world today do people suffer from locusts?
3. How are locusts dangerous to people? According to the video, how much do they eat?
4. Where did the American locusts lay their eggs? What probably happened to the locust eggs?
5. How might solving the mystery of the American locust swarm help people in Africa?

After Viewing

A | Discuss the answers to the questions in "While Viewing" with a partner.

B | Critical Thinking: Synthesizing. How might the American locust swarm have used swarm intelligence?

◄ Painted locust, Galapagos Island National Park, Ecuador

GOAL: Writing a Comparative Essay

In this lesson, you are going to plan, write, revise, and edit a comparative essay on the following topic: **Compare the ways in which two groups collaborate.**

A | **Brainstorming.** Make a list of groups that collaborate. For each one, note some details about how and why the members of the group collaborate. Think about both human and animal groups.

Groups that Collaborate	Examples of Collaboration
Humans: students, workers,	students - use social media to research a group project,
Animals: fish, bees,	

B | **Planning.** To write a comparative essay, choose the subjects you are going to compare and think of points to use to compare them (these can be points of similarity or difference). For this task, first choose two subjects from exercise **A** that you want to compare.

Subjects to compare: _____ and _____

C | **Vocabulary for Writing.** The words and phrases below can be useful when writing about collaboration. Find them in the reading passage on pages 100–105, and use context to guess their meanings. Then complete each definition with the correct word or phrase from the box.

cope with (paragraphs B, R)	**collective intelligence** (paragraphs U, V, W)
dependent on (paragraph F)	**interacting** (paragraph E)
self-organizing (paragraphs F, S)	**synchronized** (paragraph B)

1. If two activities are _____, they are made to happen together, at the same time.

2. _____ is the intellectual power of a group of people, as opposed to an individual.

3. To _____ a situation or problem is to manage to deal with it.

4. If you are _____ something or someone, you need that object or person in order to succeed or be able to survive.

5. A _____ system creates its own order without a leader or a controlling mechanism.

6. When people are _____, they are doing something together and having an effect on each other together.

Free Writing. Write for five minutes. Describe an example of human collaborative behavior. Try to use some of the words in exercise **C**.

D | Read the information in the box. Then complete the sentences (1–5). Change the underlined words and phrases to the correct parallel form. (There may be more than one possible answer.)

Language for Writing: Using Parallel Structure

When you are listing items or comparing them, the items must follow the same grammatical pattern. This is called **parallel structure**. Parallel structure applies to adjectives, noun phrases, verb phrases, and clauses.

Adjectives:
The robots will be able to penetrate **dangerous** and **unpredictable** environments.

Noun phrases:
Both **anti-globalization protests** and **crowd funding activities** are examples of collective intelligence.

Verb phrases:
The boids were programmed to **avoid** crowding, **fly** in the same direction, and **stay** close to each other.

Clauses:
Human groups make good decisions **when members act responsibly** and **when they maintain independence**.

You may need to paraphrase ideas using a different part of speech.

Example: It's important for individuals in groups to make their own decisions. They should act in a responsible way.

Parallel restatement: It's important for individuals in groups **to make** their own decisions and **to act** in a responsible way.

In this case, *they should act* becomes *to act* in order to match the first verb in the list; *in a responsible way* becomes *responsibly*.

1. Micro-robots are almost undetectable because they are tiny. They also <u>move quickly</u>.

   Micro-robots are almost undetectable because they are tiny and _____.

2. The ants continue to go in the same direction. They continue <u>communicating</u> with each other.

   The ants continue to go in the same direction and _____ with each other.

3. Examples of swarm intelligence that artificial systems have simulated include fish schooling. There are systems that also simulate <u>the way animals herd</u> and <u>birds flock</u>.

   Examples of swarm intelligence that artificial systems have simulated include fish schooling, _____, and _____.

4. Non-dominant wolves are responsible for looking after the young. They also must <u>help</u> the pack find food.

   Non-dominant wolves are responsible for looking after the young and _____ the pack find food.

5. Bees and ants are similar in terms of how they assign roles to each other and how they communicate with each other. <u>Avoiding predators is another similarity</u>.

   Bees and ants are similar in terms of how they assign roles to each other, how they communicate with each other, and _____.

E | Look back at your Free Writing. Did you write any sentences using parallel structures? If not, add some to your sentences.

Writing Skill: Organizing a Comparative Essay

There are two main ways to organize a comparative essay: the **block method** and the **point-by-point method**.

With the **block method**, you discuss all the points of comparison about one subject and then discuss those same points about the other subject. The outline looks like this:

> Introduction + Thesis Statement
> 1st Body Paragraph: Subject A
> > Point 1
> > Point 2
> > Point 3
> 2nd Body Paragraph: Subject B
> > Point 1
> > Point 2
> > Point 3
>
> Conclusion

Writing Skill: Organizing a Comparative Essay *(continued)*

With the **point-by-point method**, you discuss each subject in terms of the points of comparison you've chosen. If there are three points of comparison, the outline looks like this:

Introduction
Thesis Statement
1st Body Paragraph: Point 1
                          Subject A
                          Subject B
2nd Body Paragraph: Point 2
                          Subject A
                          Subject B
3rd Body Paragraph: Point 3
                          Subject A
                          Subject B
Conclusion

Remember to use a variety of linking phrases to introduce your points. For example:

To show similarity: *in the same way, likewise, similarly, both, the same is true for . . . , have . . . in common*

To show contrast: *on the other hand, whereas, however, although, in contrast*

F | **Critical Thinking: Analyzing.** Look at the notes for a comparative essay on behavior and discuss these questions with a partner.

1. What two subjects are being compared?

2. What are possible points of comparison?

3. How would you make a block outline for these notes? How would you make a point-by-point outline?

4. The writer has not found all the details and examples necessary to develop the body paragraphs. What other details would you look for to add to either outline?

Notes

Humans and some nonhuman primates cooperate and share with each other.

Humans live in groups; orangutans live alone, but other nonhuman primates (e.g., chimpanzees, apes) live in groups; humans share food (e.g., ??); monkeys do not.

Humans can learn from experience; chimpanzees cannot—they learn by observation; human parents teach children; pass on knowledge verbally and by demonstration; chimpanzees also pass on knowledge—not verbally but by demonstration.

Humans create and use tools for specific purposes; chimpanzees do, too (e.g., sticks to catch ants for food); apes observed using tree trunks as bridges to cross streams.

A | Planning. Follow the steps to make notes for your essay.

Step 1 Look at your notes in exercise **A**, page 111. What points can you use to compare your two subjects? Choose at least three.

Step 2 Complete the thesis statement in the space below.

Step 3 Choose an organizational method for your essay and write it in the space below.

Step 4 Depending on your organizational method, complete the outline in the space below.

Step 5 Write a topic sentence for each body paragraph. Remember to relate these to the key concepts of the thesis statement in your introduction.

Step 6 For each paragraph, note some examples or details that illustrate your comparison.

Step 7 Note some ideas for a conclusion.

Thesis Statement: _____

Organization Method (Block or point-by-point): _____

1st Body Paragraph

Topic sentence: _____

_____

Examples: _____

_____

_____

2nd Body Paragraph

Topic sentence: _____

_____

Examples: _____

_____

_____

(for point-by-point method)
3rd Body Paragraph

Topic sentence: _____

_____

Examples: _____

_____

_____

Ideas for Conclusion: _____

B | Draft 1. Use your outline to write a first draft of your essay.

C | **Critical Thinking: Analyzing.** Work with a partner. Read the following essay, which compares the behavior of two insects. Then follow the steps to analyze the essay.

Both honeybees and ants are social insects that live in groups called colonies. They survive by means of their collective intelligence. Their decision-making power is distributed throughout the group; that is, no one ant or bee makes decisions for the group. Instead, they work together. As Deborah M. Gordon, a biologist at Stanford University, says, "Ants aren't smart. Ant colonies are." The same is true for bee colonies. Although bees and ants are quite different physically, they have a lot in common in terms of their social behavior. Specifically, honeybees and ants have similar roles within the colony, both have communication systems, and both have the capacity for learning.

Both individual ants and bees have specific roles within their communities. Ants live in colonies of up to a million individuals. There may be one or more queens, which are fertile females. There is also a number of fertile males. Their job is to mate with the queen. Most ants in a colony are wingless, sterile females called workers who care for the young, forage for food, and do just about every other job that helps the colony survive. Honeybee colonies, with fewer individuals than ant colonies—up to about 60,000—have roles similar to those in ant colonies. There are sterile female worker bees that perform a variety of functions, and fertile drones whose only job is to mate with the queen. The main difference in the social organizations of bees and ants is that while ant colonies can have more than one queen, there is only one queen in a bee colony.

Sophisticated communication systems that ensure survival are found among both bees and ants. Ants communicate by using chemicals called pheromones, which can alert others to danger or lead them to a food source. For example, worker ants set out in search of food. When they find a promising source, they let the rest of the colony know how to find it by leaving a trail of pheromones on the way back to the colony. The other ants pick up the message using their sense of smell. Bees, on the other hand, use movement to communicate with each other. Worker bees send messages to each other by means of a "dance." Different speeds of movement send different messages. For example, when worker bees called scouts go out to find a new home for the colony, they return and do a dance for the other worker bees that indicates the location of the new home and also how suitable it is. The faster the scouts dance, the better the new location is.

Honeybees and ants are both capable of learning. Zhang, et al (2005) found that bees can be trained to learn and remember a route to a food source. The researchers also found that bees can be taught to recognize camouflaged objects and use the concepts of "sameness" and "difference" to accomplish certain tasks. Ants have also shown the ability to learn. Recent research has shown that ants, in fact, teach their skills to each other. Franks and Richardson (2006) found that some ants take a partner when they go foraging for food. The leader "teaches" the route to the next ant by speeding up or slowing down so the follower doesn't get lost.

As we can see, the social behavior of honeybees and ants is quite similar. Both coordinate complex actions and accomplish crucial survival tasks by cooperating in groups consisting of a large number of individuals. Unintelligent as they may be as individuals, as groups they often show amazing brilliance as they go about their everyday activities.

References

Franks, N.R., & Richardson, T. (2006). Teaching in tandem-running ants. Nature, 439 (7073), 153.

Miller, Peter (2010). The Smart Swarm (p. 6). New York, NY: Penguin Group.

Zhang, S., Bock F., Si A., Tautz J., & Srinivasan, M.V. (2005, April 5). Visual working memory in decision making by honey bees. Proceedings of the National Academy of Sciences of the United States of America, 102 (14), 5250–5255.

Step 1 Underline the thesis statement and circle its key words.

Step 2 Underline the topic sentences of the body paragraphs. Does the order of the paragraphs reflect the order of ideas in the thesis? Did the writer use the block method or point-by-point?

Step 3 Circle the key words in the topic sentences. Do they reflect the key words in the thesis statement? Are they repetitions or paraphrases?

Step 4 What details in the body paragraphs does the writer use to develop the key concepts in each of the topic sentences?

D | Revising. Follow the steps (1–4) in exercise **C** to analyze your own essay.

E | Peer Evaluation. Exchange your first draft with a partner and follow the steps below.

Step 1 Read your partner's essay and tell him or her one thing that you liked about it.

Step 2 Complete the outline showing the ideas that your partner's essay describes. (The outline continues on page 118.)

Thesis Statement: _____

Organizational Method (Block or point-by-point): _____

1st Body Paragraph

Topic sentence: _____

_____

Examples: _____

_____

_____

2nd Body Paragraph

Topic sentence: _____

_____

Examples: _____

_____

_____

(for point-by-point method)
3rd Body Paragraph

Topic sentence: _____

_____

```
Examples: _____

_____

_____

Ideas for Conclusion: _____
```

Step 3   Compare this outline with the one that your partner created in exercise **A** on page 115.

Step 4   The two outlines should be similar. If they aren't, discuss how they differ.

F | **Draft 2.** Write a second draft of your essay. Use what you learned from the peer evaluation activity and your answers to exercise **D**. Make any other necessary changes.

G | **Editing Practice.** Read the information in the box. Then improve the parallel structure in each of the sentences (1–4).

> Remember to use parallel structure in sentences with two or more adjectives, noun phrases, or verb phrases. That is, keep the same part of speech for all items in a list, paraphrasing when necessary.

1. The robots were programmed to look for anything pink and they avoided running into each other.

2. Coyotes and wolves are similar in terms of how they choose a leader and they hunt together.

3. The robots are quick, responsive, and it is impossible to detect them.

4. Ants survive by cooperating and they make group decisions.

H | **Editing Checklist.** Use the checklist to find errors in your second draft.

Editing Checklist	Yes	No
1. Are all the words spelled correctly?		
2. Does every sentence have correct punctuation?		
3. Do your subjects and verbs agree?		
4. Have you used parallel structure correctly?		
5. Are your verb tenses correct?		

I | **Final Draft.** Now use your Editing Checklist to write a third draft of your essay. Make any other necessary changes.

ACADEMIC PATHWAYS

Lesson A: Inferring an author's attitude
Understanding verbal phrases

Lesson B: Writing introductions and conclusions
Writing a personal opinion essay

Think and Discuss

1. What are some benefits of being able to use a second or foreign language?

2. What do you think is the most difficult thing about learning a new language?

▲ Young students in Shanghai, China, read a lesson from their textbook. Globally, there are estimated to be more than one billion students learning English.

▲ Schoolchildren pose for a photo near Hustain Nuruu, Mongolia. Although Russian is still the most commonly spoken foreign language among older people in Mongolia, increasing numbers of young Mongolians are studying English.

Exploring the Theme

Read the information and discuss the questions.

1. What are two reasons that parents in many countries send their children to English–language schools at an early age?

2. At what age do you think people should begin learning a second language? Why?

3. Do you think language learning becomes easier or more difficult as you get older? In what ways?

According to many linguists, children are able to learn new languages more easily than adults. Research shows that we may be born with a natural, or innate, ability to learn language. Changes that occur in the brain as we age may make language learning progressively more difficult. This doesn't mean that older people cannot learn a language. In fact, adults have some advantages over children in a classroom setting. For example, they can already read, they have the discipline to study, and they are usually motivated to learn.

However, since children appear to have an innate language-learning ability, there is a trend worldwide for countries to introduce foreign language learning at an earlier age. In Europe, most children begin studying English between the ages of six and nine. In Korea, where English-language kindergartens are growing in popularity, children often begin learning English between the ages of three and five. And in China, some parents send children as young as two years old to private language schools to learn English. Only time will tell whether studying English at such an early age is an effective strategy.

A | Building Vocabulary. Read the following paragraph about reading fiction. Use the context to guess the meanings of the words and phrases in **blue**. Then write the correct word or phrase to complete each definition (1–7).

For many people, certain fiction books have a special meaning. A story that a person read when they were young, for example, can make them **nostalgic** for their childhoods. But why should people read fiction? Those who enjoy reading may not have ever considered that question. They simply find reading fiction **irresistible**—when they see a new novel, they want to pick it up. If you love fiction, you might feel it's impossible to feel any other way about books. **On the contrary**, some people are not interested in fiction at all. They find reading fiction **monotonous** and boring, or they feel the formal language of literature is **unintelligible**. Many people prefer reading nonfiction or the news because the language is more **straightforward** and easier to understand. However, some researchers believe they have found **definitive** proof that reading fiction is actually beneficial for the human brain. A research team at the University of Toronto led by professor Maja Djikic, for example, found that people who read literary fiction become more open-minded and creative in their thinking, and are also better able to deal with uncertainty.

1. You use "_____" when you have just said or implied that something is not true and you are going to say that the opposite is true.

2. Something that is _____ is very boring because it has a regular, repeated pattern that never changes.

3. If you describe something as "_____," you approve of it because it is easy to do or understand.

4. Something that is _____ provides a firm conclusion that cannot be questioned.

5. When you feel _____, you think affectionately about the past.

6. If you describe something as "_____," you mean that it is so good or attractive that you cannot stop yourself from liking it or wanting it.

7. If something is _____, it is impossible to understand because it is not written or pronounced clearly or because its meaning is confused or complicated.

B | Building Vocabulary. Complete the definitions (1–5) with words from the box. Use a dictionary to help you.

| contemporaries | cryptic | excluded | integral | perpetual |

1. A(n) _____ remark or message contains a hidden meaning or is difficult to understand.

2. A(n) _____ act, situation, or state is one that seems never to end or change.

3. If someone is _____ from a place or an activity, that person is prevented from entering it or joining it.

4. Someone's _____ are people who are or were alive at the same time as that person is or was.

5. Something that is a(n) _____ part of something is an essential part of that thing.

Word Link

con = *together, with*: **con**done, **con**sensus, **con**temporary, **con**vene

Word Link

crypt = *hidden*: **crypt**, **crypt**ic, en**crypt**

C | Using Vocabulary. Answer the questions. Share your ideas with a partner.

1. Are there any types of food or drink that you find **irresistible**?
2. Do any books, songs, or foods make you **nostalgic** for the past? Explain.
3. For what reasons might someone be **excluded** from an activity or a place?

D | Brainstorming. Discuss your answers to this question in small groups: What are some different ways to learn new words or phrases in a foreign language?

studying song lyrics _____

_____

_____

E | Predicting. Read the first and last paragraphs of the reading passage on pages 124–127. What kind of reading is this? Circle your answer and check your prediction as you read the rest of the passage.

a. a scientific article

b. a personal essay

c. a short fiction story

The Secret Language

by Daisy Zamora

▲ A replica Mississippi steamboat heads out from New Orleans.

> ## Language can be a barrier— but also a window through which we experience new visions of the world.

track **2-01**

A THE FIRST WORDS I HEARD IN ENGLISH were from my grandmother Ilse Gamez, who I remember as a magical presence in my childhood. Everything about her seemed legendary to me. Among the stories she used to tell, my favorites were about her life in New Orleans, where she and her family arrived from Europe and where she spent her childhood until she was 14, when they set sail again, bound for Nicaragua, fulfilling her parents' wish to return **definitively** to their country of origin. Her stories of New Orleans were filled with references and names in English (frequently also in French), and those mysterious words, so different from the ones I heard in everyday speech, produced in me an **irresistible** fascination. They sounded like strange music, an exotic melody coming from faraway fantastic places where life had an agitation,[1] a rhythm, an acceleration[2] unknown and unheard-of in the peaceful world I shared with my parents, sisters, and brothers. We were all part of an enormous family that included grandparents, great-aunts, great-uncles, uncles, aunts, and first cousins, as well as a second and third level of blood relatives, followed immediately by all the other people in the category of relatives included in the family universe and its state of **perpetual** expansion.

B The English I heard from my grandmother Ilse had nothing to do with the English I was taught in kindergarten through songs teaching us to count from one to ten, or the language that appeared in the English textbooks we studied in the second and third grade of primary school: "See Dick. See Jane. See Spot. See Puff. See Spot run. See Puff jump." For me, that English lacked charm, instead sounding like the noise of my shoes crunching in the gravel of the schoolyard during recess. But that other English, the one my grandmother and her sisters spoke, possessed multiple and varied registers[3] that always amazed me. Sometimes it sounded like the trill of a bird, light and crystalline, and at other times flowed in dense, thick amber[4] like honey. It would

rise in high notes with the lonely, **nostalgic** sound of a flute, or swirl in a whirlpool like the frenzied crowds I imagined rushing around the streets of a big metropolis . . .

C Before long, my ears began to discern another way of speaking the language. It was not the **cryptic** and fantastic English full of attractions and mystery that I loved to listen to, nor the tiresome, repetitious one that sounded like a cart struggling over cobbled streets. No, this other English expressed things in a different way that was not enigmatic[5] and seductive, nor dumb and **monotonous**, but dramatic and direct: whatever the characters said, happened simultaneously. That is to say, a word was an act; words and action occurred at the same time. An activity was named at the very moment it took place. For example, a character that was evidently crying, would say: "I'm crying." Another one, obviously hiding something, would declare: "I'll hide this!"

D It was the English I started to learn from cartoons on television, where the characters expressed thoughts, emotions, and feelings in a **straightforward** way: "Out! Help! Stop it! Don't go away! I'll be back! Let's go!" I learned phrases and words that communicated necessity in a fast, precise manner. The language of cartoons also introduced me to metaphors. The first time I heard characters in a downpour shouting their heads off with the phrase "The sky is falling, the sky is falling!" I believed it was the proper way to say in English, "It's a downpour," or "It's raining very hard."

---

[1] If someone is in a state of **agitation**, he or she is very worried or upset.

[2] An **acceleration** is an increase in speed.

[3] A **register** is a variety of language used in a specific situation.

[4] **Amber** is a hard yellowish substance that is often used as jewelry.

[5] Someone or something that is **enigmatic** is mysterious and difficult to understand.

◀ Mardi Gras celebrations on Bourbon Street in the French Quarter of New Orleans

E I had no choice but to learn yet another kind of English from cowboy movies, because my cousins constantly used it in their games. Also, in a mechanical way, I learned by heart the English names for all the plays in baseball, the most popular sport in Nicaragua.

F Gradually, the English that was so dull to me in the first grades of school expanded and deepened, with readings transforming it into a beautiful language that kept growing inside, becoming more and more a part of my consciousness, invading my thoughts and appearing in my dreams. Understanding the language and speaking it in a natural way became **integral** to my being, my way of appreciating literature, especially poetry, and enjoying the lyrics of my favorite songs, which I was able to repeat perfectly.

G Literature classes were my favorite. To act as a character in any of Shakespeare's plays, or to read an O. Henry short story out loud to my classmates, or a chapter of Robert Louis Stevenson's *Treasure Island*, or a sonnet[6] by Elizabeth Barrett Browning, brightened my day. At the school library, I discovered, among other authors, Walt Whitman, Emily Dickinson, and Edna St. Vincent Millay, then Carl Sandburg and William Carlos Williams. Further along, I encountered William Blake, the sisters Brontë, Jane Austen, and Ernest Hemingway. Years later, while at university, I read the Americans William Faulkner, Ezra Pound, and Gertrude Stein, and the Irish authors William Butler Yeats and James Joyce.

H Along with my intense reading, I also became a music lover and put together a rather substantial collection of Frank Sinatra and Beatles records—my favorites, although my interests included many other groups and singers in English. From that deep relationship with the language, I wound up with what I considered a broad and complex knowledge of English, the sounds of which captivated me in the first years of life.

I But my true encounter with living English (that is, the one spoken in everyday life) happened in the United States, where I went to spend my school vacations in

---

[6] A **sonnet** is a special type of poem with 14 lines and regular rhymes.

Middletown, Connecticut. My first impression of the country was completely idyllic. My aunt and uncle's house, where I would stay for three months, was a beautiful and comfortable three-story building, an old New England manor with a gorgeous garden out back, an orchard, a stable with horses, and a pond full of trout. A dense woods of birch and a variety of pine and spruce trees, crisscrossed by narrow paths dotted with wildflowers, went around the edge of that peaceful pond in a landscape that seemed like it was lifted from a fairy tale. Those vacations are part of the happy memories of my life because I also had the unforgettable experience of going to New York City for the first time and visiting the 1964 World's Fair. However, what is most deeply imprinted in my memory of that first visit to the U.S. is the shock I received from the language I had believed I understood and spoke correctly.

Almost immediately, I realized that my English, that is, the English through which I expressed myself, sounded strange to everybody. My cousins, not to mention their friends, listened to me with surprise or mocking looks. In turn, their English was almost **unintelligible** to me because they spoke, of course, in teenage slang. When one of my cousins couldn't stand it anymore, she told me that I was a weirdo, that I spoke like a philosopher, some sort of Socrates or something, and asked me to make an effort to try to talk like normal people so I could make some friends. She didn't have a clue about the extreme anguish I was going through trying to understand what was being said around me, trying to decipher everything I misunderstood, assuming one thing

for another. Desolate, I thought about the abundant literature I had read up to then, and the songs I had worked so hard to memorize. It was all worthless for learning to speak practical English that would help me establish bonds with boys and girls my own age. **On the contrary**, the vocabulary I learned from books, especially from the poetry that taught me to love the language, had no place in the everyday speech of my **contemporaries**.

To be accepted by everybody, I started paying extreme attention to how I expressed myself and to the words I chose. I anxiously searched for ways to adapt my way of speaking, imitating what I heard from others, so I wouldn't be **excluded** from their conversations or activities. I understood that if I didn't do that, I would be left on the fringes of the main current, the mainstream where all U.S. teenagers lived, with space only for themselves. The barrier was not easy to cross, and when I couldn't do it, my consolation was to take refuge in the library of the house, where I read, during that first vacation, an English translation of Fyodor Dostoevsky's *Crime and Punishment*.

I was 14 years old when I went to the States for the first time—the same age as my grandmother Ilse when she watched New Orleans fade into the distance from the deck of a steamship—and ever since then I've understood what it means to live in direct contact with a language through the people who speak it, through their culture, and through their vision of the world.

▼ The 1964 World's Fair in New York City

Writers of the World

During her first vacation overseas, Daisy Zamora describes seeking refuge in her family library, where the literary treasures included an English translation of Dostoevsky's *Crime and Punishment*. Today, as shown below, Dostoevsky remains one of the world's most translated authors. Several other of Zamora's favorite writers appear in this Top 50: Shakespeare, Stevenson, and Hemingway have been translated from English into many other languages.

In this UNESCO compilation of the most translated authors, size of last name corresponds to the number of translations (listed below name). Color indicates language of original publication.

■ English ■ German ■ French ■ Russian ▨ Danish
▨ Ancient Greek ▨ Italian/Latin/Polish ▨ Swedish

Dostoyevsky is an alternate spelling of *Dostoevsky*

A | Identifying Main Ideas. In the reading on pages 124–127, Zamora describes the different ways she experienced English. Write the correct paragraph letter(s) next to each method (1–6).

A/B	B	C/D	F/G	H	I/J

1. _____ by reading literature

2. _____ by encountering native speakers in the U.S. (her cousins)

3. _____ as a child, from her family (grandmother)

4. _____ from TV and movies

5. _____ from her school

6. _____ by listening to music

B | Identifying Key Details. Match each type of English (1–5) with Zamora's description of it.

1. her grandmother's English   _____ a. impossible to understand

2. the English in primary school   _____ b. mysterious words

3. the English in cartoons   _____ c. a fast, precise manner

4. the English of literature   _____ d. lacked charm

5. the English of her cousins   _____ e. brightened her day

CT Focus: Inferring an Author's Attitude

An author's use of language can help us understand his or her **attitude** toward, or feelings about, a subject. For example, in personal essays or narratives, writers often use figurative or sensory language to convey their feelings now or in the past. When Zamora describes her grandmother as "a magical presence in my childhood," we can infer that she had—and probably still has—a warm and loving feeling toward her grandmother, even though she doesn't state that explicitly.

C | Critical Thinking: Inferring an Author's Attitude. Write answers to the questions (1–4) and discuss your answers with a partner.

1. How does Zamora describe her grandmother's English? What does she compare it to? What can we tell about her feelings about this language?

   _____

   _____

   _____

2. What does Zamora tell us about the English she learned at school? What two sounds does she compare it to? What can we infer about her feelings about this type of language?

_____

_____

_____

3. What adjectives and phrases does Zamora use to describe her childhood vacation home in Connecticut? What does she compare the landscape to? What can we infer about her feelings toward that place today?

_____

_____

_____

4. How does Zamora describe her experience of speaking with teenagers in the United States? Who does Zamora's cousin compare her to? What can we infer about how Zamora felt at that time?

_____

_____

_____

D | **Identifying Meaning from Context.** Find and underline the following phrases in the reading passage on pages 124–127. Use context to help you identify the meaning of each phrase (1–8). Then match each phrase with its definition.

1. _____ Paragraph A: **unheard-of**

2. _____ Paragraph B: **had nothing to do with**

3. _____ Paragraph D: **shouting their heads off**

4. _____ Paragraph H: **wound up with**

5. _____ Paragraph J: **not to mention**

6. _____ Paragraph J: **didn't have a clue**

7. _____ Paragraph J: **had no place in**

8. _____ Paragraph K: **on the fringes of the main current**

a. didn't know anything about
b. yelling loudly
c. left out or excluded from the most popular group
d. was completely unrelated to
e. eventually had
f. nonexistent
g. plus; in addition
h. didn't belong in

E | **Critical Thinking: Analyzing Types of Language.** Find one example of teenage language from the reading. Add four more examples of English words or phrases that teenagers say. Then discuss how the English found in literature and textbooks is different from teenage English. Complete the chart and share your ideas in a small group.

Teenage Language	How Is the Language in Literature Different?	How Is the Language in Textbooks Different?

F | **Personalizing.** Write an answer to the question below. Then share your answer in a small group.

How does being a language learner help you understand Zamora's essay?

_____

_____

_____

_____

_____

_____

Reading Skill: Understanding Verbal Phrases

Verbals are forms of verbs that are used as other parts of speech. The three kinds of verbals are present participles (*going, speaking*), past participles (*scared, surprised*), and infinitives (*to speak, to try*). A verbal phrase is a phrase that begins with a verbal. Writers often use verbal phrases to vary their sentence patterns and to combine short sentences. Verbal phrases are sometimes separated from the rest of the sentence with commas.

***Speaking slowly**, she gave me directions to the train station.* =
She spoke slowly. She gave me directions to the train station.

*I had a whole conversation in Spanish, **surprised I was able to communicate at all**.* =
I had a whole conversation in Spanish. I was surprised I was able to communicate at all.

***To learn Japanese quickly**, I didn't allow myself to speak English for a month.* =
I wanted to learn Japanese quickly. I didn't allow myself to speak English for a month.

A | **Analyzing.** Underline the verbal phrases in these sentences from the reading. Some sentences have more than one verbal phrase. Then write answers to the questions. Share your answers with a partner.

Example: For me, that English lacked charm, <u>instead sounding like the noise of my shoes crunching in the gravel of the schoolyard during recess.</u>

What does the verbal phrase describe? _____ the type of English _____

1. The first time I heard characters in a downpour shouting their heads off with the phrase "The sky is falling, the sky is falling!"

    Who does the verbal phrase describe? _____

2. Gradually, the English that was so dull to me in the first grades of school expanded and deepened with readings transforming it into a beautiful language that kept growing inside, becoming more and more a part of my consciousness, invading my thoughts and appearing in my dreams.

    What activity does the first verbal phrase describe? _____

    What do the second and third verbal phrases describe? _____

3. She didn't have a clue about the extreme anguish I was going through trying to understand what was being said around me, trying to decipher everything I misunderstood, assuming one thing for another.

    Who do the three verbal phrases describe? _____

4. To be accepted by everybody, I started paying extreme attention to how I expressed myself and to the words I chose.

    What does the verbal phrase do: ask a question, give a reason, or describe a thing? _____

Kenyans in New York

▲ A tour bus drives through Times Square in New York City.

Before Viewing

A | **Using a Dictionary.** Here are some words and phrases you will hear in the video. Match each word or phrase with the correct definition. Use your dictionary to help you.

| grab (something) | graze like cows | stretch (our) legs |

1. _____ (*informal*) eat snacks throughout the day in place of full meals
2. _____ walk around after sitting for a long period of time
3. _____ get; pick up quickly

B | **Thinking Ahead.** Imagine you are from a small rural community and you are arriving in a large city for the first time. What things might you find surprising? Make a list with a partner.

While Viewing

A | Watch the video about two Kenyans visiting New York City. As you watch, check your answers to exercise **B**, above. Circle the topics that are mentioned in the video.

B | Read questions 1–4. Think about the answers as you view the video.

1. What are some things that surprised the two visitors from Kenya?
2. What new words and phrases did the Kenyans pick up from their guide?
3. How does one Kenyan compare an ATM with a goat?
4. Do you think these men would find your hometown more or less surprising than New York City?

After Viewing

A | Discuss your answers to the questions 1–4 above with a partner.

B | **Critical Thinking: Synthesizing.** Consider the challenges that the Kenyans and Daisy Zamora had when they came to the United States for the first time. In what ways were their experiences similar and different? Who do you think had more difficulty adapting? Why?

GOAL: Writing a Personal Opinion Essay

In this lesson, you are going to plan, write, revise, and edit an essay on the following topic:
Write an opinion essay about the best way to learn a language.

Language for Writing: Adding Information with Verbal Phrases

You can add information to your sentences and vary your sentence patterns by using verbal phrases.

A present or past participial verbal phrase consists of a verbal with an adverb or an adverbial phrase (a phrase that modifies a verb). You can use a present or past participial verbal phrase like an adjective. It can modify a noun, a pronoun, or a whole clause.

pronoun   present participial verbal phrase
He looked totally confused, **staring at the teacher with his mouth open**.

past participial verbal phrase   pronoun
***Totally confused**, he stared at the teacher with his mouth open.*

An infinitive verbal phrase consists of an infinitive verb with an object or other modifier. Infinitive verbal phrases often express reasons or purposes. They can also modify a whole clause.

infinitive verbal phrase   clause
***To improve his grade**, he hired a tutor.*

infinitive verbal phrase   clause   infinitive verbal phrase
To improve his grade**, he hired a tutor **to help him study.

(Do not use a comma if the infinitive phrase comes at the end of the sentence.)

A | Circle the correct verbal phrase to complete each sentence (1–4).

1. **To teach / Teaching / Taught** their children to read, parents have to make it a point to read aloud books that are interesting to their children.

2. **To excite / Exciting / Excited** by the events in a story, children have a purpose for listening as someone reads to them—they need to find out what happens next.

3. **To look / Looking / Looked** for meaning as they listen, children begin to learn that reading has value.

4. **To increase / Increasing / Increased** vocabulary, children need to hear and read words they don't know.

B | Analyzing. Find the features (a–f) in the following introduction and conclusion. Underline them and write the correct letter next to each feature. Share your answers with a partner.

a. thesis statement

b. general information about the topic

c. surprising statement, interesting question, quotation, or story

d. restatement of thesis

e. explanation of how points fit together

f. final thought

Writing Skill: Writing Introductions and Conclusions

The first paragraph of an essay—the introductory paragraph—includes the thesis statement and general information about the essay topic. To grab the reader's attention, you can start with a surprising statement, an interesting question, a quotation, or a brief story.

The last, or concluding, paragraph of an essay should give the reader a sense of completeness. The conclusion usually includes a restatement of the thesis, an explanation of how the points made in the paper fit together, and a final thought about the topic. This final thought can take the form of a provocative question or a prediction about the future.

Introduction:

Nelson Mandela once said, "If you talk to a man in a language he understands, that goes to his head. If you talk to him in his own language, that goes to his heart." In other words, you can only truly communicate with another person if you speak that person's language. While the ability to communicate with someone who speaks a different language is a great benefit of language learning, I believe that studying a second language can improve our lives in other ways.

Conclusion:

Learning anything new can increase our knowledge and experience of life. However, language learning benefits us in several ways, even if we never plan to use a second language. Studying a second language can improve our reading skills and listening skills in our own language. Having better reading and listening skills can make us better students. Studies show that language learning can also improve our memories and our problem-solving skills. These abilities can help us in school, at work, and in life in general. Moreover, scientists have recently discovered that studying a second language can actually change the brain's shape. These changes can help us become better thinkers. Considering all these benefits of learning a new language, why would anyone choose not to study a second language?

C | **Brainstorming.** Refer back to your ideas for exercise **D** on page 123. Choose the three best methods for learning English. Complete the chart below with reasons that each method is effective. Include some examples from your own experience. Share your ideas with a partner.

Methods			
Reasons and Examples			

D | **Vocabulary for Writing.** You can use phrases such as "I think," "I believe," and "In my opinion" to introduce your opinion. However, varying your phrases can add interest to your writing. Some of the phrases below can introduce personal opinions, and some can introduce general opinions. Write each phrase in the correct column in the chart.

As far as I'm concerned,	It is thought that	Some people say that
In my experience,	. . . is generally considered to be . . .	Speaking for myself,
It is accepted that	Personally, I think	

Personal Opinion	General Opinion

A | **Planning.** Decide which of the methods you listed on page 123 is best. Follow the steps to make notes for your essay.

Step 1 Make notes for your introduction in the outline.

Step 2 Write your thesis statement.

Step 3 For each topic sentence, write one reason why the method you chose is effective.

Step 4 For each body paragraph, note examples or details that support your topic sentence. Include an example of a personal experience in at least one paragraph.

Step 5 Make notes for your conclusion.

Introduction: _____

_____

Thesis statement: _____

1st body paragraph:

Topic sentence: _____

_____

Examples or details: _____

_____

2nd body paragraph:

Topic sentence: _____

_____

Examples or details: _____

_____

3rd body paragraph:

Topic sentence: _____

_____

Examples or details: _____

_____

Conclusion:

Restatement of thesis: _____

Final thought: _____

B | **Draft 1.** Use your outline to write a first draft of your essay.

C | Critical Thinking: Analyzing. Work with a partner. Read the following opinion essay, which discusses the best way to teach children to read. Then follow the steps to analyze the essay.

Author Emilie Buchwald once said, "Children are made readers on the laps of their parents." I agree with her statement, and I think that some children very easily begin reading on their own as a result of having been read to by their parents. But, in my experience, it's not always that straightforward. Many children have difficulty with reading comprehension or are not interested in reading because they think it's boring. I believe that to teach these children to read, parents, teachers, and other responsible adults have to make it a point to read aloud books that are interesting to the children and are slightly above the children's reading level.

When books are interesting, children understand that reading can be exciting and, as a result, they pay attention. Excited by the events in a story, children have a purpose for listening as someone reads to them—they need to find out what happens next. That purpose can increase reading comprehension. When children begin reading on their own and are given books that they will enjoy, they have a purpose for reading, which will motivate them to try to understand what they're reading.

Even books without exciting stories can be interesting if children can connect the books to their own lives. Relatable characters and events give children something to discuss after a book is finished. This shows children that books can teach them something. Looking for meaning as they listen along, children begin to learn that reading has value. Traditionally, it was thought that children have to first learn to read, and then read to learn. In other words, children have to learn the sounds of letters first and then learn that the letters can form words with meaning. Personally, I think that it's never too early to start equating reading with learning. As far as I'm concerned, children as young as two or three years old can begin to understand that books can teach them something.

When children start to read by themselves, it can still be helpful to read to them, especially if the books that are read to them are a bit higher than their reading level. To increase vocabulary, children need to hear and read words that they don't know. Confused or puzzled by unfamiliar words, children will push themselves to learn because the words are relevant to the story. When parents or teachers realize that they've just read an unfamiliar word, they should resist explaining the definition right away. Rereading the surrounding sentences slowly, they encourage children to try to use context to guess the meaning of the word, teaching them an important skill they can use throughout their reading lives.

When children are encouraged to see books and stories as tools that can excite them, teach them, and take them to new worlds, they are motivated to read. This motivation goes a long way toward creating strong readers. Reading interesting books that are higher than a child's reading level can help build a strong desire to read and an understanding of what words have to offer. Surfing the Internet, reading information on social networking sites, and clicking on links to read entertaining blog posts, people read more these days than they ever have in the past. In the future, the need for strong reading skills will probably increase. Therefore, understanding the value of reading at a very young age can only benefit children in the future.

Step 1 Underline the thesis statement.

Step 2 Circle the surprising statement, interesting question, quotation, or story in the introduction.

Step 3 Underline the topic sentences of the body paragraphs.

Step 4 Circle each reason in the body paragraphs.

Step 5 Label the features of the conclusion (restatement of thesis, explanation, final thought).

D | **Revising.** Follow steps 1–5 in exercise **C** to analyze your opinion essay.

E | **Peer Evaluation.** Exchange your first draft with a partner and follow these steps.

Step 1 Read your partner's essay and tell him or her one thing that you liked about it.

Step 2 Complete the outline showing the ideas that your partner's essay describes.

Introduction: _____

_____

Thesis statement: _____

1st body paragraph:

Topic sentence: _____

_____

Examples or details: _____

_____

2nd body paragraph:

Topic sentence: _____

_____

Examples or details: _____

_____

3rd body paragraph:

Topic sentence: _____

_____

Examples or details: _____

_____

Conclusion:

Restatement of thesis: _____

Final thought: _____

Step 3 Compare this outline with the one that your partner created in exercise **A** on page 137.

Step 4 The two outlines should be similar. If they aren't, discuss how they differ.

F | Draft 2. Write a second draft of your essay. Use what you learned from the peer evaluation activity and your answers to exercise **D**. Make any other necessary changes.

G | Editing Practice. Read the information in the box and find and correct one mistake with verbal phrases in each sentence (1–5). Then write the letter for the type of mistake you find.

When you use verbal phrases, remember:
- verbal phrases modify nouns, pronouns, or whole clauses.
- to separate a verbal phrase from a clause with a comma.
- you don't need a comma if an infinitive verbal phrase comes at the end of a sentence.

Types of mistakes:

a. no noun, pronoun, or clause after the verbal phrase
b. unnecessary comma
c. missing comma

1. _____ Taking classes every night, learned a lot quickly.

2. _____ You can take private lessons, to learn a new language.

3. _____ Living in a bilingual household I learned Spanish easily.

4. _____ To improve your pronunciation you have to practice.

5. _____ Watching TV in English, learned a lot of natural language.

H | Editing Checklist. Use the checklist to find errors in your second draft.

Editing Checklist	Yes	No
1. Are all the words spelled correctly?		
2. Does every sentence have correct punctuation?		
3. Do your subjects and verbs agree?		
4. Have you used verbal phrases correctly?		
5. Did you vary your phrases for introducing an opinion?		
6. Are your verb tenses correct?		

I | Final Draft. Now use your Editing Checklist to write a third draft of your paper. Make any other necessary changes.

Resources and Development

ACADEMIC PATHWAYS

Lesson A: Identifying a writer's point of view
Understanding cohesion (II)
Lesson B: Researching and note-taking
Writing an expository essay

◀ A woman in
Iringa, Tanzania,
uses her solar
light to chase
away hyenas.

Think and Discuss

1. What factors are important for a country's economic development?
2. What resources does your country have? What resources does it lack?

141

Exploring the Theme

A. Look at the map and key. Then answer the questions.

  1. What regions have the highest concentrations of low-income people? What regions have the highest concentrations of high-income people?

  2. What makes the average incomes of China and India fall into the lower middle-class range?

B. Read the information on development and discuss your answers to the questions.

  1. What does development mean, in terms of economics?

  2. How do developing and developed countries differ?

  3. What is one way to rate a country's level of development?

NORTH AMERICA

New York

Los Angeles

Mexico City

AMAZON

BASIN

SOUTH AMERICA

Rio de Ja

São Paulo

Buenos Aires

○ City with population of 10 million or more

0 mi   1000
0 km   1000

MAP DATA: OAK RIDGE NATIONAL LABORATORY
LANDSCAN 2009 (POPULATION DENSITY)

Global Development

Where and How We Live

The map shows population density; the brightest points are the highest densities. Each country is colored according to its average annual gross national income per capita, using categories established by the World Bank. Some nations—such as economic powerhouses China and India—have an especially wide range of incomes. But as the two most populous countries, both are lower middle class when income is averaged per capita.

LOW INCOME LEVEL		LOWER MIDDLE		UPPER MIDDLE		HIGH	
$995 or less a year		$996 to $3,945		$3,946 to $12,195		$12,196 or more	
100 1,000 10,000		100 1,000 10,000		100 1,000 10,000		100 1,000 10,000	
People per square mile		People per square mile		People per square mile		People per square mile	

Defining Development

In economics, **development** is often used to refer to a change from a traditional economy to one based on technology. A traditional economy usually centers on individual survival. Families and small communities often make their own food, clothing, housing, and household goods. The economies of developing countries often rely heavily on agriculture. Developing countries also rely on raw materials, which can be traded to developed countries for finished goods. These raw materials include oil, coal, and timber.

Developed countries have economies that are more diverse. Their economies rely on many different people and organizations performing specialized tasks. Agriculture and raw materials represent only part of the economy of a developed country. Other sectors include manufacturing, banking and finance, and services such as hairdressing and plumbing. This vast economy results in a great variety of goods and services.

One way to rate a country's level of development is by the total value of goods and services the country produces, divided by the number of people in the country. This is called the gross national income (GNI) per capita.

A | Building Vocabulary. Read the following paragraph. Use the context to guess the meanings of the words in **blue**. Then write each word next to its definition (1–6).

    For people in developing nations, solar-powered devices can offer several **distinct** advantages. The availability of low-cost solar lamps, for example, means longer working hours—and therefore more employment opportunities—as well as better security at night. In recognition of this move toward solar energy, an organization in Uganda—Solar Sister—is turning local women into solar entrepreneurs. Solar Sister participants sell solar-powered products such as lamps and phone chargers. The women can start with only **rudimentary** business skills, because Solar Sister provides training. In addition, women can start a business with no initial financial **investment**, because Solar Sister provides products for them to sell when they begin. The women can then repay the cost of their starter products once their businesses get going. A successful entrepreneur can make up to $540 in **annual** income. One success story is a Ugandan woman named Grace. **Revenue** from her solar sales business tripled the family income, **thereby** allowing all of her children to attend school.

1. _____: yearly

2. _____: noticeable, important; separate

3. _____: use of money for income or profit

4. _____: money that a company earns

5. _____: basic; not at a high level

6. _____: by this means

▲ A student uses a solar light to study.

B | Building Vocabulary. Complete the definitions (1–6) with the words and phrase from the box. Use a dictionary to help you.

> denied   evolutionary   military intervention
> minority   orientation   tensions

1. The _____ of a thing is its position relative to something else.

2. _____ occurs when armed forces—such as an army—go into a place to solve a conflict.

3. If you are _____ something, you cannot do it or have it.

4. "_____" describes a process of gradual change and development.

5. _____ are feelings that occur where there is a possibility of violence or conflict.

6. A _____ is a smaller number or part of things in a larger group.

C | Using Vocabulary. Answer the questions. Share your ideas with a partner.

1. What kinds of **tensions** do you hear about currently in the news?

2. What do you think is the minimum **annual** income that people in your country need to live well?

3. Do you think **military intervention** can ever be the best way to resolve a political conflict? Why, or why not?

D | Brainstorming. Discuss your answers to these questions in small groups.

What do you know about Africa? What comes to mind when you think about Africa?

E | Predicting. Look at the image on pages 146–147. Then read the first and last sentences of each paragraph of the reading passage (pages 146–151). Discuss your answers to these questions (1–3) with a partner. Check your ideas as you read the rest of the passage.

1. Describe the location and geographical orientation of the continent of Africa. How does its orientation appear to be different from that of other continents?

2. What topics will the article probably discuss? Geography? History? Both geography and history?

3. Will the article discuss problems? Solutions? Both problems and solutions?

Word Partners

Use **tension** with verbs, nouns, and adjectives:
(*v.*): **ease** tension, **relieve** tension;
(*n.*): **source of** tension; (*adj.*): **racial** tension, **ethnic** tension

THE SHAPE OF
AFRICA
by Jared Diamond

The hope for Africa's future lies with its abundant human and natural resources.

track 2-02

A

ASK SOMEONE TO TELL YOU quickly what they associate with Africa and the answers you'll get will probably range from "cradle of humankind" and "big animals" to "poverty" and "tribalism." How did one continent come to embody such extremes?

B

Geography and history go a long way toward providing the explanations. Geographically, Africa resembles a bulging sandwich. The sole continent to span both the north and south temperate zones,[1] it has a thick tropical core lying between one thin temperate zone in the north and another in the south. That simple geographic reality explains a great deal about Africa today.

C

As to its human history, this is the place where some seven million years ago the **evolutionary** lines of apes and protohumans[2] diverged. It remained the only continent our ancestors inhabited until around two million years ago, when *Homo erectus* expanded out of Africa into Europe and Asia. Over the next 1.5 million years, the populations of those three continents followed such different evolutionary courses that they became **distinct** species. Europe's became the Neandertals, Asia's remained *Homo erectus*, but Africa's evolved into our own species, *Homo sapiens*. Sometime between 100,000 and 50,000 years ago, our African ancestors underwent some further profound change. Whether it was the development of complex speech or something else, such as a change in brain wiring, we aren't sure. Whatever it was, it transformed those early *Homo sapiens* into what paleoanthropologists[3] call "behaviorally modern" *Homo sapiens*. Those people, probably with brains similar to our own, expanded again into Europe and Asia. Once there, they exterminated or replaced or interbred with Neandertals and Asia's hominins and became the dominant human species throughout the world.

[1] **Temperate zones** are areas between the tropics and the polar circle.
[2] A **protohuman** is an early human ancestor.
[3] **Paleoanthropologists** are scientists who study human fossils.

In effect, Africans enjoyed not just one but three huge head starts over humans on other continents. That makes Africa's economic struggles today, compared with the successes of other continents, particularly puzzling. It's the opposite of what one would expect from the runner first off the block. Here again, geography and history give us answers.

It turns out that the rules of the competitive race among the world's humans changed radically about 10,000 years ago, with the origins of agriculture. The domestication of wild plants and animals meant our ancestors could grow their own food instead of having to hunt or gather it in the wild. That allowed people to settle in permanent villages, to increase their populations, and to feed specialists—inventors, soldiers, and kings—who did not produce food. With domestication came other advances, including the first metal tools, writing, and state societies.

The problem is that only a tiny **minority** of wild plants and animals lend themselves to domestication, and those few are concentrated in about half a dozen parts of the world. As every schoolchild learns, the world's earliest and most productive farming arose in the Fertile Crescent of southwestern Asia, where wheat, barley, sheep, cattle, and goats were domesticated. While those plants and animals spread east and west in Eurasia, in Africa they were stopped by the continent's north-south **orientation**. Crops and livestock tend to spread much more slowly from north to south than from east to west because different latitudes require adaptation to different climates, seasonalities, day lengths, and diseases. Africa's own native plant species—sorghum, oil palm, coffee, millets, and yams—weren't domesticated until thousands of years after Asia and Europe had agriculture. And Africa's geography kept oil palm, yams, and other crops of equatorial Africa from spreading into southern Africa's temperate zone. While South Africa today boasts[4] the continent's richest agricultural lands, the crops grown there are mostly northern temperate crops, such as wheat and grapes, brought directly on ships by European colonists. Those same crops never succeeded in spreading south through the thick tropical core of Africa.

[4] To **boast** is to possess a feature that is a source of pride.

▼ Betsileo woman carrying a bundle of rice in Madagascar

▲ Botswana's San people, or Bushmen, are some of the world's last surviving hunter-gatherers.

The domesticated sheep and cattle of Fertile Crescent origins took about 5,000 years to spread from the Mediterranean down to the southern tip of Africa. The continent's own native animals—with the exception of guinea fowl and possibly donkeys and one breed of cattle—proved impossible to domesticate. History might have turned out differently if African armies, fed by barnyard-giraffe meat and backed by waves of cavalry[5] mounted on huge rhinos, had swept into Europe to overrun its mutton-fed soldiers mounted on puny horses. That this didn't happen was no fault of the Africans; it was because of the kinds of wild animals available to them.

Ironically, the long human presence in Africa is probably the reason the continent's species of big animals survive today. African animals co-evolved with humans for millions of years, as human hunting prowess gradually progressed from the **rudimentary** skills of our early ancestors. That gave the animals time to learn a healthy fear of man and, with it, a healthy avoidance of human hunters. In contrast, North and South America and Australia were settled by humans only within the last tens of thousands of years. To the misfortune of the big animals of those continents, the first humans they encountered were already fully modern people, with modern brains and hunting skills. Most of those animals—woolly mammoths, saber-toothed cats, and in Australia marsupials[6] as big as rhinoceroses—disappeared soon after humans arrived. Entire species may have been exterminated before they had time to learn to beware of hunters.

Unfortunately, the long human presence in Africa also encouraged something else to thrive—diseases. The continent has a well-deserved reputation for having spawned some of our nastiest ones: malaria, yellow fever, East African sleeping sickness, and AIDS. These and many other human illnesses arose when microbes causing disease in animals crossed species lines to evolve into a human disease. For a microbe already adapted to one species, to adapt to another can be difficult and require a lot of evolutionary time. Much more time has been available in Africa, cradle of humankind, than in any other part of the planet. That's half the answer to Africa's disease burden; the other half is that the animal species most closely related to humans—those whose microbes required the least adaptation to jump species—are the African great apes and monkeys.

[5] A **cavalry** is a group of soldiers who ride horses.
[6] **Marsupials** are animals such as kangaroos. Female marsupials carry their babies in pouches on their bellies.

Africa continues to be shaped in other ways by its long history and its geography. Of mainland Africa's ten richest countries—the only ones with **annual** per capita gross domestic products over $3,500—nine lie partly or entirely within its temperate zones: Egypt, Libya, Tunisia, Algeria, and Morocco in the north; and Swaziland, South Africa, Botswana, and Namibia in the south. Gabon is Africa's only tropical country to make the list. In addition, nearly a third of the countries of mainland Africa (15 out of 47) are landlocked, and the only African river navigable[7] from the ocean for long distances inland is the Nile. Since waterways provide the cheapest way to transport cumbersome[8] goods, geography again thwarts Africa's progress.

All these factors can lead to the question: "Is the continent, or at least its big tropical core, doomed eternally to wars, poverty, and devastating diseases?"

I'd answer, "Absolutely not." On my own visits to Africa, I've been struck by how harmoniously ethnic groups live together in many countries—far better than they do in many other parts of the globe. **Tensions** arise in Africa, as they do elsewhere, when people see no other way out of poverty except to fight their neighbors for dwindling resources. But many areas of Africa have an abundance of resources: The rivers of central Africa are great generators of hydroelectric power; the big animals are a major source of ecotourism **revenue** in eastern and southern Africa; and the forests in the wetter regions, if managed and logged sustainably, would be renewable and lucrative[9] sources of income.

[7] A **navigable** river is wide enough for a boat to travel along safely.
[8] If something is **cumbersome**, it is large and heavy and therefore difficult to carry or handle.
[9] A **lucrative** activity, job, or business is very profitable.

" History might have turned out differently if African armies, fed by barnyard-giraffe meat and backed by waves of cavalry mounted on huge rhinos, had swept into Europe . . . "

As for Africa's health problems, they can be greatly alleviated with the right planning and funding. Within the past half century, several formerly poor countries in Asia recognized that tropical diseases were a major drain on their economies. By investing in public health measures, they have successfully curbed those diseases, and the increased health of their people has led to far healthier economies. Within Africa itself, some international mining and oil companies have been funding successful public health programs throughout their concession areas[10] because they realized that protecting the health of their workers was an excellent business **investment** for them.

What's the best case for Africa's future? If the continent can overcome its health problems and the corruption that plagues many of its governments and institutions, then it could take advantage of today's globalized, technological world in much the same way that China and India are now doing. Technology could give Africa the connections that its geography, particularly its rivers, long **denied** it. Nearly half of all African countries are English speaking, an advantage in trade relations, and an educated, English-speaking workforce could well attract service jobs to many African countries.

If Africa is to head into a bright future, outside investment will continue to be needed, at least for a time. The cost of perpetual aid to or **military intervention** in Africa is thousands of times more expensive than solving health problems and supporting local development, **thereby** heading off [11] conflicts. Not only Africans but the rest of us will be healthier and safer if Africa's nations increasingly take their places as peaceful and prospering members of the world community.

[10] A **concession area** is a place where someone is given the right to sell a product or run a business.
[11] If you **head off** an event, you keep it from happening.

▼ Cape Town Stadium, seen here from Table Mountain, was built for the 2010 Soccer World Cup and has become a symbol of modern Africa.

A | **Identifying Main Ideas.** Skim the reading again. Write the correct paragraph letter (B, C, D, E, F, G, H) next to each main idea (1–7).

1. ＿＿＿ The co-evolution of animals and humans affected the survival of some species in Africa.

2. ＿＿＿ Humans have been in Africa for a very long time.

3. ＿＿＿ Africa's geographical orientation affected the spread of agriculture on the continent.

4. ＿＿＿ It's a mystery why the long human history of Africa hasn't been an advantage.

5. ＿＿＿ Africa's geographic location explains the extremes that exist on the continent.

6. ＿＿＿ The development of agriculture impacts a culture.

7. ＿＿＿ Animal domestication took a long time to spread across Africa.

B | **Identifying Main Ideas.** Complete the main idea statements for paragraphs I, J, and K. Then write the main ideas of paragraphs L, M, and N using the paraphrasing strategies you learned in Unit 4.

1. Paragraph I: The long human presence in Africa led to ＿＿＿＿＿＿＿＿＿＿＿＿＿＿＿.

2. Paragraph J: The richest countries in Africa lie in ＿＿＿＿＿＿＿＿＿＿＿＿＿＿＿.

3. Paragraph K: Africa has hope because of ＿＿＿＿＿＿＿＿＿＿＿＿＿＿＿.

4. Paragraph L: ＿＿＿＿＿＿＿＿＿＿＿＿＿＿＿＿＿＿＿＿＿＿＿＿

＿＿＿＿＿＿＿＿＿＿＿＿＿＿＿＿＿＿＿＿＿＿＿＿＿＿＿＿

5. Paragraph M: ＿＿＿＿＿＿＿＿＿＿＿＿＿＿＿＿＿＿＿＿＿＿＿＿

＿＿＿＿＿＿＿＿＿＿＿＿＿＿＿＿＿＿＿＿＿＿＿＿＿＿＿＿

6. Paragraph N: ＿＿＿＿＿＿＿＿＿＿＿＿＿＿＿＿＿＿＿＿＿＿＿＿

＿＿＿＿＿＿＿＿＿＿＿＿＿＿＿＿＿＿＿＿＿＿＿＿＿＿＿＿

C | **Critical Thinking: Identifying Chronology.** Find these events in paragraph C. Put each event (a–f) in the correct place in the time line.

a. "behaviorally modern" *Homo sapiens* appear in Africa
b. *Homo erectus* evolves into three distinct species: Neandertals in Europe, *Homo erectus* in Asia, *Homo sapiens* in Africa
c. apes and protohumans split
d. *Homo erectus* moves to Europe and Asia
e. *Homo sapiens* wipe out Neandertals and *Homo erectus* and become dominant species
f. *Homo sapiens* move into Europe and Asia

D | Identifying Key Details. Write answers to the questions.

1. What are the "head starts" that Diamond refers to in paragraph D?

_____

_____

2. What are some effects of the development of agriculture?

_____

_____

3. What blocked the spread of agriculture in Africa?

_____

_____

4. Why did many animal species survive in Africa, unlike other places such as Australia?

_____

_____

5. Why is the proximity to great apes and monkeys a problem in Africa?

_____

_____

6. What two geographical conditions affect the wealth of Africa?

_____

_____

7. How does Diamond describe the potential of Africa's resources?

_____

_____

8. What actions may give Africa a better future?

_____

_____

E | **Identifying Meaning from Context.** Find and underline the following words and phrases in the reading passage on pages 146–151. Use context to help you identify the meaning of each word or phrase. Match each word or phrase with its definition.

1. _____ Paragraph B: **go a long way toward**

2. _____ Paragraph D: **head starts**

3. _____ Paragraph F: **lend themselves to**

4. _____ Paragraph I: **spawned**

5. _____ Paragraph J: **landlocked**

6. _____ Paragraph K: **struck by**

7. _____ Paragraph L: **a (major) drain on**

8. _____ Paragraph M: **plagues**

a. a use of something such as resources that most people feel is not a good use

b. caused to happen

c. surrounded by other countries and not having access to bodies of water

d. help a great deal

e. advantages in a competition

f. continually causes problems

g. impressed by

h. are suitable for, or adapt easily to

CT Focus: Identifying Point of View

It's important to identify a writer's attitude, or **point of view**, toward his or her topic in order to fully understand the main ideas. Look for clues to the point of view in how the writer presents advantages and disadvantages. Does one receive more weight than the other? Look also at language use. Point of view can be indicated directly through word choice—for example, by the use of words and expressions with positive or negative connotations.

F | **Critical Thinking: Analyzing a Writer's Point of View.** Analyze Diamond's point of view by discussing your answers to the following questions.

1. In paragraph K, Diamond answers his own question, "Absolutely not." Why did Diamond choose to add *absolutely* to his answer?

2. What aspects of Africa today does Diamond describe in paragraph K? What word does Diamond use to describe the way ethnic groups live together in Africa?

3. What word does Diamond use to describe the number of resources in Africa? Why did he use this word instead of *a lot of*?

4. In general, how does Diamond describe Africa's future in paragraphs K–M? In a positive way or in a negative way? How do you know?

5. What is Diamond's point of view overall? Is his attitude about Africa's future basically optimistic or pessimistic?

Reading Skill: Understanding Cohesion (II)

A piece of writing has cohesion when all of its parts are connected logically and flow smoothly from one idea the next. In Unit 1, you saw how writers use pronouns, demonstratives, and synonyms. Another cohesive device is the repetition of key words.

Often, writers use key words early in a piece of writing when they are stating the thesis. Then they refer to the key words later on as they develop the supporting information for their thesis. This helps the reader to follow the flow of ideas. The references to the key words may be repetitions or paraphrases.

Example of a thesis for an essay on problems and solutions in the state of California:

California's economy has been affected by <u>population growth</u> and <u>taxation policies</u>.
                                                              key phrase   key phrase

Example of repetition of a key word or phrase in a body paragraph:

Dramatic <u>population growth</u> in the 2000s has led to . . .
                   repetition

Example of paraphrasing of a key word or phrase in a body paragraph:

The <u>reduction of property taxes</u> in the 1970s had a long-range effect on . . .
             paraphrase

A | Analyzing. Answer the questions to analyze the use of key word repetition in "The Shape of Africa."

1. Complete the key words in Diamond's thesis.

   Africa has been shaped by its _____ and _____ .

2. Where does he repeat or paraphrase these key words? List examples from the text. Note the paragraph where you find each one.

   the long human presence (H)

B | Critical Thinking: Evaluating. Discuss these questions with a partner.

Does the organization of Diamond's article, especially the use of repetition and paraphrasing, help you to understand his ideas? Why, or why not?

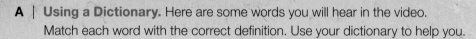
The Encroaching Desert

Before Viewing

A | Using a Dictionary. Here are some words you will hear in the video. Match each word with the correct definition. Use your dictionary to help you.

▲ A scorching sun casts long shadows as camels cross salt flats in Djibouti.

| hectare | monsoon | nomadic | sterile |

1. _____: not able to produce living things, such as plants

2. _____: a measurement of area, equal to 2.471 acres or 10,000 square meters

3. _____: moving from place to place; not having a permanent home

4. _____: seasonal, heavy rainfall

B | Thinking Ahead. What do you remember from Unit 1 about *desertification*? Work with a partner to write an explanation of it in your own words.

_____

_____

_____

While Viewing

Read questions 1–4. Think about the answers as you view the video.

1. What was the Sahara desert like 4,000 years ago?

2. What role did monsoon rains play in the Sahel in the past?

3. On what other continent is desertification a problem?

4. What is happening to 5–6 million hectares of farmland every year?

After Viewing

A | Discuss your answers to questions 1–4 above with a partner.

B | Critical Thinking: Synthesizing. How might Jared Diamond explain the role desertification plays in the conditions that exist in Africa today?

GOAL: Writing an Expository Essay

In this lesson, you are going to plan, write, revise, and edit an essay on the following topic: *Choose a country or region and explain how it has been affected by its history and geography.*

A | Brainstorming. Make a list of two or three countries or regions that interest you. What do you know about key events in their history and important aspects of their geography? List facts in the chart. Then select the country or region you will research.

Countries/Regions	History	Geography

B | Vocabulary for Writing. The words and phrases below can be useful when writing about geography and history. Find them in the reading passage on pages 146–151, and use context to guess their meanings. Then match each word or phrase to its definition.

1. _____ : **embody** (paragraph A)

2. _____ : **span** (paragraph B)

3. _____ : **underwent** (paragraph C)

4. _____ : **concentrated in** (paragraph F)

5. _____ : **be shaped in** (paragraph J)

6. _____ : **per capita gross domestic products** (paragraph J)

a. to extend over a large area

b. experienced; suffered (from)

c. to be influenced in

d. to be a symbol of

e. the economic output of a country by person

f. located in one place instead of being distributed

Free Writing. Write for five minutes about one aspect of the country or region you chose in exercise **A**, such as its location or its resources. Try to use some of the words and phrases from exercise **B**.

C | Read the information in the box. Then write quotes and paraphrases using a different reporting verb and phrase in each sentence.

Language for Writing: Referring to Sources

When you use other people's ideas in your writing, you either quote them directly or you paraphrase them. Try to paraphrase as much as possible, but use direct quotations when the original words are particularly effective. Use the following words and phrases to refer to sources.

According to Diamond, *"The long human presence in Africa is probably the reason the continent's species of big animals survive today."*

As Diamond says, *"The long human presence in Africa is probably the reason the continent's species of big animals survive today."*

Diamond says that *"the long human presence in Africa is probably the reason the continent's species of big animals survive today."*

Diamond says that *the fact that humans have been in Africa for a very long time probably explains why many animal species still exist on the continent.*

It's common to use *that* after reporting verbs in academic writing. Note that when you use *that* in a quote, it must fit grammatically into the sentence.

Vary your style by using different reporting verbs, such as the following:
says, states, claims, believes, explains, points out, suggests, reports, concludes, argues.

Choose a reporting verb that matches the meaning you intend. For example, if you are reporting on research, you might say, "X concludes that." If you are reporting on a persuasive idea, you might say, "X argues that." If you are reporting on an opinion, you might use "X thinks/believes/feels that."

See page 90 for more on reporting verbs and phrases.

1. Write a quote that answers this question: What may have happened to the large animals that disappeared in Australia and North and South America? (paragraph H)

   _____

   _____

2. Write a quote that expresses Diamond's opinion on how people get along with each other in Africa. (paragraph K)

   _____

   _____

3. Rewrite your paraphrase of the main idea of paragraph L (page 152) using a reporting verb.

   _____

4. Rewrite your paraphrase of the main idea of paragraph M (page 152) using a reporting verb.

   _____

Writing Skill: Researching and Note-taking

When researching information online for an essay, you may need to choose and evaluate sources quickly and efficiently. You will also need to note the most relevant information. Use these tips to make your research and note-taking more effective.

Researching

- Limit your search results by using precise key words with quotation marks around them.

- Scan the URLs in your search results to quickly eliminate sites that don't appear to be relevant.

- Avoid encyclopedia sites as your main source, when possible. You will write a better essay if you use original sources. However, encyclopedia sites may be a good place to find original sources—check the References section at the end of each article.

- When you go to a source site, preview the content: Read the title and the subheads, look at the pictures, and read the captions. As you preview, ask yourself: Is the site trustworthy? Is the information accurate? Is it current? Is the information thorough?

Note-taking

- Avoid plagiarism by having index cards handy or a note-taking document open while you are doing online research. When you find information that is useful, write the ideas in your own words. Never cut and paste text from websites!

- In your notes, include all correct source information: the correct names of people and the publications you will refer to in your essay.

- For ideas that you will quote directly, write the source of the quotation and the exact words that you will quote.

- Label your notes with a *P* for information that you have paraphrased and a *Q* for information you have quoted.

D | **Critical Thinking: Researching.** Work with a partner. Look at the following research questions and discuss your answers to these questions: What key words should you use for an online search? What types of websites would give you the best information?

1. What are some ways to improve agricultural production in Africa?

2. What languages are spoken in Africa?

3. What are some examples of how outside aid has helped Africa?

E | **Critical Thinking: Note-Taking.** Compare the following notes on an original text. Which is the better version? Why? Share your answer with a partner.

The impacts of slavery on Africa are widespread and diverse. Computerized calculations have projected that if there had been no slave trade, the population of Africa would have been 50 million instead of 25 million in 1850.

— From National Geographic Encyclopedia:
http://education.nationalgeographic.com/education/encyclopedia/

a. Slavery has had a huge impact on Africa. There would have been 50 million inhabitants in Africa instead of only 25 million in 1850 if there had been no slave trade.

b. Slavery had several damaging effects on Africa; for example, it reduced the population by 50 percent in the 19th century.

F | **Critical Thinking: Applying.** Research information on one of the countries or regions you chose in exercise **A**. Take notes on the following points.

1. Find background information on the country or region. What is it like today?

_____

_____

_____

_____

2. Find out about the geography of the country or region. How does its geography affect its current situation? Find out where it is located, what its climate is like, what its main resources are, and so on.

_____

_____

_____

_____

3. Find out about the history of the country or region. What are the key events? How does its history affect its current situation?

_____

_____

_____

_____

A | **Planning.** Use your research notes to plan your essay. Follow the steps.

Step 1 Choose three aspects of the geography and history of the country / region that you want to discuss. Write a thesis statement in the outline.

Step 2 Write a topic sentence for each of your body paragraphs. Remember to reflect your key concepts in your topic sentences.

Step 3 For each body paragraph, write two to three examples or details that explain the ideas in your topic sentences.

Step 4 Note some ideas for an introduction and a conclusion for your essay.

Thesis statement:

What are three key aspects of the country's/region's geography/history that affect the way it is today?

_____

1st body paragraph: one aspect of its geography/history

Topic sentence: _____

_____

Explanation and examples: _____

_____

_____

2nd body paragraph: another aspect of its geography/history

Topic sentence: _____

_____

Explanation and examples: _____

_____

_____

3rd body paragraph: third aspect of its geography/history

Topic sentence: _____

_____

Explanation and examples: _____

_____

_____

Ideas for introduction and conclusion: _____

_____

B | **Draft 1.** Use your outline to write a first draft of your essay.

C | Critical Thinking: Analyzing. Work with a partner. Read the essay, which explains how geography and history have influenced Singapore. Then follow the steps to analyze the essay.

Singapore is a collection of small islands in Southeast Asia. The majority of the population is concentrated on the mainland, a diamond-shaped island 30 miles (49 km) wide and 15.5 miles (25 km) long. Singapore boasts the world's largest concentration of millionaires, is culturally diverse, and frequently ranks in the top ten in work- and personal-life satisfaction surveys. What makes Singapore the place that it is today? Its geographical location, its lack of natural resources (especially fresh water), and its recent immigration history have all played a part in shaping this small island nation.

Thanks to its geography, trade is one of the most important aspects of Singapore's economy. The country lies to the south of Malaysia, from which it is separated by a narrow body of water called the Johor Strait. Its southern coast is on the Singapore Strait, which separates it from Indonesia. Its advantageous location made it a key stopping-off point for ships traveling from Asia to Europe. As a result, Singapore became an important center for international trade. In the 1970s, the government invested in building ports along the coast. This made it even easier for ships to come and go. Today, the Port of Singapore is one of the busiest in the world. This has helped Singapore to become the 14th largest exporter and the 15th largest importer in the world.

The lack of natural resources, especially fresh water, has also shaped Singapore. Having a rain forest climate, Singapore receives over 90 inches of rainfall a year. However, because it has little land to retain the water, the supply of fresh drinking water for Singapore's citizens is very limited. As a result, Singapore must import water from nearby countries. In addition, the country has built water-recycling and desalination plants. Water-recycling plants transform wastewater into drinking water, and desalination plants make use of the abundant seawater that surrounds the island. According to the Public Utilities Board (PUB), Singapore's national water agency, current and planned plants will meet up to 55 percent of the demand for fresh water by 2060.

Singapore's recent history of immigration goes a long way toward explaining its rich cultural diversity. For many years, the government of Singapore had liberal immigration policies. The country needed foreign workers partly due to its low birthrate: there are only .78 births per woman, which is below the replacement rate of 2.1. By 2005, 40 percent of the population was made up of residents from other parts of Asia, North America, and Europe. Although there has been some opposition to these liberal immigration policies in recent history, many experts believe that immigration is necessary to maintain a strong workforce and to offset an aging population. In a *Forbes* magazine interview, investor and Singapore resident Jim Rogers argued that if Singapore cannot get enough labor through immigration, inflation may result, with an overall detrimental effect on the country's economy. As Rogers pointed out, "Every country in history that has a backlash against foreigners is going to go into decline."

As with many countries, Singapore has been shaped by its geography and history. Since gaining its independence from Malaysia in 1965, the tiny city-state has gone from a poor trading port to one of the wealthiest states in the world. And it shows: High-rise condos and skyscrapers dominate the landscape, and shoppers peruse the latest designer goods in its many upscale malls and boutiques. Although Singapore is a small country with a declining birthrate and few natural resources, its advantageous location in the heart of Southeast Asia will continue to make it attractive to immigrants, tourists, and investors alike.

Step 1 Underline the thesis statement and circle the key words.

Step 2 Underline the topic sentences of the body paragraphs. Does the order of the body paragraphs reflect the order of the ideas in the thesis?

Step 3 Circle the key words in the topic sentences. Do they reflect the key words in the thesis statement?

Step 4 What details in the body paragraphs does the writer use to develop the key concepts in each of the topic sentences?

Step 5 Where has the writer referred to sources? Which reporting verbs and phrases has the writer used?

D | Revising. Follow the steps in exercise **C** to analyze your own essay.

E | Peer Evaluation. Exchange your first draft with a partner and follow these steps.

Step 1 Read your partner's essay and tell him or her one thing that you liked about it.

Step 2 Complete the outline showing the ideas that your partner's essay describes.

Thesis statement:

What are three key aspects of geography/history that affect the way the country/region is today?

_____

1st body paragraph: one aspect of its geography/history

Topic sentence: _____

_____

Explanation and examples: _____

_____

_____

2nd body paragraph: another aspect of its geography/history

Topic sentence: _____

_____

Explanation and examples: _____

_____

_____

3rd body paragraph: third aspect of its geography/history

Topic s entence: _____

_____

Explanation and examples: _____

_____

_____

Ideas for introduction and conclusion: _____

_____

Step 3 Compare this outline with the one that your partner created in exercise **A** on page 161.

Step 4 The two outlines should be similar. If they aren't, discuss how they differ.

F | **Draft 2.** Write a second draft of your essay. Use what you learned from the peer evaluation activity and your answers to exercise **D**. Make any other necessary changes.

G | **Editing Practice.** Read the information in the box. Then find and correct one mistake with quotes or paraphrases in each sentence (1–4).

> When you refer to sources, remember to:
>
> - use correct punctuation. With quotes, use quotation marks and a comma to separate a person's exact words from the rest of the sentence. Use a comma after the phrase that includes *According to*.
> - make sure that sentences referring to sources are grammatical. For example, do not use *that* with "As X says ~~that~~ . . ."

1. Susan Sontag said that To photograph is to confer importance.
2. According to Griffiths photography has influenced our notion of what is beautiful.
3. Diamond asks, What's the best case for Africa's future?"
4. As Kolbert says that, "Probably the most obvious way humans are altering the planet is by building cities."

H | **Editing Checklist.** Use the checklist to find errors in your second draft.

Editing Checklist	Yes	No
1. Are all the words spelled correctly?		
2. Does every sentence have correct punctuation?		
3. Do your subjects and verbs agree?		
4. Have you used reporting verbs and phrases correctly?		
5. Are your verb tenses correct?		

I | **Final Draft.** Now use your Editing Checklist to write a third draft of your essay. Make any other necessary changes.

Living Longer

Think and Discuss

1. What daily habits can contribute to good health?

2. How do you think a person's genes can affect their health?

▲ An 89-year-old fisherman from Okinawa Island, Japan, shows off his muscles.

Exploring the Theme

Look at the map and the chart, and read the information below. Then discuss the questions.

1. What are the main causes of death in North America and Europe?

2. Where in the world are communicable diseases and injuries the main causes of death?

3. What is the life expectancy in your country? What are the main causes of death there?

4. Why do the main causes of death differ around the world?

5. How does income relate to life expectancy?

Causes of Mortality

In the developing world, communicable diseases—such as HIV/AIDS and cholera—are the most common cause of unnatural death. In the world's poorest countries, and particularly in sub-Saharan Africa, a lack of adequate health care and an overabundance of infectious diseases, parasites, and malaria cut lives short. In wealthier, more developed countries, people have more access to health care and nutritious food sources, and they live longer as a result. People in these countries most often die of noncontagious diseases such as diabetes, heart disease, and cancer.

Comparing Income and Life Expectancy

Life expectancy refers to the length of time a typical person is expected to live. In Europe, Central Asia, and North America, high incomes result in longevity, with the average person living for almost 80 years. The area of the world with the lowest income is also the area with the shortest life expectancy. The average life expectancy in sub-Saharan Africa is just over 40 years.

COMPARING INCOME AN[

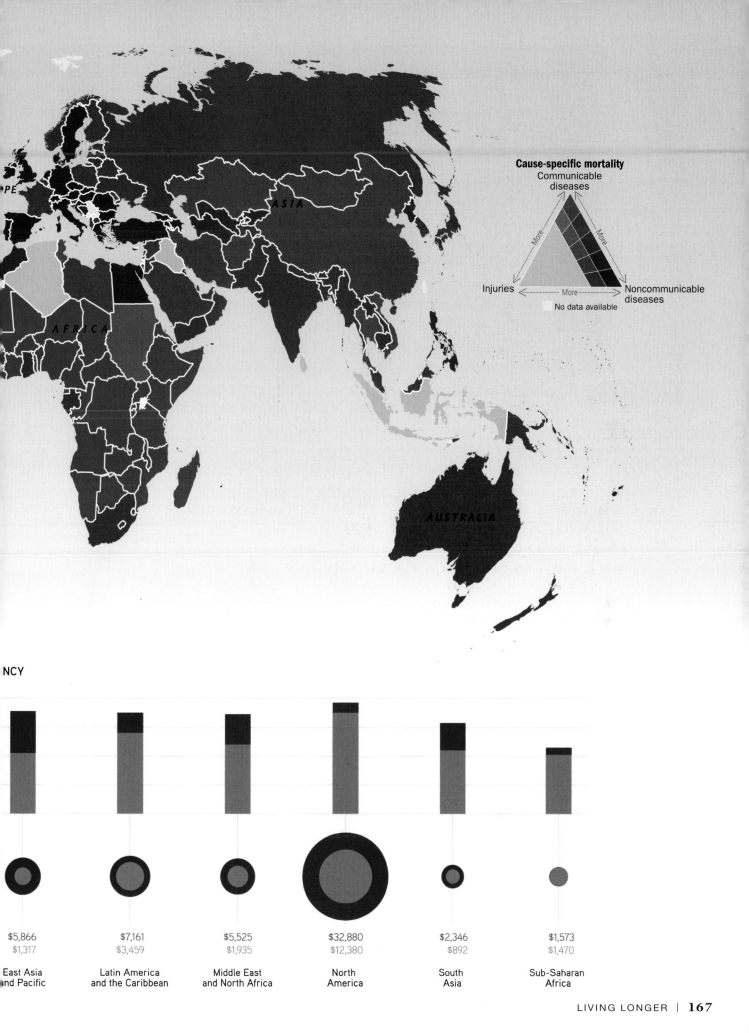

Cause-specific mortality

Communicable diseases

Injuries ← More → Noncommunicable diseases

☐ No data available

NCY

$5,866	$7,161	$5,525	$32,880	$2,346	$1,573
$1,317	$3,459	$1,935	$12,380	$892	$1,470
East Asia and Pacific	Latin America and the Caribbean	Middle East and North Africa	North America	South Asia	Sub-Saharan Africa

A | **Building Vocabulary.** Read the following paragraphs about losing weight. Use the context to guess the meanings of the words and phrase in **blue**. Then write the correct word or phrase to complete each sentence (1–7).

When people want to lose weight, they often skip meals and try to eat smaller amounts of food. They're usually hungry as a result, but it seems like the logical thing to do. Eating and losing weight seem to be two **contradictory** ideas. However, studies show that eating when you're hungry can actually help you lose weight, and, **conversely**, skipping meals can make you gain weight. Why? We have **mechanisms** in our bodies that let us know when we're hungry and when we're full. "Overhunger" can interfere with those mechanisms, and research shows that when people skip a meal and let themselves be overly hungry, they tend to eat more than they need to at their next meal.

The **implication** of this research isn't that you can eat anything you want when you're hungry and still lose 10 pounds; you also need to embrace certain dietary **restrictions**. For example, maintain a low intake of fats and simple carbohydrates such as white bread and pastries. Instead, eat lean proteins and plenty of fruits and vegetables. It's also important to be aware of what you eat. Write down everything you eat—and when you eat it—in a food diary. That way, you can easily **reconstruct** your food intake. Doing so can help you **gain insight into** what is making you gain weight or what is keeping you from losing weight.

Word Link

struct = to build:
con**struct**, de**struct**ive,
in**struct**, recon**struct**,
structure

1. If two or more facts, ideas, or statements are _____, they state or imply that opposite things are true.

2. You say "_____" to indicate that the situation you are about to describe is the opposite or reverse of the one you have just described.

3. If you _____ a complex situation or problem, you gain an accurate and deep understanding of it.

4. The _____ of a statement, an event, or situation is what it suggests is the case.

5. If you _____ an event that happened in the past, you try to get a complete understanding of it by combining a lot of small pieces of information.

6. You can refer to things that limit what you can do as _____.

7. A(n) _____ is a process or system that enables something to take place.

B | **Building Vocabulary.** Complete the definitions (1–5) with the words from the box. Use a dictionary to help you.

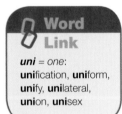

Word Link

uni = one:
unification, **uni**form,
unify, **uni**lateral,
union, **uni**sex

distinction	intact	outnumbers	ratio	unification

1. _____ is the process by which two or more countries join together and become one country.

2. If one group _____ another, the first group has more people or things in it than the second group.

3. If something has a _____ , it has a particular importance or quality.

4. Something that is _____ is complete and has not been damaged or changed.

5. A(n) _____ is a relationship between two things in numbers or amounts.

C | Using Vocabulary. Answer the questions. Share your ideas with a partner.

1. What are some common dietary **restrictions** that people have? Which ones are voluntary?
2. In your regular diet, do healthy foods **outnumber** unhealthy foods, or vice versa?
3. What do you think is the **ratio** of vegetarians to non-vegetarians in your country?

D | Brainstorming. Discuss your answers to these questions in small groups.

1. What are some factors that can affect a person's life expectancy?
2. What do you think are the most important factors that influence life expectancy?

E | Predicting. Skim the reading passage and look at the photos on pages 171–177. Circle the aspects of longevity that you think the passage will discuss.

genetics	lifestyles	diet	friends
family relationships	community	happiness	socializing
scientific research	luck		

F | Critical Thinking: Predicting a Conclusion. Read paragraphs A–C of the reading passage on pages 171–177. Then write answers to the questions. Check your predictions as you read the rest of the passage.

1. What do you think Passarino and Berardelli were trying to determine?

_____

2. What do you think they discovered?

_____

CT Focus

As you read, try to **predict the author's conclusion**. Re-evaluate your prediction as you read. Thinking ahead will help give more meaning to the information you read.

Reading Skill: Asking Questions as You Read

Asking yourself questions as you read can give you a deeper understanding of the information in the text. It can also help you make inferences about the writer's intent. Engaging with a text by asking questions is almost like having a conversation with the writer.

As you read, predict answers to your questions. Note the answers that you discover as you progress through a text. For example, after reading paragraph A of the reading on page 172, you might ask, "Why are Passarino and Berardelli going to Molochio?" You might predict that they are going there to learn about the culture, to talk to a centenarian, or to learn what it's like to be a centenarian. After reading paragraph B, you learn that the two men are going to talk with centenarian Salvatore Caruso. Then you might ask, "Why do they want to talk to Caruso?"

A | Asking Questions as You Read. As you read the passage on pages 171–177, complete the chart.

Paragraphs	Information That You Learned or That Surprised You	Your Questions	Possible Answers to Your Questions	Answers Given Later in the Text
A–D		Why are Passarino and Berardelli going to Molochio? Why do they want to talk to centenarians?		
E–H				
I–K				
L–M				
N–P				

Beyond 100

by Stephen S. Hall

▲ An 83-year-old woman practices yoga
in Solana Beach, California.

Our genes harbor many secrets to a long and healthy life. And now scientists are beginning to uncover them.

track 2-03

ON A CRISP JANUARY MORNING, with snow topping the distant Aspromonte mountains and oranges ripening on the nearby trees, Giuseppe Passarino guided his silver minivan up a curving mountain road into the hinterlands of Calabria, mainland Italy's southernmost region. As the road climbed through fruit and olive groves, Passarino, a geneticist at the University of Calabria, chatted with his colleague Maurizio Berardelli, a geriatrician. They were headed for the small village of Molochio, which had the **distinction** of numbering four centenarians— and four 99-year-olds—among its 2,000 inhabitants.

Soon after, they found Salvatore Caruso warming his 106-year-old bones in front of a roaring fire in his home on the outskirts of the town. Known in local dialect as "U' Raggiuneri, the Accountant," Caruso was calmly reading an article about the end of the world in an Italian version of a supermarket tabloid.[1] A framed copy of his birth record, dated November 2, 1905, stood on the fireplace mantle.

Caruso told the researchers he was in good health, and his memory seemed prodigiously **intact**. He recalled the death of his father in 1913, when Salvatore was a schoolboy; how his mother and brother had nearly died during the great influenza pandemic of 1918–19; how he'd been dismissed from his army unit in 1925 after accidentally falling and breaking his leg in two places. When Berardelli leaned forward and asked Caruso how he had achieved his remarkable longevity, the centenarian said with an impish smile, "*No Bacco, no tabacco, no Venere*—No drinking, no smoking, no women." He added that he'd eaten mostly figs and beans while growing up and hardly ever any red meat.

Passarino and Berardelli heard much the same story from 103-year-old Domenico Romeo—who described his diet as "*poco, ma tutto*—a little bit, but of everything"—and 104-year-old Maria Rosa Caruso, who, despite failing health, regaled[2] her visitors with a lively version of a song about the local patron saint.[3]

On the ride back to the laboratory in Cosenza, Berardelli remarked, "They often say they prefer to eat only fruits and vegetables."

"They preferred fruit and vegetables," Passarino said drily, "because that's all they had."

Although eating sparingly may have been less a choice than an involuntary circumstance of poverty in places like early 20th-century Calabria, decades of research have suggested that a severely restricted diet is connected to long life. Lately, however, this theory has fallen on hard scientific times. Several recent studies have undermined the link between longevity and caloric **restriction**.

In any case, Passarino was more interested in the centenarians themselves than in what they had eaten during their lifetimes. In a field historically marred[4] by exaggerated claims and dubious entrepreneurs hawking[5] unproven elixirs,[6] scientists studying longevity have begun using powerful genomic technologies, basic molecular research, and, most important, data on small, genetically isolated communities of people to **gain** increased **insight into** the maladies of old age and how they might be avoided. In Calabria, Ecuador, Hawaii, and even in the Bronx, studies are turning up molecules and chemical pathways that may ultimately help everyone reach an advanced age in good, even vibrant, health.

---

[1] A **tabloid** is a newspaper that has small pages, short articles, and a lot of photographs. Tabloids are usually considered to be less serious than other newspapers.

[2] If you **regale** people with songs or stories, you entertain them.

[3] The **patron saint** of a place, an activity, or a group of people is a saint who is believed to give them special help and protection.

[4] If something is **marred**, it is spoiled or damaged.

[5] **Hawking** something is selling it, usually on the street.

[6] An **elixir** is a liquid that is considered to have magical powers.

◀ A 107-year-old Calabrian man has helped produce olive oil throughout his life.

In Calabria, the hunt for hidden molecules and **mechanisms** that confer longevity on people like Salvatore Caruso begins in places like the *Ufficio Anagrafe Stato Civile* (Civil Registry Office) in the medieval village of Luzzi. The office windows here offer stunning views of snow-covered mountains to the north, but to a population geneticist the truly breathtaking sights are hidden inside the tall file cabinets ringing the room and on shelf after shelf of precious ledgers numbered by year, starting in 1866. Despite its well-earned reputation for chaos and disorganization, the Italian government, shortly after the **unification** of the country in 1861, ordered local officials to record the birth, marriage, and death of every citizen in each *comune*, or township.

Since 1994, scientists at the University of Calabria have combed through these records in every one of Calabria's 409 *comuni* to compile an extraordinary survey. Coupling family histories with simple physiological[7] measurements of frailty

and the latest genomic technologies, they set out to address fundamental questions about longevity. How much of it is determined by genetics? How much by the environment? And how do these factors interact to promote longevity—or, **conversely,** to hasten the aging process? To answer all those questions, scientists must start with rock-solid demographic[8] data.

"Here is the book from 1905," explained Marco Giordano, one of Giuseppe Passarino's young colleagues, opening a tall green ledger. He pointed to a record, in careful cursive, of the birth of Francesco D'Amato on March 3, 1905. "He died in 2007," Giordano noted, describing D'Amato as the central figure of an extensive genealogical tree. "We can **reconstruct** the pedigrees[9] of families from these records."

[7] **Physiology** is the study of how bodies function.

[8] **Demographic** information is information about people in a particular society or age group.

[9] Someone's **pedigree** is his or her background or ancestors.

Cross-checking the ledger entries against meticulously detailed registry cards (pink for women, white for men) going back to the 19th century, Giordano, along with researchers Alberto Montesanto and Cinzia Martino, has reconstructed extensive family trees of 202 nonagenarians and centenarians in Calabria. The records document not only siblings of people who lived to 100 but also the spouses of siblings, which has allowed Passarino's group to do a kind of historical experiment on longevity. "We compared the ages of D'Amato's brothers and sisters to the ages of their spouses," Giordano explained. "So they had the same environment. They ate the same food. They used the same medicines. They came from the same culture. But they did not have the same genes." In a 2011 paper, the Calabrian researchers reported a surprising conclusion: Although the parents and siblings of people who lived to at least 90 also lived longer than the general population, a finding in line with earlier research, the genetic factors involved seemed to benefit males more than females.

The Calabrian results on gender offer yet another hint that the genetic twists and turns that confer longevity may be unusually complex. Major European studies had previously reported that women are much likelier to live to 100, **outnumbering** male centenarians by a **ratio** of four or five to one, with the **implication** that some of the reasons are genetic. But by teasing out details from family trees, the Calabrian researchers discovered an intriguing paradox: The genetic component of longevity appears to be stronger in males—but women may take better advantage of external factors such as diet and medical care than men do.

Getting to 100 candles

Centenarians reach that milestone because they're healthier, by virtue of genetics, common sense, or luck. In people with an average life span, diseases of old age strike earlier and last longer.

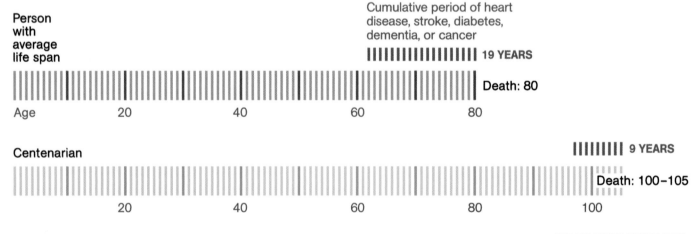

Person with average life span

Cumulative period of heart disease, stroke, diabetes, dementia, or cancer

|||||||||||||||||| 19 YEARS

Death: 80

Age   20   40   60   80

Centenarian

|||||||| 9 YEARS

Death: 100–105

20   40   60   80   100

NGM ART. SOURCE: THOMAS PERLS, NEW ENGLAND CENTENARIAN STUDY, BOSTON UNIVERSITY

In the dimly lit, chilly hallway outside Passarino's university office stand several freezers full of tubes containing centenarian blood. The DNA from this blood and other tissue samples has revealed additional information about the Calabrian group. For example, people who live into their 90s and beyond tend to possess a particular version, or allele, of a gene important to taste and digestion. This allele not only gives people a taste for bitter foods like broccoli and field greens, which are typically rich in compounds known as polyphenols that promote cellular health, but also allows cells in the intestine to extract nutrients more efficiently from food as it's being digested.

Passarino has also found in his centenarians a revved-up[10] version of a gene for what is called an uncoupling protein. The protein plays a central role in metabolism—the way a person consumes energy and regulates body heat—which in turn affects the rate of aging.

"We have dissected five or six pathways that most influence longevity," says Passarino. "Most of them involve the response to stress, the metabolism of nutrients, or metabolism in general—the storage and use of energy." His group is currently examining how environmental influences—everything from childhood diet to how long a person attends school—might modify the activity of genes in a way that either promotes or curtails longevity.

[10] If something is **revved up**, it is more active than usual.

▼ A 96-year-old man uses his all-terrain vehicle to run errands on Ikaria Island, Greece.

The Cost of Care

The United States spends more on medical care per person than any country, yet life expectancy is shorter than in most other developed nations and many developing ones. Lack of health insurance is a factor in life span and contributes to an estimated 45,000 deaths a year. Why the high cost? The U.S. has a fee-for-service system that pays medical providers piecemeal for appointments, surgery, and the like. That can lead to unneeded treatment that doesn't reliably improve a patient's health. Says Gerard Anderson, a professor at Johns Hopkins Bloomberg School of Public Health who studies health insurance worldwide, "More care does not necessarily mean better care."

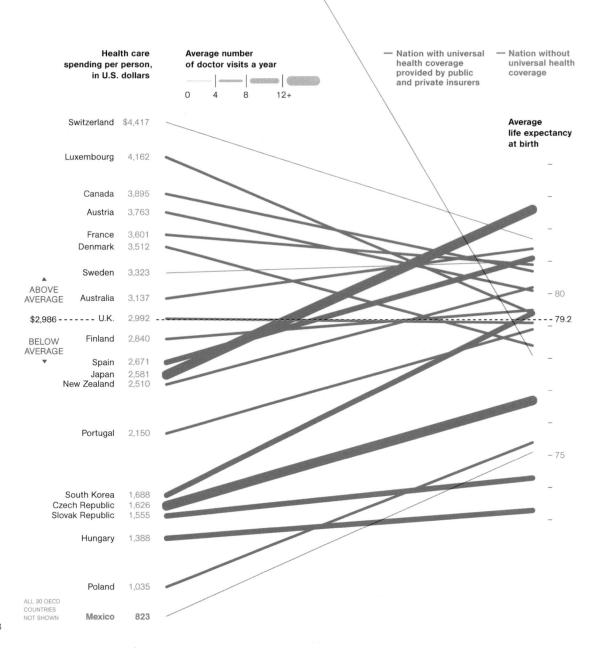

United States $7,290

Health care spending per person, in U.S. dollars

Average number of doctor visits a year

0   4   8   12+

— Nation with universal health coverage provided by public and private insurers

— Nation without universal health coverage

Average life expectancy at birth

Country	Spending
Switzerland	$4,417
Luxembourg	4,162
Canada	3,895
Austria	3,763
France	3,601
Denmark	3,512
Sweden	3,323
Australia	3,137
U.K.	2,992
Finland	2,840
Spain	2,671
Japan	2,581
New Zealand	2,510
Portugal	2,150
South Korea	1,688
Czech Republic	1,626
Slovak Republic	1,555
Hungary	1,388
Poland	1,035
Mexico	823

▲ ABOVE AVERAGE

$2,986 - - - - - - -

BELOW AVERAGE ▼

— 80

79.2

— 75

ALL 30 OECD COUNTRIES NOT SHOWN

Yoga exercise is believed to be one contributing factor to longevity.

AROUND THE WORLD, STUDIES are being done to determine the causes of longevity and health in old age. If nothing else, the plethora of new studies indicates that longevity researchers are pushing the scientific conversation to a new level. In October 2011, the Archon Genomics X Prize launched a race among research teams to sequence the DNA of a hundred centenarians (dubbing the contest "100 over 100").

But genes alone are unlikely to explain all the secrets of longevity, and experts see a cautionary tale[11] in recent results concerning caloric restriction. Experiments on 41 different genetic models of mice, for example, have shown that restricting food intake produces wildly **contradictory** outcomes. About half the mouse species lived longer, but just as many lived less time on a restricted diet than they would have on a normal diet. And last August, a long-running National Institute on Aging experiment on primates concluded that monkeys kept on a restricted-calorie

diet for 25 years showed no longevity advantage. Passarino made the point while driving back to his laboratory after visiting the centenarians in Molochio. "It's not that there are good genes and bad genes," he said. "It's certain genes at certain times. And in the end, genes probably account for only 25 percent of longevity. It's the environment, too, but that doesn't explain all of it either. And don't forget chance."

Which brought to mind Salvatore Caruso of Molochio, 107 years old and still going strong. Because he broke his leg 88 years ago, he was unfit to serve in the Italian Army when his entire unit was recalled during World War II. "They were all sent to the Russian front," he said, "and not a single one of them came back." It's another reminder that although molecules and mechanisms yet unfathomed[12] may someday lead to drugs that help us reach a ripe and healthy old age, a little luck doesn't hurt either.

[11] A **cautionary tale** is one that is intended to give a warning to people.

[12] If something is **unfathomed**, it is not understood or explained, usually because it is very strange or complicated.

A | Understanding Main Ideas. Write answers to the questions about the main ideas in "Beyond 100."

1. Why is Calabria a good place to study longevity?

_____

_____

2. What are some of the main points scientists have learned about longevity?

_____

_____

_____

_____

B | Identifying Key Details. Work with a partner. Find information in the reading passage to answer these questions.

1. Why did the researchers compare centenarians with their spouses and siblings?

_____

_____

2. What tools did the researchers use to make family trees of people in Calabria?

_____

_____

3. What are two ways that genetics can contribute to longevity?

_____

_____

4. What evidence shows that caloric restriction may not lead to longevity?

_____

_____

C | Identifying Supporting Examples. Complete the chart on the next page with information about how three factors affect the lives of each individual or group. If the information is not included in the reading, leave the space blank.

	Genetics	External Factors	Chance
Domenico Romeo			
Maria Rosa Caruso			
Salvatore Caruso			
Men, in general			
Women, in general			

D | **Identifying Meaning from Context.** Find and underline the following words in the reading passage on pages 171–177. Use context to help you match each word with its definition.

1. _____ Paragraph C: **prodigiously**
2. _____ Paragraph C: **impish**
3. _____ Paragraph G: **undermined**
4. _____ Paragraph H: **dubious**
5. _____ Paragraph I: **breathtaking**
6. _____ Paragraph I: **chaos**
7. _____ Paragraph L: **meticulously**
8. _____ Paragraph L: **nonagenarians**
9. _____ Paragraph M: **paradox**

a. a state of complete disorder and confusion

b. largely, impressively

c. disrespectful or naughty in a playful way

d. not completely honest, safe, or reliable

e. made something less strong or less secure

f. very carefully and with great attention to detail

g. extremely beautiful or amazing

h. a situation that involves two things that seem to contradict each other

i. people who are between 90 and 99 years old

E | Identifying Meaning from Context. Find and underline the following phrases on pages 171–177. Use the context to help you match each phrase with the best meaning. (Some of these phrases have similar meanings.)

1. _____ Paragraph G: **fallen on hard times**
2. _____ Paragraph H: **turning up**
3. _____ Paragraph J: **combed through**
4. _____ Paragraph M: **teasing out**
5. _____ Paragraph S: **brought to mind**

a. looked very carefully at information in order to find something
b. begun a difficult period
c. made someone think of something
d. successfully uncovering something that is difficult to get
e. separating out particular facts from a great deal of information

F | Understanding Infographics. Write answers to the questions about the infographic on page 176.

1. Which country spends the most per person on health care? The least?

   Most: _____   Least: _____

2. Which countries have the highest number of annual doctor visits? The lowest?

   Highest: _____

   Lowest: _____

3. Which country has the longest life expectancy? The shortest?

   Longest: _____   Shortest: _____

G | Critical Thinking: Making Inferences. Based on the infographic on page 176, what inferences can be made about the relationship between health care spending and longevity? What can be inferred about the relationship between doctor visits and longevity?

_____

_____

_____

H | Personalizing. Write an answer to the following question and share your answer with a partner.

Would you like to live to be a centenarian? Why, or why not?

_____

_____

_____

VIEWING

Secrets of a Long Life

◀ A 104-year-old woman in Okinawa, Japan.

Before Viewing

A | Using a Dictionary. Here are some words you will hear in the video. Match each one with the correct definition. Use your dictionary to help you.

1. _____: sitting down a lot of the time and not doing much exercise
2. _____: having deep religious beliefs
3. _____: the state of being extremely overweight
4. _____: disconnect yourself from all forms of technology for a period of time

> devout
> obesity
> sedentary
> unplug

B | Thinking Ahead. What are some habits that can help people live longer? Make a list with a partner.

While Viewing

A | Watch the video about longevity. As you watch, check your answers to exercise **B** in "Before Viewing." Circle the topics that are mentioned in the video.

B | Read questions 1–4. Think about the answers as you view the video.

1. What habits do the people of Sardinia, Okinawa, and Loma Linda have in common?
2. How is the reason for longevity in Loma Linda different from the reason for longevity in Sardinia and Okinawa?
3. In which places is the culture of longevity disappearing? Why?
4. The culture of longevity is not disappearing in one of the places. Why?

After Viewing

A | Discuss your answers to questions (1–4) above with a partner.

B | Critical Thinking: Synthesizing. Discuss your answers to the questions (1–3) in a small group.

1. The narrator of the video is surprised that both men and women in Sardinia live long lives. How might Giuseppe Passarino and Maurizio Berardelli (from the reading on pages 171–177) explain this phenomenon?
2. The narrator states that people in Okinawa may live longer because they practice caloric restriction. How might Passarino and Berardelli respond to this statement?
3. Which is more recent, the video or the article? How do you know?

GOAL: Writing an Argumentative Research Paper

In this lesson, you are going to plan, write, revise, and edit a research paper on the following topic: *Should scientists spend time, money, and resources to help people live 100 years or longer?*

Writing Skills: Planning a Research Paper

In an essay, the writer usually presents his or her own views about a topic and may or may not refer to sources. A research paper is different because it must include information from outside sources, such as journals, books, and websites.

An argumentative research paper involves expressing an opinion on a topic and then using researched examples and evidence to support the thesis. There are several steps involved in planning an argumentative research paper.

Choose a topic: Pick something that you can research and that you can argue about. (In this unit, the topic is chosen for you.) Consider a possible thesis statement or question, but be flexible. You may change your mind after you do some research.

Brainstorm ideas: Make a T-chart to brainstorm ideas that answer your question or ideas that support your possible argument and the opposite argument.

Do research: Take notes on relevant information that supports your potential thesis. Use index cards so it's easy to organize your notes later. Your teacher may specify a minimum number of sources. (Review Researching and Note-taking in Unit 7, page 159).

Draft a thesis statement: Decide what your overall argument, or thesis statement, will be.

Make an outline: Ask: *What is the best way to convince my readers that my argument is valid? What idea do I want to share first? What do I want to share next? What evidence supports each idea?* Draft a basic outline of your paper and organize your note cards to follow your outline. Then complete your outline with information from your note cards.

A | Critical Thinking: Evaluating. Check (✓) the statements that are possible argumentative research topics.

☐ 1. Cigarette advertisements are no longer permitted in some countries.

☐ 2. Alcohol advertisements on television are harmful.

☐ 3. There would be fewer auto accidents if the legal driving age were changed to 21.

☐ 4. The legal driving age is different all over the world.

☐ 5. Cigarette smoking around children should be made illegal.

☐ 6. In the past, tobacco was used medicinally.

B | Critical Thinking: Evaluating. Check (✓) the four pieces of evidence that best support the following thesis: "Cigarette smoking around children should be made illegal."

☐ 1. A lot of people smoke cigarettes around their children.

☐ 2. Some cigarette advertisements target children.

☐ 3. According to James Garbarino of Cornell University, "More young children are killed by parental smoking than by all unintentional injuries combined."

☐ 4. A recent study shows that the children of smokers are more likely to become smokers than children whose parents don't smoke.

☐ 5. A recent German study showed that teenagers who are exposed to tobacco ads are more likely to start smoking than teens who don't see these ads.

☐ 6. World Health Organization statistics show that tobacco use kills six million people a year.

☐ 7. According to the World Health Organization, 600,000 nonsmokers die from secondhand smoke every year.

C | Brainstorming. Consider the following question: *Should scientists spend time, money, and resources so that people can live 100 years or longer? Or would the money be better spent elsewhere?* Explore the question by completing the T-chart with your own ideas.

Yes, scientists should spend time, money, and resources for this.	No, scientists should not spend time, money, and resources for this.
This research may help us all be healthier.	If most people live to 100, who will take care of all the elderly people?

D | **Researching and Note-taking.** Research the topic and take notes. Decide on your thesis statement and add ideas to your T-chart in exercise **C**.

Language for Writing: Explaining the Significance of Evidence

Evidence doesn't stand on its own. In other words, as a writer, you have to show your readers why a piece of evidence is important. After you have provided a piece of evidence from your research, explain how that evidence supports your argument. You can introduce your explanation with the following phrases:

This research shows that . . .   This supports the idea that . . .

As this evidence shows, . . .   This demonstrates . . .

For example: *A recent German study showed that teenagers who are exposed to tobacco ads are more likely to start smoking than teens who don't see these ads.* **This research shows that** *tobacco advertisements negatively affect teenagers, encouraging them to start smoking and potentially increasing their chances of having tobacco-related medical problems such as lung cancer and stroke.*

E | **Applying.** Write an explanation for each piece of evidence that supports the following thesis statement: "Cigarette smoking around children should be made illegal."

1. According to James Garbarino of Cornell University, "More young children are killed by parental smoking than by all unintentional injuries combined."

_____

_____

_____

2. According to the World Health Organization, 600,000 nonsmokers die from secondhand smoke every year.

_____

_____

_____

3. World Health Organization statistics show that tobacco use kills six million people a year.

_____

_____

_____

4. A recent study shows that the children of smokers are more likely to become smokers than children whose parents don't smoke.

_____

_____

A | Planning. Follow the steps to make an outline for your research paper.

Step 1 Write notes about the background of your topic. For example, what are scientists doing? Why are they doing it?

Step 2 Write your thesis statement from exercise **D** on page 184 in the outline.

Step 3 Choose three arguments from your T-chart on page 183 to support your thesis. It is often a good idea to present your strongest argument last.

Step 4 Write a topic sentence for each of your body paragraphs. Remember to reflect your key concepts in your topic sentences.

Step 5 For each body paragraph, write one or two pieces of evidence that support the ideas in your topic sentences. Include reasons why the evidence is significant.

Step 6 Write ideas for your conclusion.

Introductory paragraph:

Give some background about the topic (e.g., what scientists are currently doing to gather information about longevity). What is your thesis statement?

_____

_____

1st body paragraph: What is one argument in support of your thesis?

Topic sentence: _____

Explanation and examples: _____

_____

_____

2nd body paragraph: What is a second argument in support of your thesis?

Topic sentence: _____

Explanation and examples: _____

_____

_____

3rd body paragraph: What is the strongest argument in support of your thesis?

Topic sentence: _____

Explanation and examples: _____

_____

_____

Concluding paragraph: Review your main points and your thesis statement.

_____

_____

B | Draft 1. Use your outline to write a first draft of your paper.

C | Critical Thinking: Analyzing. Work with a partner. Read the research paper, which argues that it should be illegal to smoke around children. Then follow the steps to analyze it.

One way to cite your sources is to include the last name of the author and the year in parentheses. If you introduce your information with the author's name, you include only the year in parentheses. This paper uses the APA (American Psychological Association) style.

In the 1500s, when Europeans began using tobacco, people were not aware of the dangers of smoking. In fact, according to the article "Tobacco: From Miracle Cure to Toxin," doctors often prescribed tobacco as medicine, believing it could cure cancer and many other diseases (Wexler, 2006). But in the early 20th century, people began to suspect that tobacco was dangerous rather than helpful. These days, it is widely accepted that cigarette smoking is dangerous and can cause medical problems such as lung cancer and stroke. In some countries, tobacco companies are required to include health warnings on their cigarette packs. Right now, many people believe that secondhand smoke is dangerous, but not everyone agrees. Therefore, there are no laws protecting nonsmokers from secondhand smoke. As history has shown, we have been wrong about the safety of tobacco in the past and people suffered as a result. For that reason, new laws should be created that make it illegal to smoke around children.

You can use the background information in your opening paragraph to lead your reader to your thesis statement.

Research shows that secondhand smoke endangers nonsmokers' lives. The World Health Organization (WHO) states that 600,000 nonsmokers die from secondhand smoke every year. Approximately 28 percent of these people are children. According to the WHO's statistics, 40 percent of children have at least one smoking parent (2013). It's true that secondhand smoke is everywhere, and making smoking illegal around children won't protect them from all secondhand smoke. Nevertheless, as James Garbarino of Cornell University states, "More young children are killed by parental smoking than by all unintentional injuries combined" (Lang, 1998). If children were not forced to breathe their parents' secondhand smoke, their exposure to tobacco smoke would decrease dramatically. This demonstrates that enacting laws that prohibit people from smoking around children would have a positive impact on children's health and life expectancy.

You can introduce opposing arguments in your research paper and then refute them.

Of course, secondhand smoke endangers everyone, not just children. However, laws should be enacted to protect children specifically because they can't protect themselves. If an adult doesn't want to be around secondhand smoke, he or she can just walk away. However, children don't always have that option. Children of smokers are especially in danger of suffering from secondhand smoke because smoking occurs in their homes every day. Secondhand smoke might be in every breath that they breathe. In addition, secondhand smoke affects infants differently than it does adults. According to WHO, while secondhand smoke can cause serious heart and lung diseases in adults, it can cause sudden death in infants (2013).

In addition to endangering children's health, exposure to smoking encourages children to smoke as teenagers and adults. According to an article in *Medical News Today*, a study showed that the children of smokers were "more than two times as likely to begin smoking cigarettes on a daily basis between the ages of 13 and 21 than were children whose parents didn't use tobacco" (Schwarz, 2005). This greatly increases the child's chances of an early death. WHO statistics show that tobacco use kills six million people a year (2013). These statistics combined show that exposure to smoking is deadly for children, and lives would be saved if smoking around children were illegal.

Cigarette smoking is so popular that it will probably never completely disappear, even though people are aware of the dangers. However, there are things we can do in order to protect nonsmokers, especially children. Making it illegal to smoke around children would result in fewer children dying from secondhand smoke and fewer children becoming smokers. Perhaps most importantly, it would protect those who can't protect themselves.

Reference List

Lang, Susan S. (1998, Spring). Child protection expert says parental smoking is abuse. Human Ecology Forum, 26, 22. Retrieved from http://www.redwoods.edu/instruct/jjohnston/English1A/readings/smoking/smokingisabuse.htm

Schwarz, Joel. (2005, September 28). Children whose parents smoked are twice as likely to begin smoking between ages 13 and 21 as offspring of nonsmokers. University of Washington. Retrieved from http://www.washington.edu/news/2005/09/28/children-whose-parents-smoked-are-twice-as-likely-to-begin-smoking-between-ages-13-and-21-as-offspring-of-nonsmokers/

Wexler, Thomas A. (2006, June 12). Tobacco: from miracle cure to toxin. YaleGlobal Online. Retrieved from yaleglobal.yale.edu/about/tobacco.jsp

World Health Organization. (2013, July). Tobacco: fact sheet N° 339. Retreived from www.who.int/mediacentre/factsheets/fs339/en/

Step 1   Underline the thesis statement.

Step 2   Check (✓) the sentences that provide opposing viewpoints.

Step 3   Underline the topic sentences of the body paragraphs.

Step 4   Circle each piece of evidence in the body paragraphs.

Step 5   Underline the main points that are reviewed in the conclusion.

D | **Revising.** Complete steps 1–5 in exercise **C** on your own research paper.

E | **Peer Evaluation.** Exchange your first draft with a partner and follow these steps.

Step 1   Read your partner's research paper and tell him or her one thing that you liked about it.

Step 2   Complete the outline showing the ideas that your partner's research paper describes.

Introductory paragraph:

Give some background about the topic (e.g., what scientists are currently doing to gather information about longevity). What is your thesis statement?

_____

_____

1st body paragraph: What is one argument in support of your thesis?

Topic sentence: _____

Explanation and examples: _____

_____

_____

2nd body paragraph: What is a second argument in support of your thesis?

Topic sentence: _____

Explanation and examples: _____

_____

_____

3rd body paragraph: What is the strongest argument in support of your thesis?

Topic sentence: _____

Explanation and examples: _____

_____

_____

Concluding paragraph: Review your main points and your thesis statement.

_____

_____

Step 3   Compare this outline with the one that your partner created in exercise **A** on page 185.

Step 4   The two outlines should be similar. If they aren't, discuss how they differ.

F | **Draft 2.** Write a second draft of your paper. Use what you learned from the peer evaluation activity and your answers to exercise **D**. Make any other necessary changes.

G | **Editing Checklist.** Use the checklist to find errors in your second draft.

Editing Checklist	Yes	No
1. Are all the words spelled correctly?		
2. Does every sentence have correct punctuation?		
3. Do your subjects and verbs agree?		
4. Are your verb tenses correct?		
5. Have you used explanation phrases correctly?		

H | **Final Draft.** Now use your Editing Checklist to write a third draft of your research paper. Make any necessary changes.

Memorable Experiences

◄ Hitchhiking
travelers signal for
a lift to Moscow on
the Russian Steppe.

Think and Discuss

1. What is your most memorable travel experience? What made it memorable?
2. In what ways can travel teach us important lessons about life?

Exploring the Theme

Great thinkers and writers have been describing the value of travel for centuries. Read some of their thoughts on travel, meeting people, and gaining new experiences. Then discuss them using the following questions.

1. What does each quotation mean? Explain it in your own words.

2. Which quotation do you most agree with? Are there any that you disagree with? Explain your answers.

3. Do you know any quotations that are similar to these in your native language? If so, share them with your classmates.

For many people, traveling is more than just moving from one place to another. Travel can be a kind of education, one that is acquired through experiences—experiences with new and unfamiliar people, places, and customs. How we deal with these experiences and what we learn from them can often have more value than an education at one of the world's greatest universities.

There are no foreign lands. It is the traveler only who is foreign.

Robert Louis Stevenson, American writer

There are no strangers here; Only friends you haven't yet met.

William Butler Yeats, British poet

Travelers climb the immense sand ▲ dunes in the Sossuvlei region of Namibia's Namib-Naukluft Park.

Traveling—it leaves you speechless, then turns you into a storyteller.

Ibn Battuta,
Moroccan and Berber explorer

No one realizes how beautiful it is to travel until he comes home and rests his head on his old, familiar pillow.

Lin Yutang, Chinese writer

WE LIVE IN A WONDERFUL WORLD THAT IS FULL OF BEAUTY, CHARM AND ADVENTURE. THERE IS NO END TO THE ADVENTURES WE CAN HAVE IF ONLY WE SEEK THEM WITH OUR EYES OPEN.

Jawaharlal Nehru, Indian prime minister

To awaken quite alone in a strange town is one of the pleasantest sensations in the world.

Freya Stark, British explorer

Perhaps travel . . . by demonstrating that all peoples cry, laugh, eat, worry, and die, can introduce the idea that if we try and understand each other, we may even become friends.

Maya Angelou, American poet

A traveler without observation is a bird without wings.

Moslih Eddin Saadi, Persian poet

A | Building Vocabulary. Use the context to guess the meanings of the words in **blue**. Then write the words next to their definitions (1–7).

Word Usage

Ensure and **insure** both mean "to make certain." *Insure* can also mean to protect against loss: "Travelers should insure their belongings against theft."

> Why do we remember some events more clearly than others? Studies show that being in a heightened emotional state when an event occurs may **ensure** better retention of the event. One type of emotional memory is a flashbulb memory. A flashbulb memory often happens when people are **confronted** with a shocking event. For example, years after the September 11, 2001 attacks, many people can remember exactly what they were doing when they heard about them.

> As strange as it may seem, when I remember the **massive** 7.1 earthquake that occurred in San Francisco in 1989, I have very positive feelings. I was only six years old at the time, and I recall not being the least bit afraid. Because the electricity was off, I didn't see any frightening images on TV. My parents were calm and positive. The neighbors all got together to share their food so it wouldn't spoil. It was like one big party. When I went back to school, though, I realized that other kids were very traumatized by the event. I think this taught me a valuable lesson: Your own experience with reality often **transcends** what other people tell you about it.

> Should parents take their children out of class to go on trips during the school year? Many U.S. elementary schools don't think so. However, a recent study shows that children benefit when they are **exposed** to new cultures and experiences through travel. A recent survey showed that school-aged children who took time off from class for travel had higher grade point averages and were more likely to attend college than other children. Although in most cases schools do not give children time off for travel, some schools will allow it if students complete school **assignments** while on the road. In addition, many parents **devise** assignments for their children such as keeping a journal or photo log, which have the added benefit of creating lasting memories.

1. _____: introduced to an experience

2. _____: goes beyond normal limits or boundaries

3. _____: challenged by or forced to deal with something

4. _____: tasks or work that people have to do, usually of an academic nature

5. _____: to have an idea for something and design it

6. _____: very large

7. _____: make certain that something happens

B | **Building Vocabulary.** Complete the definitions (1–5) with the words from the box.

| compelled | conceived | desperate | intervene | assumptions |

1. If you make _____ about someone, you form an opinion about him or her without any real proof.

2. If you are _____, you are in such a bad situation that you are willing to try anything to change it.

3. If you _____ in a situation, you become involved in it and try to change it.

4. If you feel _____ to do something, you feel that you must do it because it is the right thing to do.

5. If a plan has been _____, it has been thought of.

C | **Using Vocabulary.** Answer the questions. Share your ideas with a partner.

1. Have you ever felt **compelled** to make a big change in your life? Explain your answer.

2. If you saw two people fighting on the street, would you **intervene**? Why, or why not?

3. Can you think of a time when you **made assumptions about** people that were not correct? Explain your answer.

Word Partners
Use **assumption** with adjectives and verbs: (*adj.*) **common** assumption, **underlying** assumption; (*v.*): **challenge an** assumption, **make an** assumption

D | **Brainstorming.** Can you think of examples when your first impressions of a place turned out to be wrong? Share your ideas in a small group.

_____

_____

_____

E | **Predicting.** Read paragraphs A and B on page 195. What do you think will happen next in the story? Note your ideas below. Then check your predictions as you read the rest of the passage.

_____

_____

_____

Welcome Stranger

by Sebastian Junger

▲ A lone truck travels down a dirt track
near the town of Gillette, Wyoming, USA.

> Author Sebastian Junger learns that first impressions are often wrong—and other hard-won lessons from the road.

track **2-04**

MY PLAN WAS TO CROSS MONTANA, Idaho, and Washington before it got too cold, then work my way down to Los Angeles and return home across the desert and the Deep South. I figured I'd make it back by Christmas. My first night was spent in a blizzard in the South Dakota Badlands, the second in the desolate little town of Gillette, Wyoming. The next morning, I limped out to the highway and stood in the shrieking wind under a high, cold, cloudless sky with my thumb jabbed out. Freight liners barreled[1] past me. Locals drove by in pickups and threw beer bottles that exploded against the frozen pavement.

After two or three hours, I saw a man working his way toward me along the on-ramp from town. He wore filthy canvas coveralls and carried a black lunch box, and as he got closer, I could see that his hair was matted in a way that occurs only after months on the skids. Gillette was a hard-bitten mining town that had fallen on bad times, and I thought that anyone walking out to the highway looking like that on a 20-degree (minus 6-degree Celsius) day was probably pretty **desperate**. I put my hand on the pepper spray[2] in my pocket and turned to face him. My backpack was on the pavement by my feet. I was ready.

"You been out here long?" he asked.

I nodded.

"Where you headed?"

"California."

"Warm out there."

"Yup."

"You got enough food?"

I thought about this. Clearly, he didn't have any, and if I admitted that I did, he'd ask for some. That in itself wasn't a problem, but it would mean opening my backpack and revealing all my obviously expensive camping gear. I felt alone and **exposed** and ripe for pillage,[3] and I just didn't want to do that. Twenty years later, I still remember my answer: "I got some cheese."

---

[1] If a vehicle or a person is **barreling**, it is moving very quickly.

[2] **Pepper spray** is a chemical compound in an aerosol that is used as a self-defense weapon.

[3] **Pillage** is stealing other people's property using violent methods. If someone is **ripe for pillage**, he or she is in a situation in which it is likely that another person will take something from him or her.

E
"You won't make it to California with just a little cheese," he said. "You'll starve." At first, I didn't understand. What was he saying, exactly? I kept my hand on the pepper spray.

F
"Believe me," he said, "I know. Listen, I'm living in a car back in town, and every day I walk out to the mine to see if they need me. Today they don't, so I won't be needing this lunch of mine."

G
I began to sag with understanding. In his world, whatever you have in your bag is all you've got, and he knew "a little cheese" would never get me to California.

H
"I'm fine, really," I said. "I don't need your lunch."

I
He shook his head and opened his box. It was a typical church meal—a bologna sandwich, an apple, and a bag of chips—and I kept protesting, but he wouldn't hear of it. I finally took his lunch and watched him walk back down the on-ramp toward town. I learned a lot of things in college, I thought, and I learned a lot from the books I'd read on my own. I had learned things in Newfoundland and in Europe and in Mexico and in my hometown of Belmont, Massachusetts, but I had to stand out there on that frozen piece of interstate to learn true generosity from a homeless man.

J
The lessons were piling up.[4] You had to be wary when you traveled, I realized, but you also had to be open. You had to protect yourself, but you couldn't be so suspicious that you'd lie to avoid giving food to a stranger. These were lessons from the harsher parts of the world, but I started to think that maybe they were applicable anywhere. It seemed as though there must be a way of traveling that made you ready for anything. The starting point was respect; if you didn't lead with that, even with street-corner thugs,[5] nothing was going to turn out well. So you start with respect and see where it goes; if it doesn't work, you switch to something else. On a highway on-ramp in Wyoming, everyone is equal, more or less. No one has a past, no one has a future, and things pretty much come down to how you treat one another. There's a certain liberty in that; there's a certain justice.

[4] If things are **piling up**, they are increasing in number.
[5] **Thugs** are violent people or criminals.

◄ Men are dwarfed by the landscape—and the coal trucks—in Wyoming.

A snowy path ► leads toward the Sierra de Gredos mountains, Spain.

Obviously, the more money you spend when you're traveling, the less likely you are to find yourself in those situations. And yet. I once said "sir" to a doorman at a fancy hotel, and a friend asked me why I'd done that. I can't remember my answer exactly, but I suspect that it related to that guy out on the highway. He's always with me, in a way, reminding me not to **make assumptions about** people, reminding me to keep my heart open. Everyone has a role in the world, and who is to say which role is more worthy or admirable than any other.

That became a cornerstone[6] of my journalism. Since every person I've interviewed has led a life unique to them, they have something to say about the world that I couldn't get from anyone else. That gives them a value that **transcends** any job or social rank they might have. I began to see that you could divide up the world in many different ways, and some of those ways actually put a homeless man from Wyoming at the top. He might not have known it, but I do, and the point of much of my work has been to communicate that.

I kept traveling, and I kept learning. Once, I caught a bus up into a wild and remote part of western Spain called the Sierra de Gredos because I'd heard there were still wolves up there . It was a hasty plan **conceived** the night before in a barroom in Salamanca, and as soon as I stepped off the bus, I realized that I was in over my head: It was snowing hard, and the mountain town where I found myself seemed completely deserted. There wasn't even a hotel. In the quickly gathering dusk, I started walking back down the road looking for a place to spend the night. The only plan I could **devise** was to build a fire and try to keep myself awake until dawn, but after five or ten minutes of walking, I saw a lone pair of headlights coming down the mountainside. The car made its way slowly along the switchbacks,[7] and when it approached me, the driver stopped and rolled down the window. "Get in," he said. "No one walks in these mountains at night. You'll die."

---

[6] The **cornerstone** of something is the basic part of it on which its existence, success, or truth depends.

[7] A **switchback** is a road that goes up a steep hill in a series of sharp bends.

An hour later, I was back in that bar in Salamanca. What sense of responsibility, I wondered, had **compelled** that man to stop? He had no idea whether or not I was dangerous, and yet he took a risk to **ensure** that a complete stranger would be OK. It seemed as though he understood there to be some sort of general citizenship in the world, and that if a fellow citizen were threatened, it was his duty—everyone's duty—to **intervene**.

As I got older, I traveled less for its own sake and more for journalism **assignments**. I found myself covering wars in West Africa and Afghanistan and the Balkans—situations that were far more dangerous than the aimless trips of my youth. However, those early trips undoubtedly affected me more than I'd realized at the time. They may not have taught me the specific skills of my new trade, but it was in places like Spain and Mexico where I first learned how to comport myself [8] in the world.

Many years later, I **confronted** the daunting task of walking into a fishermen's bar in Gloucester, Massachusetts, and asking the bartender—a woman named Ethel Shatford—about the death of her son. A local boat, the *Andrea Gail*, had gone down in a **massive** storm in 1991, and the book I wrote about her was eventually published as *The Perfect Storm*. The Crow's Nest was the sort of bar where everyone turns to look at a stranger as soon as he walks in. I ignored the stares, took a seat at the bar, and ordered a beer from Ethel.

[8] If you **comport yourself** in a particular way, you behave that way.

I had no idea how to begin, but I had help. They were all still with me, I realized—the man in Wyoming and the rest of the people I've met on my travels—they were still there, guiding and informing me, whispering their lessons in my ear. And in one way or another, they all had something to tell me about how I should approach Ethel Shatford.

Just tell her, I finally thought. Tell her she knows something about the world that a lot of other people might need to hear.

◄ A monument in Gloucester, Massachusetts, honors the memory of fishermen who died at sea.

THEY THAT GO DOWN TO THE SEA IN SHIPS
1623 — 1923

A | Identifying Purpose. Write answers to the questions. Share your ideas with a partner.

1. What do you know about the writer of "Welcome Stranger"?

   _____

   _____

2. What was the writer's purpose? Why did he name the article "Welcome Stranger"?

   _____

   _____

3. What do you think is the overall message of the article?

   _____

   _____

B | Identifying Purpose and Structure. What is the purpose of each of the main parts of "Welcome Stranger"? Match each part of the reading with its purpose.

a. A–I

b. J–L

c. M–N

d. O

e. P–R

1. _____ to show how past lessons helped the writer accomplish a difficult task in the present

2. _____ to describe a second travel experience and the lesson it contained

3. _____ to connect the past with the present

4. _____ to describe an experience of meeting someone while traveling

5. _____ to reflect on the meaning of a travel experience and others like it

C | Identifying Key Details. Answer the questions about "Welcome Stranger." Note the paragraphs in which you find the answers.

1. What was Junger's first impression of the man he sees on the on-ramp? Paragraph: _____

   _____

   _____

2. How did Junger interpret the homeless man's questions? Paragraph: _____

   _____

   _____

3. Why was Junger surprised by the homeless man? Paragraph: _____

_____

_____

4. What are Junger's "rules" for traveling? What is the most important rule, according to Junger?
Paragraph: _____

_____

_____

5. What does the incident with the doorman illustrate? Paragraph: _____

_____

_____

6. What became the cornerstone of Junger's journalism? How has it helped him in his work?
Paragraph: _____

_____

_____

7. What situation taught Junger that some people will take a risk to help others?
Paragraph: _____

_____

_____

8. How did Junger's lessons help him interview Ethel Shatford? Paragraph: _____

_____

_____

D | Identifying Meaning from Context. Find and underline the following phrases in
the reading passage on pages 194–198. Use context to help you match each phrase with
its definition.

1. _____ Paragraph A: **work my way (down to)**   a. not make assumptions
2. _____ Paragraph B: **on the skids**   b. use as a starting point
3. _____ Paragraph J: **lead with (something)**   c. confronting a situation that I'm not prepared for
4. _____ Paragraph K: **keep my heart open**
5. _____ Paragraph M: **in over my head**   d. seemingly difficult or frightening job
6. _____ Paragraph P: **daunting task**   e. in a bad situation, especially economically
     f. travel toward

E | **Critical Thinking: Making Inferences.** Work with a partner. Use clues in "Welcome Stranger" to make inferences about Junger. Underline any words in the story that help you answer the questions (1–5).

1. Why does Junger initially refuse the homeless man's lunch?

   _____

   _____

2. Why do you think Junger was hitchhiking across the United States instead of driving or taking some other form of transportation?

   _____

   _____

3. How old do you think Junger is at the time the story takes place?

   _____

   _____

4. Why do you think Junger was carrying pepper spray?

   _____

   _____

5. What kind of person is Junger? What are some adjectives you might use to describe him?

   _____

   _____

F | **Critical Thinking: Personalizing.** Discuss the questions with a partner.

Have you ever been in any situations like the ones Junger describes in "Welcome Stranger"? If so, how were your experiences similar to his? If not, would you like to go on trips like the ones he describes? Why, or why not?

Reading Skill: Analyzing a Personal Narrative

When you analyze a narrative, you think about the following components:

- the **setting**: where the narrative takes place
- the **theme**: the main idea or the purpose of the narrative. For example, the theme of a story might be that hard work pays off or that you can't run away from your problems.
- the **mood**: the feeling the narrative communicates. Writers often communicate mood through word choice. For example, a writer can convey a positive mood by describing people or events as *delightful* or *joyful*.
- the **characters**: who the narrative is about
- the **plot**: the events, or anecdotes, that form the narrative's storyline

A | Analyzing. Discuss these questions about "Welcome Stranger" with a partner.

1. **Setting**: Where (in what places) does the narrative take place?

2. **Theme**: What is the theme of "Welcome Stranger"? In other words, what is the main idea of the story?

3. **Mood**: What is the mood of the narrative? What feelings does Junger communicate? What words help to convey the mood?

4. **Characters**: Who are the most important characters in the narrative? How would you describe the following characters?
   - Junger (narrator)
   - the homeless man

B | Retelling an Anecdote. There are two main anecdotes—short stories that illustrate an idea— in the story of "Welcome Stranger": the one with the homeless man and the one that takes place in Spain. Choose one and note the main events on the time line. Explain to a partner what happens first, second, third, and so on.

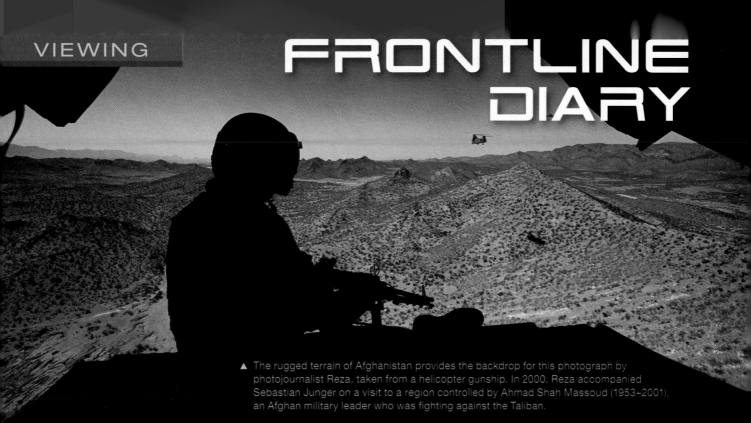

FRONTLINE DIARY

▲ The rugged terrain of Afghanistan provides the backdrop for this photograph by photojournalist Reza, taken from a helicopter gunship. In 2000, Reza accompanied Sebastian Junger on a visit to a region controlled by Ahmad Shah Massoud (1953–2001), an Afghan military leader who was fighting against the Taliban.

Before Viewing

A | Using a Dictionary. Here are some words and phrases you will hear in the video. Match each one with the correct definition. Use a dictionary to help you.

1. _____: take someone or something into a place secretly
2. _____: difficult or impossible to get to
3. _____: not understood or known about
4. _____: a state of disorder and confusion

> chaos
> inaccessible
> shrouded in mystery
> smuggle

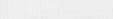 **B | Thinking Ahead.** What do you know about Afghanistan today? What do you know about its history? Share your ideas in a small group.

While Viewing

Read questions 1–4. Think about the answers as you view the video.

1. How does the narrator describe Afghanistan?
2. How do Junger and Reza get into the country? What makes the trip into Afghanistan dangerous?
3. On the first day at Massoud's headquarters, how does Junger describe breakfast?
4. In the feast scene at the end, how does Junger describe the Afghan people?

After Viewing

 A | Discuss your answers to questions 1–4 above with a partner.

B | Critical Thinking: Synthesizing. What assumptions do you think Junger had about Afghanistan before his visit? How do you think his feelings changed? How does this experience compare with those he recounts in "Welcome Stranger"?

GOAL: Writing an Extended Personal Narrative

In this lesson, you are going to plan, write, revise, and edit an essay on the following topic: *Describe a past experience that taught you a valuable life lesson.*

A | **Brainstorming.** Think of some lessons you have learned in life that you can connect with past experiences. Describe the experiences to your partner. Then discuss your answers to the questions.

1. Which experience is the most interesting?
2. Which one do you remember the best?
3. Which one do you remember the most details about?

B | **Vocabulary for Writing.** The following time words and phrases can be useful when writing a narrative. They help you show the order in which events occur. Write five sentences about the experiences you discussed in exercise **A** using these words and phrases.

after	after that	at first	before	during
eventually	finally	from . . . to . . .	later	meanwhile
next	the next time	now	one day	then
until	when	whenever	while	

_____

_____

_____

_____

_____

Free Writing. Write for five minutes. Describe one of the life lessons that you discussed in exercise **A**. Why was it an important lesson?

C | Read the information in the box. Then write sentences (1–4) using the cues with the simple past, the past perfect, and the past continuous. Sometimes more than one answer is possible.

Language for Writing: Reviewing Past Forms

When you write a narrative, you often use a variety of past verb forms. Use the simple past to describe events that were completed in the past.

> Freight liners <u>barreled</u> past me.

Combine the past continuous with the simple past to describe progressive events that occurred at the same time as completed past events, or that were interrupted by past events.

> It <u>was snowing</u> hard and the mountain town where I <u>found</u> myself <u>seemed</u> completely deserted.

> I <u>was walking</u> along the ramp when a man <u>stopped</u> his car and <u>offered</u> me a ride.

Use the past perfect to describe events that were completed in the past prior to other past events.

> Gillette <u>was</u> a hard-bitten mining town that <u>had fallen</u> on bad times.
>   second event   first event

Example
event in progress: we / drive in the desert

interrupting event: we / see an old man by the road

(when) _We were driving in the desert when we saw an old man by the road._

Or: _When we were driving in the desert, we saw an old man by the road._

1. event in progress: I / hike up a dusty trail

   interrupting event: I / encounter a rattlesnake

   (when) _____

2. first event: Belmont / become a busy working-class town

   second event: I / be born

   (by the time) _____

3. first: I / not really know the importance of trust

   second: I / started to spend a lot of time traveling

   (until) _____

4. first: we / go on vacation to Wyoming three times

   second: we / moved there last year

   (before) _____

Writing Skill: Using Sensory Details

Sensory details are details that show how things look, feel, smell, taste, or sound. Sensory details can enrich your writing style. They make sentences in narrative and descriptive writing more interesting because they help the reader experience what the writer is describing.

The next morning, I <u>limped</u> out to the highway and stood in the <u>shrieking</u> wind under a <u>high, cold, cloudless</u> sky with my thumb <u>jabbed</u> out.

Words like *limped* and *jabbed* convey body movements; they help you see how the narrator moved. *Shrieking* conveys how loud the wind sounded. *High, cold,* and *cloudless* paint a picture of how the sky looked.

D | **Critical Thinking: Analyzing.** Discuss in a small group the underlined sensory details in the sentences (1–6) from "Welcome Stranger." What do they convey? How do they help you more clearly understand what Junger is describing?

1. My first night was spent in a blizzard in the South Dakota Badlands, the second in the <u>desolate</u> little town of Gillette, Wyoming.

2. Freight liners <u>barreled</u> past me.

3. Locals drove by in pickups and threw beer bottles that <u>exploded</u> against the frozen pavement.

4. After two or three hours, I saw a man <u>working his way</u> toward me along the on-ramp from town.

5. He wore <u>filthy canvas</u> coveralls and carried a black lunch box, and as he got closer, I could see that his hair was <u>matted</u> in a way that occurs only after months <u>on the skids</u>.

6. In the <u>quickly gathering</u> dusk, I started walking back down the road looking for a place to spend the night.

E | **Critical Thinking: Applying.** Rewrite five of the sentences from your Free Writing using sensory details.

A | **Planning.** Follow the steps to make notes for your narrative.

Step 1 Look back at exercise **A** on page 204 and choose the story you want to tell.

Step 2 Write a thesis statement for your narrative in the space below. Answer the questions.

Step 3 Think about the beginning, the middle, and the end of your story. Use a time line like the one on page 202, if necessary. Then answer the questions to write a topic sentence for each of your body paragraphs.

Step 4 Note some ideas for an introduction. Include details that set the scene for your narrative, such as the time and place of your story.

Step 5 Think about ways to analyze and reflect on your life lesson for your conclusion. Restate your thesis and add some new information.

Introduction: Where/When did this happen? _____

Thesis statement: What did you learn? Why is this event important?

_____

1st body paragraph: What happened first?

Topic sentence: _____

Explanation and examples: _____

_____

_____

2nd body paragraph: Then what happened?

Topic sentence: _____

Explanation and examples: _____

_____

_____

3rd body paragraph: What happened after that?

Topic sentence: _____

Explanation and examples: _____

_____

_____

Optional additional body paragraphs: What happened after that?

Topic sentence: _____

Explanation and examples: _____

_____

_____

Conclusion: How/Why are these events important to you?

_____

_____

B | **Draft 1.** Use your outline to write a first draft of your narrative.

C | **Critical Thinking: Analyzing.** Work with a partner. Read the essay, which is a personal narrative. Then follow the steps to analyze the narrative.

When I was a child, my father had a saying: "All work is noble." What he meant was that it didn't matter what your job was—the important thing was to do your best at whatever you did. My parents weren't wealthy. They worked hard all their lives at honest, necessary jobs that I thought were dull. They provided a good life for me. Thanks to their efforts, I was able to go to college. But I wanted to do something different with my life, something glamorous—I was too special to take just any sort of job! But my attempts to get my dream job helped me to understand my father's words: "It doesn't matter what you do, just do the best you can."

It was January, in the middle of one of the coldest winters the East Coast had experienced in years. I had set out for New York to get a job as a graphic designer. I had studied design in college, and I had a great portfolio filled with samples of my work. I had a little money that I received as a graduation present. It was enough to get me there and to support myself for about a month. I was sure it would be enough—I would be offered a fantastic job immediately, or so I thought.

After a few weeks, though, I found myself wandering around the streets, down to my last few dollars. I had been to countless design offices, only to be turned away by one patronizing office flunky after another. I didn't get one interview. No one saw my work samples. I only had enough money for a couple more nights at the hostel where I was staying. I hadn't eaten since the previous day. I had no prospects and all the wrong clothes. How had I gotten to this point, I wondered as I shivered in my thin California jacket. But this was typical for me at the time. When I was in my early 20s, I thought I knew everything. It never occurred to me that I should have contacted design companies in advance, let alone checked the weather!

When I was just about to give up, I called my parents. I hadn't called them the entire time I was there—I was waiting until I had some good news. I felt that I should be supporting myself at this point in my life and not relying on other people—especially my parents—in any way. When I reached them, they suggested that I get a job working in a restaurant just until I could get something else. At first, I balked. I didn't come to New York to be a waiter. I could do that anywhere! I felt angry. I was disappointed in myself. But I was hungry, and I refused to go home feeling ashamed and defeated.

I decided that I wasn't going to give up. After that call, I gave some serious thought to what my parents had said. Earlier, I had noticed a posh-looking café near one of the design offices, and I headed over there. When I entered, I could see it was a popular place. There was a massive lunch crowd. A few harried waiters were dashing around carrying orders. I asked a woman at the front desk if they were hiring. She turned out to be the owner. She said they were shorthanded, and she offered me a job on the spot. To my surprise, I found that I was very good at being a waiter. I was completely amazed that I enjoyed serving people. I started making big tips right away and soon found a place to live. The main thing was that I felt good about myself—I was able to survive in a big city, and I didn't have to depend on my parents. Later, the owner learned that I had a design background. She paid me extra to design menus for the café. That work led to a part-time job at an advertising company.

A few weeks before, I never would have considered taking a job as a waiter, but there I was. I eventually got the design job of my dreams, but that winter I learned not to make assumptions about work. As my dad said, "All work is noble."

Step 1 What information does the introduction include to set up the story?

Step 2 Underline the thesis statement. Does it explain the lesson that the writer learned?

Step 3 Underline the time words and expressions that the writer used in the body paragraphs. Is the order of the events clear?

Step 4 Circle any sensory details in the narrative. Do they give you a clear picture of what the writer experienced?

Step 5 Does the writer analyze or reflect on the lesson in the conclusion?

D | Revising. Follow steps 1–5 in exercise **C** to analyze your own narrative.

E | Peer Evaluation. Exchange your first draft with a partner and follow these steps.

Step 1 Read your partner's narrative and tell him or her one thing that you liked about it.

Step 2 Complete the outline showing the information and events that your partner's narrative describes.

Introduction: Where/When did this happen? _____

Thesis statement: What did you learn? Why is this event important?

_____

1st body paragraph: What happened first?

Topic sentence: _____

Explanation and examples: _____

_____

_____

2nd body paragraph: Then what happened?

Topic sentence: _____

Explanation and examples: _____

_____

_____

3rd body paragraph: What happened after that?

Topic sentence: _____

Explanation and examples: _____

_____

_____

Optional additional body paragraphs: What happened after that?

Topic sentence: _____

Explanation and examples: _____

_____

_____

Conclusion: How/Why are these events important to you?

_____

Step 3 Compare this outline with the one that your partner created in exercise **A** on page 207.

Step 4 The two outlines should be similar. If they aren't, discuss how they differ.

F | **Draft 2.** Write a second draft of your narrative. Use what you learned from the peer evaluation activity and your answers to exercise **D**. Make any other necessary changes.

G | **Editing Practice.** Read the information in the box. Then find and correct one mistake in each sentence (1–4).

> When you use past forms, remember to use:
>
> - the past continuous for progressive actions in the past and the simple past for events that were completed: *I was walking along the trail when I met another hiker.*
> - the correct past participles in sentences with the past perfect. Memorize irregular past participles such as *buy* ➞ *bought*. See page 250 for a list of past forms.

1. As soon as I arrived in Mexico City, I realized I had forgot all the Spanish I had ever learned.
2. I waited at the bus stop when a friendly-looking older man stopped and asked me if I wanted a ride.
3. I learned that I had not apply for a passport early enough to go on my trip at the end of the month.
4. I was looking for the exit when suddenly all the lights were going out.

H | **Editing Checklist.** Use the checklist to find errors in your second draft.

Editing Checklist	Yes	No
1. Are all the words spelled correctly?		
2. Does every sentence have correct punctuation?		
3. Do your subjects and verbs agree?		
4. Have you used past forms correctly?		

I | **Final Draft.** Now use your Editing Checklist to write a third draft of your narrative. Make any other necessary changes.

Imagining the Future

Think and Discuss

1. Do you think humans will ever live on another planet? Why, or why not?
2. Why do you think some people are fascinated with the idea of visiting other planets?

▲ An early science-fiction illustration by artist and explorer Anthony Fiala (1869–1950) depicts an imaginary trip to Mars.

Exploring the Theme

Read the information below and discuss the questions.

1. Why were a lot of science-fiction stories written in the 17th and 18th centuries?
2. Which of the books, television shows, and movies mentioned below have you read or seen? What others do you know about?
3. In what ways is modern science fiction different from that of previous centuries? How do you think science fiction will evolve in the future?

The origins of today's science-fiction tales can be traced back at least 2,000 years. The ancient Hindu epic *Ramayana* describes machines that can fly into space. The Greek playwright Aristophanes, who was alive at around the same time, also wrote about traveling through the air to other worlds—a dream that continues to inspire writers and filmmakers today.

8th–10th Centuries

In *One Thousand and One Nights*, also known as *The Arabian Nights*, the character Bulukiya travels through space to strange worlds in search of the herb of immortality.

17th and 18th Centuries

The period in Europe known as "The Age of Reason" was a time of great scientific discovery. Two notable stories of the period are English author Francis Godwin's *The Man in the Moone* (1638) and French writer Voltaire's *Micromégas* (1752), which suggested that people from other planets might be more advanced than people on Earth.

19th Century

Further scientific discoveries inspired stories of exploration under the sea, inside the earth, through time, and in outer space. Some of the most popular were Jules Verne's *From the Earth to the Moon* (1865) and H. G. Wells's *The War of the Worlds* (1898).

Early 20th Century

The creation of magazines devoted to science-fiction stories and the development of film technology led to a boom in science-fiction stories, ranging from Buck Rogers to Fritz Lang's 1927 movie *Metropolis*.

1940s to Today

Some of the best-known sci-fi stories—including Ray Bradbury's *The Martian Chronicles* (1950)— were written during the "Golden Age of Science Fiction" in the 1940s and 50s. Since then, the genre has evolved with TV shows, such as *Star Trek* and *The X-Files*, and movies about space exploration and invasion, such as *District 9* and *Avatar*.

▲ Michael Whelan's artwork for
The Martian Chronicles portrays
an imaginary alien landscape.

A | **Building Vocabulary.** Read the following paragraphs about science fiction. Use the context to guess the meanings of the words and phrase in **blue**. Then write the correct word or phrase to complete each sentence (1–6).

THE POWER OF SCIENCE FICTION

Ever since people first gazed up at the **flickering** stars, we have wondered what might be "out there." This fascination with distant worlds is still with us today. When we watch movies such as *Star Trek* or *Star Wars* and their many **sequels**, we can visit worlds that **look familiar** and strange at the same time. The alien **invasion** movie *Independence Day* speculated on our first encounters with intelligent—but unfriendly—beings. Science fiction also allows us to imagine the eventual **destiny** of our own planet: In the movie *Wall-E*, for example, a robot continues to clean up the Earth's trash, centuries after the last traces of humanity have **vanished** from our world.

James Cameron's *Avatar* ▶ envisaged a human-alien clash of civilizations on a distant planet.

1. If people or things _____ to you, they appear to be similar to someone or something that you know.

2. If people or things have _____, they have disappeared suddenly or in a way that cannot be explained.

3. A(n) _____ occurs when a foreign enemy enters a place, such as a country, by force.

4. _____ to a book or movie continue its story.

5. _____ refers to whatever will happen in the future, especially when it is considered to be controlled by someone or something else.

6. If a light or flame is _____, it is shining unsteadily.

B | Building Vocabulary. Complete the definitions (1–6) with the words or phrase from the box. Use a dictionary to help you.

dwindle	flee	in proportion	literally	resembles	stunned

1. If one thing or person _____ another, the two things or people are very similar to each other.

2. If you _____ a person or thing, you escape from that person or thing.

3. If you are _____ by something, you are extremely shocked or surprised by it.

4. If one thing increases or decreases _____ to another thing, it changes to the same degree as the second item.

5. You use "_____" to emphasize that what you are saying is true, even though it seems exaggerated or surprising.

6. If things _____, they become smaller, weaker, or fewer in number.

Word Link

liter = letter:
al**liter**ation, il**liter**ate, **liter**al, **liter**ally

Word Partners

Use **flee/fled** with nouns:
(*n.*) fled **the scene**; (*from + n.*) fled **from the situation**, (*to + n.*) fled **to safety**

C | Using Vocabulary. Answer the questions. Share your ideas with a partner.

1. Think of a movie or television show that portrays life on a distant planet. In what ways does the world **resemble** our own world? How is it different?

2. What technology that we use today do you think will **vanish** in 10, 20, or 50 years? What kinds of technology do you think we will have instead?

3. What do you think is the **destiny** of our own planet? What will it be like 1,000 years from now?

D | Brainstorming. Discuss these questions in a small group.

1. What are some reasons that someone might want to write stories about space exploration?

2. What are some reasons that humans might want to live on another planet?

E | Predicting. Skim the reading passages on pages 216–222 and answer the questions. As you read, check your predictions.

1. What kind of reading is the first passage (pages 216–218)?

   a. a fictional story
   b. an autobigraphical essay
   c. an explanatory article

2. What kind of reading is the second passage (pages 219–222)?

   a. a set of fictional stories
   b. extracts from an autobiography
   c. explanatory articles

MY MARS

by Ray Bradbury

"That was the day Mars took me home—and I never really came back."

track 2-05

A **WHEN I WAS SIX YEARS OLD,** I moved to Tucson, Arizona, and lived on Lowell Avenue, little realizing I was on an avenue that led to Mars. It was named for the great astronomer Percival Lowell, who took fantastic photographs of the planet that promised a spacefaring future to children like myself.

B Along the way to growing up, I read Edgar Rice Burroughs and loved his Martian books, and followed the instructions of his Mars pioneer John Carter, who told me, when I was 12, that it was simple: If I wanted to follow the avenue of Lowell and go to the stars, I needed to go out on the summer night lawn, lift my arms, stare at the planet Mars, and say, "Take me home."

C That was the day that Mars took me home—and I never really came back. I began writing on a toy typewriter. I couldn't afford to buy all the Martian books I wanted, so I wrote the **sequels** myself.

D When I was 15, a Martian disguised as an American boy went to see the film *Things to Come*, by H. G. Wells, about a dark, war-torn future Earth. In the final scene the protagonist,[1] Cabal, and his friend Passworthy watch the first moon rocket disappear into the heavens carrying their two grown children toward a brighter **destiny**. Cabal looks toward the dust at his feet then up at the stars, saying to Passworthy and to the audience, "Is it this or that? All the universe or nothing? Which shall it be? Which shall it be?"

E This Martian staggered out of the theater inspired to write more stories because I knew we were going to the stars.

F Some years later, I made my way to New York City on a Greyhound bus, hoping to find a publisher. I carried a bundle of manuscripts with me, and people would ask, "Is that a novel?" To which I replied, "No, I write short stories." On my last night in New York, I got a break. I had dinner with an editor from Doubleday who said to me, "I think that without realizing it, you have, in fact, written a novel."

G I asked him what he meant.

H He replied, "If you tied all your Martian landscapes together and made a tapestry of them, wouldn't they make a book that you could call *The Martian Chronicles*?"

I I was **stunned.** The small Martian in me hadn't realized that he'd been putting his hands inside my hands and moving the typewriter keys to write a book. I finished it over the next six months. I was 29—and well on my way to the stars.

[1] The **protagonist** of a story is the main character.

▲ A view from one of the *Viking* landers, which touched down on Mars in 1976

In 1976 I was invited to stay overnight at the Jet Propulsion Laboratory in Pasadena, waiting for news to come back from the *Viking 1* lander, which was going to touch down on Mars and take photographs.

It was incredibly exciting to be there, surrounded by engineers, waiting for the first pictures. There was a tall gentleman standing next to me, who I thought **looked familiar**. At last, I realized it was none other than Wernher von Braun, the man who had **fled** Germany for America to become the co-inventor of the rocket that took us to the moon and that was now taking us to the planets.

Early in the morning, the photographs began to arrive. I could hardly believe I was seeing the surface of Mars! At 9:00 A.M., ABC television put me on the air to get my reaction.

The interviewer said, "Mr. Bradbury, how do you feel about this landing? Where are the Martian cities and where are all the living beings?"

"Don't be a fool," I said. "WE are the Martians! We're going to be here for the next million years. At long last, WE ARE MARTIANS!"

That was the end of the interview.

I LIKE TO THINK of the cosmos[2] as a theater, yet a theater cannot exist without an audience, to witness and to celebrate. Robot craft and mighty telescopes will continue to show us unimaginable wonders. But when humans return to the moon and put a base there and prepare to go to Mars and become true Martians, we— the audience—**literally** enter the cosmic theater. Will we finally reach the stars?

A few years ago, I traveled back to my boyhood home in Tucson. I stood out on the lawn and looked up at the night sky—and realized the stars had never looked closer than right there on Lowell Avenue.

[2] The **cosmos** is the universe.

AUGUST 2001 THE SETTLERS

The men of Earth came to Mars

They came because they were afraid or unafraid, because they were happy or unhappy, because they felt like Pilgrims or did not feel like Pilgrims. There was a reason for each man. They were leaving bad wives or bad jobs or bad towns; they were coming to find something or leave something or get something, to dig up something or bury something or leave something alone. They were coming with small dreams or large dreams or none at all. But a government finger pointed from four-color posters in many towns: THERE'S WORK FOR YOU IN THE SKY: SEE MARS! and the men shuffled forward, only a few at first, a doublescore,[3] for most men felt the great illness in them even before the rocket fired into space. And this disease was called The Loneliness, because when you saw your home town **dwindle** to the size of your fist and then lemon-size and then pin-size and **vanish** in the fire-wake, you felt you had never been born, there was no town, you were nowhere, with space all around, nothing familiar, only other strange men. And when the state of Illinois, Iowa, Missouri, or Montana vanished into cloud seas, and, doubly, when the United States shrank to a misted island and the entire planet Earth became a muddy baseball tossed away, then you were alone, wandering in the meadows of space, on your way to a place you couldn't imagine.

So it was not unusual that the first men were few. The number grew steadily **in proportion** to the census of Earth Men already on Mars. There was comfort in numbers. But the first Lonely Ones had to stand by themselves.

[3] A score is 20 or about 20, so a **doublescore** is about 40.

FEBRUARY 2002 THE LOCUSTS

The rockets set the bony meadows afire, turned rock to lava, turned wood to charcoal, transmitted water to steam, made sand and silica into green glass which lay like shattered mirrors reflecting the **invasion**, all about. The rockets came like drums, beating in the night. The rockets came like locusts,[4] swarming and settling in blooms of rosy smoke. And from the rockets ran men with hammers in their hands to beat the strange world

T   into a shape that was familiar to the eye, to bludgeon away all the strangeness, their mouths fringed with nails so they **resembled** steel-toothed carnivores, spitting them into their swift hands as they hammered up frame cottages and scuttled over roofs with shingles to blot out the eerie stars, and fit green shades to pull against the night. And when the carpenters had hurried on, the women came in with flowerpots and chintz[5] and pans and set up a kitchen clamor to cover the silence that Mars made waiting outside the door and the shaded window.

In six months a dozen small towns had been laid down upon the naked planet, filled with sizzling neon

U   tubes and yellow electric bulbs. In all, some ninety thousand people came to Mars, and more, on Earth, were packing their grips. . . . [6]

[4] **Locusts** are large insects, similar to grasshoppers, that live mainly in hot areas and often cause serious damage to crops.
[5] **Chintz** is a cotton fabric decorated with flowery patterns.
[6] **Grips** are small suitcases.

NOVEMBER 2005 THE WATCHERS

They all came out and looked at the sky that night. They left their suppers or their washing up or their dressing for the show and they came out upon their now-not-quite-as-new porches and watched the green star of Earth there. It was a move without conscious effort; they all did it, to help them understand the news they had heard on the radio a moment before. There was Earth and there the coming war, and there hundreds of thousands of mothers or grandmothers or fathers or brothers or aunts or uncles or cousins. They stood on the porches and tried to believe in the existence of Earth, much as they had once tried to believe in the existence of Mars; it was a problem reversed. To all intents and purposes, Earth now was dead; they had been away from it for three or four years. Space was an anesthetic; seventy million miles of space numbed you, put memory to sleep, depopulated Earth, erased the past, and allowed these people here to go on with their work. But now, tonight, the dead were risen, Earth was reinhabited, memory awoke, a million names were spoken: What was so-and-so doing tonight on Earth? What about this one and that one? The people on the porches glanced sidewise at each other's faces.

At nine o'clock Earth seemed to explode, catch fire, and burn.

The people on the porches put up their hands as if to beat the fire out.

They waited.

By midnight the fire was extinguished. Earth was still there.
There was a sigh, like an autumn wind, from the porches.

"We haven't heard from Harry for a long time."

"He's all right."

"We should send a message to Mother."

"She's all right."

"Is she?"

"Now, don't worry."

"Will she be all right, do you think?"

"Of course, of course; now come to bed."

But nobody moved. Late dinners were carried out onto the night lawns and set upon collapsible tables, and they picked at these slowly until two o'clock and the light-radio message flashed from Earth. They could read the great Morse-code flashes which **flickered** like a distant firefly:

AUSTRALIAN CONTINENT ATOMIZED IN PREMATURE EXPLOSION OF ATOMIC STOCKPILE. LOS ANGELES, LONDON BOMBED. WAR. COME HOME. COME HOME. COME HOME.

Continued on page 222

They stood up from their tables.

COME HOME. COME HOME. COME HOME.

"Have you heard from your brother Ted this year?"

"You know. With mail rates five bucks a letter to Earth, I don't write much."

COME HOME.

Z "I've been wondering about Jane; you remember Jane, my kid sister?"

COME HOME.

At three in the chilly morning, the luggage-store proprietor glanced up.
A lot of people were coming down the street.

"Stayed open late on purpose. What'll it be, mister?"

By dawn the luggage was gone from his shelves.

Reading Skill: Identifying Literary Elements

Literary fiction consists of several elements. These are similar to the elements of a personal narrative (see page 202).

Plot: the action of the story—what the characters do, say, and think. Plot has a beginning, a middle, and an end. Between the beginning and the middle, action rises toward the story's climax, or most intense point. After that, the action falls toward the conclusion, or resolution, of the story.

Characters: all of the individuals in the story. These can include people, animals, or any other things that perform action or express thoughts in the story. The main character of a story is called the protagonist.

Setting: the time and place (when and where) the story takes place. However, the setting is more than just a time and location; it can also set the mood for a story.

Point of view: the perspective from which the story is told. Is the story told by a narrator outside of the story? Is it told by a character?

Theme: the story's main idea or central message. A story can have more than one theme. Sometimes the theme is stated directly, and other times it is implied.

A | **Analyzing.** Match each element below with an example from *The Martian Chronicles*.

Element

1. _____ plot
2. _____ characters
3. _____ setting
4. _____ point of view
5. _____ theme

Example

a. narrator (the writer of the story)
b. human colonists
c. the effects of colonization
d. People who have moved from Earth to Mars watch the Earth, anticipating a war. Eventually, they see parts of the Earth blow up. They decide to go back to Earth.
e. small towns set up on the surface of Mars

B | **Applying.** Complete the chart with information about a story you have read or a movie you have seen. Then describe the story to a partner.

Title	
Main Character (Protagonist)	
Setting	
Point of View	
Theme(s)	
Plot	

A | **Understanding Main Ideas.** Write answers to the questions about "My Mars" on pages 216–218. Share your ideas with a partner.

1. What events or experiences in Ray Bradbury's childhood led to his writing *The Martian Chronicles*?

   _____

   _____

   _____

2. Bradbury writes that "WE are the Martians!" (paragraph N). What does he mean?

   _____

   _____

   _____

B | **Identifying Key Details.** Write answers to the questions about "My Mars."

1. Who is John Carter? What influence did he have on Bradbury?

   _____

   _____

2. Why did Bradbury write sequels to the books that he read?

   _____

   _____

3. Why was Bradbury's visit to Pasadena in 1976 significant?

   _____

   _____

C | **Identifying Meaning from Context.** Find and underline the following words and phrases in the reading. Use context to match each word or phrase with its meaning.

1. _____ Paragraph B: **along the way**   a. walked very unsteadily

2. _____ Paragraph E: **staggered**   b. was lucky after a period of effort

3. _____ Paragraph F: **got a break**   c. after you have been hoping for it for a long time

4. _____ Paragraph J: **touch down**   d. during the course of a particular event or process

5. _____ Paragraph K: **none other than**   e. in fact; surprisingly

6. _____ Paragraph N: **at long last**   f. land (an aircraft or a spacecraft) on the ground

D | **Critical Thinking: Reading Literature Critically.** Write notes to answer the questions about the excerpts on pages 219–222. Then discuss your answers in a small group.

THE SETTLERS

1. What event causes "The Loneliness"? What real-life event can you compare with The Loneliness?

   _____

   _____

2. The narrator explains that people came to Mars "because they were afraid or unafraid, because they were happy or unhappy, . . . " How might two people with opposite reasons for leaving Earth make the same decision—to go to Mars?

   _____

   _____

   _____

THE LOCUSTS

3. Why do you think the first excerpt is titled "THE LOCUSTS"? Who or what are the locusts in the story?

   _____

   _____

4. The men from the rockets ran "with hammers in their hands to beat the strange world into a shape that was familiar to the eye." Why did they do this? In what ways do people do this in the real world?

   _____

   _____

THE WATCHERS

5. What emotions are the colonists experiencing? What do they decide to do? How do we know this?

   _____

   _____

E | Critical Thinking: Interpreting Figurative Language. Read each sentence or phrase (1–7) from the reading. What is Bradbury saying in each case? Why does he use figurative language rather than literal language? Discuss your ideas with a partner.

MY MARS

1. That was the day that Mars took me home—and I never really came back.

2. The small Martian in me hadn't realized that he'd been putting his hands inside my hands and moving the typewriter keys to write a book.

THE SETTLERS

3. And this disease was called The Loneliness, because when you saw your home town dwindle . . . you felt you had never been born, there was no town, you were nowhere, with space all around, nothing familiar, only other strange men.

THE LOCUSTS

4. The rockets came like drums, beating in the night.

5. . . . their mouths fringed with nails so they resembled steel-toothed carnivores . . .

THE WATCHERS

6. They could read the great Morse-code flashes which flickered like a distant firefly.

7. Space was an anesthetic.

F | Critical Thinking: Making Inferences. Write answers to the questions.

1. Based on what Bradbury writes in "My Mars," why do you think he told the kinds of stories that he told?

_____

_____

_____

_____

2. What is one message or warning that you think Bradbury was trying to communicate with his stories?

_____

_____

_____

_____

MISSION: MARS

Before Viewing

A | Using a Dictionary. Here are some words you will hear in the video. Match each word with the correct definition. Use your dictionary to help you.

1. _____: a deep crack in something, especially in rock or in the ground

2. _____: very large

3. _____: the land, water, or plants that you can see around you

4. _____: the force that causes things to fall toward a large object, such as a planet

> colossal
> fissure
> gravity
> scenery

 B | Thinking Ahead. If you could visit Mars, what do you think you would see? Make a list with a partner.

_____

_____

While Viewing

A | Watch the video about Mars. As you watch, check your answer to exercise **B** above. Circle the things that are mentioned.

B | Read questions 1–4. Think about the answers as you view the video.

1. What is the Valles Marineris?
2. What is significant about the fissure at the bottom of the Valles Marineris?
3. How much higher is the Mons Olympus than Mount Everest?
4. How might the gravity on Mars affect the height of the Mons Olympus?

After Viewing

 A | Discuss your answers to questions 1–4 above with a partner.

B | Critical Thinking: Synthesizing. Imagine that Ray Bradbury had today's current knowledge of Mars when he wrote *The Martian Chronicles*. How do you think the knowledge might have affected his stories?

▼ Victoria Crater, Mars

GOAL: Writing an Analysis of Literature

In this lesson, you are going to plan, write, revise, and edit a paper on the following topic:
***Write an analysis of the three excerpts from* The Martian Chronicles.**

Writing Skill: Writing Critically about Literature

When you write an analysis of a story or novel, you choose one aspect of the story or novel to focus on. Then you state an argument about that aspect, and you use quotes and paraphrases from the story as evidence to support your argument. The argument should be broad enough that you can write several paragraphs about it.

Good argument/question: In *The Martian Chronicles*, Ray Bradbury shows us that when we try to escape from our problems, we do not suddenly have perfect and happy lives.

Weak argument/question: In *The Martian Chronicles*, people decide to go to Mars to escape their problems.

In each paragraph of your analysis, you can include one or more quotes or paraphrases from the story as your evidence. Then show how each of the quotes or paraphrases is significant. In other words, show how it supports your argument or answer.

A | **Critical Thinking: Evaluating.** Check (✓) the statements that are possible topics for analysis of *The Martian Chronicles*.

- [ ] 1. The actions and feelings of the people in *The Martian Chronicles* are similar to the actions and experiences of people in real life in several ways.

- [ ] 2. In "November 2005: THE WATCHERS," the people are watching a war on Earth.

- [ ] 3. Many events in *The Martian Chronicles* are similar to events that occur in real life.

- [ ] 4. In many ways, *The Martian Chronicles* is a cautionary tale for readers.

- [ ] 5. *The Martian Chronicles* is a famous story about space exploration.

B | **Critical Thinking: Evaluating.** Check (✓) four pieces of evidence that best support the following argument: *In* The Martian Chronicles, *Ray Bradbury shows us that when we try to escape from our problems, we do not suddenly have perfect and happy lives.*

- [ ] 1. The government wanted workers to move to Mars.

- [ ] 2. "And this disease was called The Loneliness, because when you saw your home town dwindle, you were nowhere, with space all around, nothing familiar, only other strange men."

☐ 3. "The number grew steadily in proportion to the census of Earth Men already on Mars."

☐ 4. The rockets burned up and destroyed the land as they invaded Mars.

☐ 5. "the women . . . set up a kitchen clamor to cover the silence that Mars made waiting outside the door and shaded window."

☐ 6. "AUSTRALIAN CONTINENT ATOMIZED IN PREMATURE EXPLOSION OF ATOMIC STOCKPILE. LOS ANGELES, LONDON BOMBED. WAR. COME HOME. COME HOME. COME HOME."

☐ 7. "They stood up from their tables."

Language for Writing: Using a Variety of Sentence Types

One way to add interest to your writing is to include a variety of sentence types: simple, compound, and complex.

A simple sentence consists of one independent clause (one subject and verb).

The men went to Mars.

A compound sentence consists of two independent clauses joined by a coordinating conjunction (*for, and, or, but, so, nor, yet*).

People wanted to escape their problems, so they went to Mars.

A complex sentence consists of at least one independent clause and one or more dependent clauses. Dependent clauses begin with relative pronouns such as *that*, *who*, or *which*, or with subordinating conjunctions such as *because*, *although*, *before*, *after*, or *when*.

Using only simple sentences can make your writing sound abrupt or choppy. However, if you combine those sentences, your writing will sound smoother.

The men landed on Mars. They changed the landscape. They wanted it to look like Earth.

↓

After they landed on Mars, the men changed the landscape so that it looked like Earth.

C | Analyzing. What kind of sentence is each of the following? Write **S** for simple, **CD** for compound, or **CX** for complex.

1. _____ The individuals from Earth go to Mars for various reasons, but many go to leave problems behind such as "bad wives or bad jobs or bad towns."

2. _____ However, some of them eventually find that they're leaving one set of problems for another.

3. _____ In "February 2002: THE LOCUSTS," as more and more rockets land on their new home planet, they burn the planet's trees and meadows and melt the rock and sand.

4. _____ They turn Mars into a second Earth "filled with sizzling neon tubes and yellow electric bulbs."

5. _____ In a sense, they bring their problems with them because they need to be surrounded by familiar things such as "flowerpots and chintz" on this strange new planet.

D | **Brainstorming.** Brainstorm ideas from the three excerpts from *The Martian Chronicles* on pages 219–222 that support each of the arguments below.

1. The actions and feelings of the people in *The Martian Chronicles* are similar to the actions and experiences of people in real life in several ways. (Consider the following: the reasons for going to Mars, the colonization of Mars, the war, the desire to return to Earth.)

_____

_____

_____

_____

_____

2. In many ways, *The Martian Chronicles* is a cautionary tale for readers. (Consider the following: people who want to escape their problems, wars, and governments that want to colonize other countries.)

_____

_____

_____

_____

_____

Free Writing. Write for five minutes. Choose one of the arguments from exercise **A**. Write down any details and ideas that might help you support the argument.

A | **Planning.** Follow the steps to make notes for your paper.

Step 1 Decide the argument from exercise **A** (page 228) you will write about. Write your thesis statement in the outline below.

Step 2 Reread the three excerpts from *The Martian Chronicles* on pages 219–222. Underline any parts of the story that might support your thesis.

Step 3 Write the topic sentences for your three body paragraphs.

Step 4 Write notes about evidence from the excerpts that support each topic sentence. For each piece of evidence, write notes about why the evidence is significant.

Introductory paragraph: What is your argument?

_____

_____

1st body paragraph: What is one piece of evidence that supports your thesis?

Topic sentence: _____

_____

Evidence and significance of evidence: _____

_____

2nd body paragraph: What is a second piece of evidence that supports your thesis?

Topic sentence: _____

_____

Evidence and significance of evidence: _____

_____

3rd body paragraph: What is a third piece of evidence that supports your thesis?

Topic sentence: _____

_____

Evidence and significance of evidence: _____

_____

Concluding paragraph: Review your main points and your thesis statement.

_____

_____

B | **Draft 1.** Use your outline to write a first draft of your analytical paper.

C | **Critical Thinking: Analyzing.** Work with a partner. Read an analytical paper about *The Martian Chronicles*. Then follow the steps to analyze the paper.

> Use italics for the titles of books and movies.

> When you write about literature, use the present tense.

> You can weave quotes from the story into your own sentences.

> Use quotation marks around chapter titles and poem titles.

The Martian Chronicles is a novel about a time when humans on Earth start moving to and colonizing the planet Mars. The individuals from Earth go to Mars for various reasons, but many go to leave problems behind such as "bad wives or bad jobs or bad towns." However, some of them eventually find that they're leaving one set of problems for another. In *The Martian Chronicles*, Ray Bradbury shows us that when we try to escape from our problems, we don't suddenly have perfect and happy lives.

The first problem that moving to Mars causes for the migrants is a disease called "The Loneliness." As the narrator explains in "August 2001: THE SETTLERS," "this disease was called The Loneliness, because when you saw your home town dwindle to the size of your fist . . . you felt you had never been born, there was no town, you were nowhere, with space all around, nothing familiar, only other strange men." This shows that the migrants are creating new problems for themselves as they try to escape their old problems. At least on Earth, people were surrounded by familiarity—a town they knew, people they knew, and people who knew them. On their way to Mars, the "Lonely Ones" become nothing and are surrounded by nothing.

Another problem that the migrants experience is the ugliness of their own invasion of Mars. In "February 2002: THE LOCUSTS," as more and more rockets land on their new home planet, they burn the planet's trees and meadows and melt the rock and sand. And even though many of the migrants come to Mars to escape their lives on Earth, they recreate some of the less appealing things on Earth. They turn Mars into a second Earth "filled with sizzling neon tubes and yellow electric bulbs." This demonstrates that in a sense, they bring their problems with them because they need to be surrounded by familiar things such as "flowerpots and chintz" on this strange new planet.

In "November 2005: THE WATCHERS," the migrants learn that they really can't escape their own problems or their own lives. For a while, they are able to forget about Earth. After being on Mars for three or four years, "Earth now was dead" to them. However, as they watch Earth seem to "explode, catch fire, and burn" at the start of a war, they are reminded of the people and the lives they left behind. They start to wonder and worry about them. When they receive a message telling them to "COME HOME. COME HOME. COME HOME," they feel that they have to. This supports the idea that their problems haven't disappeared. They need to go back to Earth and reclaim the lives that they abandoned.

Through the actions and words of the characters in the story, Ray Bradbury's *The Martian Chronicles* shows the reader that even if you go to another planet, you can't forget about who you are or live a problem-free life. No matter where you go, you bring your problems with you, or you create new ones.

Step 1 Underline the thesis statement.

Step 2 Underline the topic sentences of the body paragraphs.

Step 3 Circle each piece of evidence in the body paragraphs.

Step 4 Underline the main points that are reviewed in the conclusion.

D | Revising. Follow the steps in exercise **C** to analyze your own analytical paper.

E | Peer Evaluation. Exchange your first draft with a partner and follow these steps.

Step 1 Read your partner's analytical paper and tell him or her one thing that you liked about it.

Step 2 Complete the outline showing the ideas that your partner's paper describes.

Introductory paragraph: What is your partner's argument?

_____

_____

1st body paragraph: What is one piece of evidence that supports the thesis?

Topic sentence: _____

_____

Evidence and significance of evidence: _____

_____

2nd body paragraph: What is a second piece of evidence that supports the thesis?

Topic sentence: _____

_____

Evidence and significance of evidence: _____

_____

3rd body paragraph: What is a third piece of evidence that supports the thesis?

Topic sentence: _____

_____

Evidence and significance of evidence: _____

_____

Concluding paragraph: Review the main points and thesis statement.

_____

_____

Step 3 Compare this outline with the one that your partner created in exercise **A** on page 231.

Step 4 The two outlines should be similar. If they aren't, discuss how they differ.

WRITING TASK: Editing

F | **Draft 2.** Write a second draft of your analytical paper. Use what you learned from the peer evaluation activity and your answers to exercise **D**. Make any other necessary changes.

G | **Editing Practice.** Use the checklist to find errors in your second draft.

Editing Checklist	Yes	No
1. Are all the words spelled correctly?		
2. Does every sentence have correct punctuation?		
3. Do your subjects and verbs agree?		
4. Have you used a variety of sentence types?		
5. Are your verb tenses correct?		

H | **Final Draft.** Now use your Editing Checklist to write a third draft of your paper. Make any other necessary changes.

◀ A Martian greets a human visitor in a scene from the TV adaptation of *The Martian Chronicles*.

UNIT 1
Man-Made Earthquakes

Narrator: Mining is a dangerous and sometimes deadly business. Each year humans extract more than 6 billion tons of coal, 2.2 billion tons of iron, and 60 million tons of aluminum from mines around the world. And the risk isn't just with the miners; sometimes it can also be deadly for communities living above the mines as well. Newcastle, Australia, is a town built on coal mining, with over a century worth of mines snaking beneath it; it also exports the largest amount of coal in the world. But, in 1989 two days after Christmas, the southeast coastal town is rocked by one of the worst natural disasters in Australian history. A magnitude 5.6 quake kills 13 people, injures 160, and creates 4 billion U.S. dollars' worth of damage in its wake. Some scientists believe the disaster isn't entirely natural; to them it seems likely the human-made mines beneath Newcastle triggered the quake.

Christian Klose: Whenever we build an excavation underground, we perturb the natural system, so pre-existing conditions, stress conditions, underground, will be disturbed by generating an excavation underground, and these stresses need to redistribute in order to get back to a balance. So, stresses that are pre-existing coming from the side or coming from the top are disturbed.

Narrator: Dr. Klose estimates that 50 percent of all human-triggered earthquakes recorded globally are induced by mines. And if an area is mined continuously for more than 200 years, stresses can multiply. Over time, miners carve a complex series of portals and tunnels to get at the mineral, removing more and more material.

UNIT 2
Tigers in the Snow

Narrator: A male tiger's hunting pattern has evolved to insure his survival in a harsh climate where food is scarce. However large his home range, he'll never share his territory with another adult male, though sometimes he'll overlap with one or more females. Once the kill has been made, it's clear the male is the dominant partner. He won't allow the female to get near until he's had enough. Only then will he allow her to approach.

Each adult female tiger needs a home range of about 200 square miles [321 kilometers] in order to thrive. Adult males need even more space, about 500 square miles [804 kilometers]. They are at the top of their food chain, but the tigers are still endangered.

Poaching and logging are two of their biggest threats. With perhaps less than 500 tigers left in Russia, the loss of even one pushes the species closer to extinction. Since the mid-nineties the steep decline of the Amur tiger has slowed down.

It is thought its fragile population has been stabilized for the moment. Any future they have, though, must happen here, in the remote mountain forests of the Siberian wilderness.

Video Scripts

UNIT 3 — Oregon Coast

Narrator: During his life Ken Kesey was at once a counterculture and literary hero, best known for his book *One Flew Over the Cuckoo's Nest.* Before he died in 2001, Kesey spoke to National Geographic about his inspiring love of the Oregon Coast.

Ken Kesey: Everybody who has come and seen the ocean for the first time, they get over there and they look and they begin to reflect, you know, whether it's a four-year-old kid or an eighty-year-old man, they, all of them go through something in their minds that I think the human has been going through for a long, long time.

It's still treacherous out there. When I'm over there working alone at night, man, you begin to think of stuff that you think, "Why am I thinking of this?" I'm thinking of ghosts and spirits and things that move in the night. It makes you think of strange and ancient magic, the coast does.

Because you just hear that continual WHOM WHOM, and it just moves you into another wavelength. When you see something over there, you see it in a different light than you do anywhere else.

It's a wonderful place to watch sunsets. Each one is different, and you will get the real theatrical play on those clouds.

All the birds will turn and watch the sun go down. And you can sit out there and watch the sky get completely dark, and every moment there's, there's stuff going on. It is a humbling thing to go over there and move along that coast. There's just something about that edge between the land and the water.

UNIT 4 — Powering Cities

Narrator: Buildings account for nearly 40 percent of all energy consumption in the United States. Our greener future depends on greener buildings. At 1 Bryant Park in New York City, architects wanted to reduce energy consumption by half! To achieve this, they took three innovative approaches: First, the ventilation system takes in air from the outside, cleans it, circulates it throughout the building, and sends it back out.

Man: Then we filter out 95 percent of the particulate, we supply it to everyone, and when it exits the building, it will be cleaner than when it came in. So you can think of this block of Manhattan operating as a giant air filter for this part of the city as the air exits back out into the city.

Narrator: Second, the building is designed to collect rainwater and reuse it throughout the tower. Not only does this cut water consumption, but it also helps keep the building cooler. The green roof at 1 Bryant Park is the collection point for rainwater. And this system helps keep the roof itself cooler.

Man: In our cities, what happens, there is something called a Heat Island Effect. This roof was 170 degrees last August . . . hot bubbling Tar Beach. And by planting these bags, we radically reduce the temperature of our roof, lowering our own little piece of New York City, lowering its temperature.

Narrator: Not a single drop of rain will go to waste. The plants absorb some of the rainwater. The rest is funneled into the building. Rainwater is collected in five tanks. The largest tank is located in the cellar. There, the water is chilled at night and used to feed the air-conditioning system during the day.

Finally, state-of-the-art windows are designed to let light in but keep the heat out.

Serge Appel: We needed to find another way to reduce the amount of sun energy that's entering into the building. So at the tops and at the bottoms of each piece of glass, we have this thing called a frit pattern, which is baked right into the glass. It's essentially paint that's baked into the glass. And it's a series of dots that fade from bottom up and from the top down. So you look right here, you can see these dots on the glass, that's the ceramic frit.

Narrator: It's creative solutions like these that helped make 1 Bryant Park one of the greenest buildings in New York. And the first skyscraper in the world to receive platinum rating from the leadership in energy and environmental design. But some say its greatest value might be as an example of what's possible!

Richard Cook: I hope that when people look at 1 Bryant Park, they think that it could be an icon of when we start thinking fundamentally differently about the environmental impact of a skyscraper.

Stuart Gaffin: By itself, usually one building won't make a difference. We really have to transform a huge number of surfaces, and systems, and technologies in order to make a dent in the climate.

Narrator: And it looks like that's exactly what is beginning to happen.

Paul Goldberger: Many of the ideas at 1 Bryant Park are already finding their way into other buildings, already. And in a few years, we'll see lots and lots of things like it.

Locust Swarm

UNIT 5

Narrator: We now head to the Central Plains region of the United States in pursuit of a mystery more than a century old. In the mid-1800s, thousands of pioneers journeyed west in search of free land and new opportunity. Then, in 1875, out of nowhere appeared the biggest swarm of locusts ever recorded. It came over the horizon like a cloud—the perfect swarm.

Not millions, not billions, but trillions of insects swept through parts of the country causing huge amounts of damage. But soon after they appeared, they disappeared. Vanished. And there's never again been a swarm of locusts in the United States. Researcher Jeff Lockwood was determined to solve this age-old mystery, which perhaps could offer hope to people in Africa and other places that are still plagued by locusts. These insects are a menace with super powers. They can leap some six feet in a single bound. They can lift 10 times their body weight with just one leg. And a swarm can eat five times what the entire population of New York City eats in one day.

Locusts start out white and wingless when they hatch from eggs. At first they can only hop, but their bodies start to stretch as they develop wings. Once they fly, they can become the most destructive insects on the planet. Yet something killed off all the locusts in the U.S., and Lockwood was determined to find out what did it.

On a glacier in the Rocky Mountains, he started to dig for clues.

Jeff Lockwood: That looks like it.

Narrator: Evidence here is frozen in time. These locusts are the same type that formed the devastating swarm in the 1800s. Researchers guessed that locusts gathered in one spot to lay their eggs. In this case, it was probably the river valleys along the Rocky Mountains. All of their eggs were in one basket, so to speak. Lockwood realized that something else happened around those same valleys all those years ago. People discovered gold . . . and to feed the miners, farmers moved in and tilled the soil where the eggs were likely laid.

The puzzle pieces fit together. As they churned the earth, the farmers probably dug up all of the locust eggs. They may have wiped out a major menace by accident. That means the key to controlling deadly airborne swarms may lie deep in the ground.

Kenyans in New York

UNIT 6

Boniface Kandari Parsulan: After long flight from Africa, we wanted to get out and stretch our legs, and then he said, "Come on, I'll show you around my village."

Rene Lopez: Follow my lead, follow my lead.

Loyapan Lemarti: Yes, boss.

Boni: Village? This not what I call a village!

Rene: Check it out.

Boni: Some people are living on top of that?

Rene: Yeah. An apartment—there on top, that's the second floor, third floor, fourth floor. So, we live on top of each other.

Boni: Because there's no place to live or what? Why do people go up there?

Rene: There's no land, so you have to live on top of each other. So? So you keep building and building and building, up, up, up, up.

Loyapan: One very important thing we need to do first. If you going to walk on the street, you must have dollar.

Rene: All right, here we go, guys. ATM. This is where I get my money.

Loyapan: Hoooo!!

Rene: Voila!

Loyapan: What's *voila*?

Rene: Well, . . .

Boni: You take someone else money?

Rene: There you go. No, I'm not takin—this is my money.

Boni: So, you always put your money here?

Rene: It's from my bank account.

Boni: So, people can break it here easily and get your money here, here?

Rene: Yes.

Boni: Why do you put your money here?

Loyapan: Where Boni and I come from, we trade things to get money. Our ATM, it's a goat. We take a goat to the market, we sell it, we get money. No dollars coming from the wall. I think dollar talk in America very much, you know. You have no dollar, you have no voice (*tsk, tsk*).

Rene: Yeah, I wish I could fully explain it to you, but I can't.

Boni: Easy money, easy money, easy!

Loyapan: What this place, Randy?

Rene: This is Washington Square Park.

Loyapan: We're walking through the, through the park. It's a lot of people sitting around eating, drinking, chilling. You know, people eat a lot here, people graze like cows, man. You know? Nonstop. Every corner you go, you see somebody sitting down eating. Randy said, "Hey, let's grab something to eat, guys."

Rene: All right, so we're gonna order a hot dog.

Boni: What kind of a dogs (*stutters*) does they sell?

Rene: Hot dogs. Beef.

Boni: Beef? Yes. OK.

Rene: Can we have one hot dog, please? With mustard and ketchup on it.

Loyapan: You can't even tell if this is a meat or what.

Boni: Randy, what's inside this hot dog? What's that, inside the hot dog?

Rene: It's ah, a smooshed-up cow.

Loyapan: Boni just like (*action*) to the hot dog, and say "Oh yeah." I want take one home to show people that what Boni ate.

Boni: Are you sure, are you sure, Randy, this is a, a cow? Is that New York style?

Rene: That's New York style. Say again. Let's hear you. (*starts skatting*) hot dog! (*skatting "boom, bap"*) hot dog!

All together: *Boom, bap, hot dog!*

The Encroaching Desert

UNIT 7

Narrator: It is hard to believe that 4,000 years ago the Sahara was a fertile region. Today, it's the largest desert in the world.

Desertification is destroying increasing amounts of farmland because of the combined actions of drought and human activity. The Sahel region of Africa, which extends from Senegal to the Sudan, is one of the regions most seriously affected by desertification.

Once, monsoon rains maintained wild vegetation that protected the ground from the sun and formed a barrier against drying winds. In the last half-century, however, previously nomadic peoples have built permanent towns and intensified their agricultural activities. The soil has been overused and become sterile. Desertification is a problem on every continent.

The Aral Sea, in Asia, has been drying up since 1954 because the rivers that once fed it have been diverted to irrigate cotton fields. In the space of 40 years, the Aral Sea lost sixty percent of its area; it is now reduced to two lakes.

On the planetary scale, it is estimated that 5 to 6 million hectares of farmland become desertified every year.

Secrets of a Long Life

UNIT 8

Residents of Sardinia, Okinawa, and Loma Linda, California, live longer, healthier lives than just about anyone else on Earth. To understand the reasons behind this, David McLain travelled to these three different cultures of longevity. He spent time in each of these places and tried to learn about their cultures of longevity. He learned about what it is they are doing to live vital and healthy lives well into their hundreds.

The first longevity hotspot he traveled to was Sardinia, Italy. What is phenomenal about this region is that men are living just as long as women. Science isn't exactly quite sure why, but one theory is that it's because women are in charge of family finances and household management, as well as child rearing. So, men have less stress as a result. Also, the Sardinians have a fanatical zeal for the family. David witnessed one family of four generations coming together to share a giant meal, which they do every weekend. David reflected, "This is what being alive and having a family is all about." This social component of longevity is incredibly important.

However, the cultures of longevity in Sardinia are rapidly disappearing. Unfortunately, the Sardinians are moving away from traditional, natural food and are leading a sedentary lifestyle. He spent time with a woman who was almost a hundred, and her great-granddaughter. Later that day he saw that same great-granddaughter eating potato chips, and wondered, "Will the next generation live as long?"

Okinawa is an archipelago in the far south of Japan. It is home to the longest-lived people on Earth. There, David met numerous people who were into their hundreds, and they were leading active and very healthy lifestyles. The 90-year-olds were biking and fishing eight miles offshore using old diving techniques on the reef. He met an amazing woman who was over a hundred. She had been in a moai.

The rough translation of the word is a group of friends who go through life together and help each other. David believes the energy and vitality that they would get from that factored into the longevity equation. The Okinawans have a wonderful word called ikigai. It translates roughly into the reason for which you wake up in the morning. All of the centenarians had ikigai, yet another reason why so many Okinawans are living so long. One of the cornerstones of Okinawan longevity is caloric restriction. Yet, interestingly, they are eating a lot of food. The trick is that the foods that they are eating are all low in caloric density. The food included beautiful miso soups filled with carrots, seaweed, onions, and potatoes. Like the Sardinians, the Okinawans grew most of the food themselves; in their gardens . . . they go to the store for very little.

Still, Okinawa is losing its longevity edge. Okinawa has the highest rate of obesity in all of Japan. For David, this was quite shocking and somewhat disturbing to see this culture of longevity disappearing right before his eyes.

One of the most surprising facts that David discovered from his research is that a community of Seventh-day Adventists outlive their American counterparts by about 10 years. What are they doing? Quite simply, the Seventh-day Adventists, who largely populate Loma Linda, California, have a religion that reinforces positive, healthy behaviors. For example, if you are a devout Seventh-day Adventist, you are a vegetarian, nondrinker, nonsmoker, and take every Saturday off to do nothing but relax and unwind. He met several incredible people including a woman who had just turned a hundred and renewed her driver's license.

Before he could go with her for a cruise, she had to go through her morning routine, where she lifts weights and rides a stationary bike. Interestingly, the Seventh-day Adventists are the only culture of longevity that he visited who are not losing their longevity edge. While photographing a baptism at the church, David thought about how this was the perfect example of the way this culture is still growing while maintaining their traditions.

Frontline Diary

Narrator: Afghanistan, remote, majestic and shrouded in mystery.

Sebastian Junger: It's one of the most inaccessible places in the world.

Narrator: It's a land of deadly violence.

Reza Deghati: We have to go, they have seen us.

Sebastian: Hate this part.

Narrator: For two journalists, one a veteran photograph, the other a best-selling writer, the danger is part of the job. They can only tell this story by jumping in to the chaos and experiencing it all— from haunting tragedies, to the inspiring optimism of people who won't give up hope, because finding Afghanistan's soul is the only way to figure out its future.

Narrator: Reza and Sebastian meet for the first time at the Munich airport.

Sebastian: Reza, Hey.

Reza: Hi, Sebastian.

Sebastian: Good to meet you.

Reza: How are you? Good to meet you.

Narrator: Their final destination—Afghanistan, a place where the odds between surviving and dying are often even money.

Narrator: Massoud has offered to smuggle Sebastian and Reza into the country, but they have to go before the sun sets.

Sebastian: That can't be the helicopter.

Reza: This is it.

Sebastian: It looks like it's been rusting for years.

Reza: No, no, this is it, this is the helicopter.

Narrator: If everything goes right it would take but an hour to reach the warzone but a lot could go wrong. An aging helicopter will be flying over Taliban airspace and will be no match for enemy jets. With no radar, they have to clear the mountains while there is still light or they will be forced to turn back. As they begin their decent they are in total darkness. They finally land with only the help of car headlights.

Sebastian: It was like being in an old truck, except it flew.

Reza: I really feel very, very, good now being here.

Narrator: Day 1, Massoud's local headquarters, Reza begins his day, just like any other, with Tai Chi. But Sebastian isn't as lucky.

Reza: Have they bring in tea? How do you feel now?

Sebastian: I feel better. The aspirin's in. It's part of the job, practically. I don't think I've ever gone to a 3rd world and not getting sick.

Narrator: At breakfast Sebastian is already gathering details for his story. This sort of beautiful formality of eating breakfast in the morning. You don't eat it out of cereal bowl and watch TV. You know there is a ritual. By mid-morning Reza and Sebastian find their way to a make-shift refugee camp along the Kokcha River. What they are about to see, won't be forgotten. Roughly 750,000 people have been driven from homes in this country, making Afghanistan the center of the world's worst refugee crisis.

Sebastian: The thing that really makes an impression sometimes is this incredible generosity of these people. You meet Afghans and they welcome you into their home; they'll give you their last crust of bread. It's very, very, moving.

Mission: Mars

Dr. Steve Squyres: You know if you are going to Mars you'd want to go for the scenery, right? I mean you're not going for the culture; you're not going for the climate, so you definitely want to go for the scenery.

One thing that people forget is that when we've landed on Mars, we have to go to places that are safe, and safe equals pretty smooth and flat.

Narrator: Here's a bit of Mars that's anything but smooth and flat. The magnificent Valles Marineris. This titanic canyon system, over two and a half thousand miles long, and six miles deep, is probably the grandest geological feature in the solar system. It's clearly the red planet's must see destination.

Dr. David Southwood: As a human being, it's the sheer gigantism of Mars that is amazing. The Valles Marineris, is, beats the Grand Canyon, hollow, and if you've ever seen the Grand Canyon you will never forget it.

Narrator: It's so colossal; the Grand Canyon would be easily swallowed by one of the smaller side branches.

Scientist 1: We're talking about something here that's the width of the United States or of Australia crossed here.

Dr. Steve Squyres: See I think the Valles Marineris would, would be the space to go. I mean build a lodge right on the rim so you can look in.

Narrator: The attraction goes beyond sheer scenic splendor. Deeper than the canyon itself, is the mystery surrounding its formation. This giant fissure, once filled by mighty lakes, has been scoured by floods of biblical proportions.

Scientist 2: You can make estimates of how much water had to have been flowing to carve these things and you get numbers like a hundred, two hundred Amazon rivers all cut loose at once—big, big amounts of water flowing across the surface.

Narrator: The other big attraction on Mars is the largest volcano, and highest mountain, in the solar system: Olympus Mons, towers at an astounding 17 miles, three times higher than Everest. Its base covers more ground than the United Kingdom, and the massive Caldera at its summit could easily swallow greater London, Paris, and New York.

Scientist 2: So things tend to be big on Mars. I think in part that's because the planet has lower gravity and so when you pile up lava you can pile it three times higher because the gravity is three times less before it'll start to collapse under its own weight.

Contents

Tips for Reading and Note Taking

Tips for Writing and Research

Reading and Writing Reference

Tips for Reading and Note Taking

Reading fluently

Why develop your reading speed?

Reading slowly, one word at a time, makes it difficult to get an overall sense of the meaning of a text. As a result, reading becomes more challenging and less interesting than if you read at a faster pace. In general, it is a good idea to first skim a text for the gist, and then read it again more closely so that you can focus on the most relevant details.

Strategies for improving reading speed:

- Try to read groups of words rather than individual words.
- Keep your eyes moving forward. Read through to the end of each sentence or paragraph instead of going back to reread words or phrases within the sentence or paragraph.
- Read selectively. Skip functional words (articles, prepositions, etc.) and focus on words and phrases carrying meaning—the content words.
- Use clues in the text—such as highlighted text (**bold** words, words in *italics*, etc.)—to help you know which parts might be important and worth focusing on.
- Use section headings, as well as the first and last lines of paragraphs, to help you understand how the text is organized.
- Use context and other clues such as affixes and part of speech to guess the meaning of unfamiliar words and phrases. Try to avoid using a dictionary if you are reading quickly for overall meaning.

Thinking critically

As you read, ask yourself questions about what the writer is saying, and how and why the writer is presenting the information at hand.

Important critical thinking skills for academic reading and writing:

- Analyzing: Examining a text in close detail in order to identify key points, similarities, and differences.
- Evaluating: Using evidence to decide how relevant, important, or useful something is. This often involves looking at reasons for and against something.
- Inferring: "Reading between the lines"; in other words, identifying what a writer is saying indirectly, or *implicitly*, rather than directly, or *explicitly*.
- Synthesizing: Gathering appropriate information and ideas from more than one source and making a judgment, summary, or conclusion based on the evidence.
- Reflecting: Relating ideas and information in a text to your own personal experience and preconceptions (i.e., the opinions or beliefs you had before reading the text).

Note taking

Taking notes of key points and the connections between them will help you better understand the overall meaning and organization of a text. Note taking also enables you to record the most important ideas and information for future use such as when you are preparing for an exam or completing a writing assignment.

Techniques for effective note taking:

- As you read, underline or highlight important information such as dates, names, places, and other facts.
- Take notes in the margin—as you read, note the main idea and supporting details next to each paragraph. Also note your own ideas or questions about the paragraph.
- On paper or on a computer, paraphrase the key points of the text in your own words.
- Keep your notes brief—include short headings to organize the information, key words and phrases (not full sentences), and abbreviations and symbols. (See next page for examples.)
- Note sources of information precisely. Be sure to include page numbers, names of relevant people and places, and quotations.
- Make connections between key points with techniques such as using arrows and colors to connect ideas and drawing circles or squares around related information.
- Use a graphic organizer to summarize a text, particularly if it follows a pattern such as cause-effect, comparison-contrast, or chronological sequence.
- Use your notes to write a summary of the passage in order to remember what you learned.

Useful abbreviations

approx.	approximately	impt	important
ca.	about, around (date / year)	incl.	including
cd	could	info	information
Ch.	Chapter	p. (pp.)	page (pages)
devt	development	para.	paragraph
e.g./ex.	example	ppl	people
etc.	and others / and the rest	re:	regarding, concerning
excl.	excluding	res	research
govt	government	wd	would
hist	history	yr(s)	years(s)
i.e.	that is; in other words	C20	20th century

Useful symbols

→	leads to / causes
↑	increases / increased
↓	decreases / decreased
& or +	and
∴	therefore
b/c	because
w/	with
=	is the same as
>	is more than
<	is less than
~	is approximately / about

Learning vocabulary

More than likely, you will not remember a new word or phrase after reading or hearing it once. You need to use the word several times before it enters your long-term memory.

Strategies for learning vocabulary:

- Use flash cards. Write the words you want to learn on one side of an index card. Write the definition and/or an example sentence that uses the word on the other side. Use your flash cards to test your knowledge of new vocabulary.
- Keep a vocabulary journal. When you come across a new word or phrase, write a short definition of the word (in English, if possible) and the sentence or situation where you found it (its context). Write another sentence of your own that uses the word. Include any common collocations. (See the Word Partners boxes in this book for examples of collocations.)
- Make word webs (or "word maps").
- Use memory aids. It may be easier to remember a word or phrase if you use a memory aid, or *mnemonic*. For example, if you want to learn the idiom *keep an eye on someone*, which means to "watch someone carefully," you might picture yourself putting your eyeball on someone's shoulder so that you can watch the person carefully. The stranger the picture is, the more you will remember it!

Common affixes

Some words contain an affix at the start of the word (*prefix*) and/or at the end (*suffix*). These affixes can be useful for guessing the meaning of unfamiliar words and for expanding your vocabulary. In general, a prefix affects the meaning of a word, whereas a suffix affects its part of speech. See the Word Link boxes in this book for specific examples.

Prefix	Meaning	Example
auto-	self	automatic
com-	with	complementary
con-	together, with	contemporary
contra-	against	contradictory
crypt-	hidden	cryptic
de-	not	decentralized
equi-	equal	equivalent
ex-	away, from, out	excluded
hypo-	below, under, less	hypothetical
in-	within	intrinsic
inter-	between	intervene
ir-	not	irresistible
liter-	letter	literally
mani-	hand, by hand	manipulative
maxi-	largest	maximum
mono-	one	monotonous
per-	through	perspective
pro-	for, forward	proportions
re-	back, again	redefine
revol-	turn	revolution
simu-	like	simulation
sub-	under, below, instead of	substitutes
trans-	across	transcends
un-	not	unintelligible
uni-	one	unification

Suffix	Part of Speech	Example
-able	adjective	unpredictable
-al	adjective	annual
-ant	adjective	relevant
-ar	adjective	familiar
-ary	adjective	rudimentary
-ate	verb	eliminate
-ate	adjective	desperate
-ed	adjective	excluded
-ence	noun	conference
-ible	adjective	irresistible
-ic	adjective	cryptic
-ism	noun	mechanism
-ist	noun	economist
-ity	noun	minority
-ive	adjective	massive
-ize	verb	decentralize
-ly	adverb	conversely
-ment	noun	investment
-sion	noun	depression
-tion	noun	implication
-y	noun	destiny

Tips for Writing and Research

Features of academic writing

There are many types of academic writing (descriptive, argumentative/persuasive, narrative, etc.), but most types share similar characteristics.

Generally, in academic writing you should:

- write in full sentences.
- use formal English. (Avoid slang or conversational expressions such as *kind of*.)
- be clear and coherent—keep to your main point; avoid technical words that the reader may not know.
- use signal words and phrases to connect your ideas. (See examples on page 248.)
- have a clear point (main idea) for each paragraph.
- be objective—most academic writing uses a neutral, impersonal point of view, so avoid overuse of personal pronouns (*I*, *we*, *you*) and subjective language such as *nice* or *terrible*.
- use facts, examples, and expert opinions to support your argument.
- show where the evidence or opinions come from. (*According to the 2009 World Database Survey,. . . .*)
- show that you have considered other viewpoints.

Generally, in academic writing you should <u>not</u>:

- use abbreviations or language used in texting. (Use *that is* rather than *i.e.*, and *in my opinion*, not *IMO*.)
- use contractions. (Use *is not* rather than *isn't*.)
- be vague. (*Many years ago, someone proposed that people had introduced a new era.* → *In the 1870s, an Italian geologist named Antonio Stoppani proposed that people had introduced a new era, which he labeled the Anthropozoic.*)
- include several pronoun references in a single sentence. (*He thinks it's a better idea than the other one, but I agree with her.*)
- start sentences with *or*, *and*, or *but*.
- apologize to the reader. (*I'm sorry I don't know much about this, but . . .*) In academic writing, it is important to sound confident about what you are saying!

Proofreading tips

Capitalization

Remember to capitalize:

- the first letter of the word at the beginning of every sentence.
- proper names such as names of people, geographical names, company names, and names of organizations.
- days, months, and holidays.
- the word *I*.
- the first letter of a title such as the title of a movie or a book.
- the words in titles that have meaning (content words). Don't capitalize *a*, *an*, *the*, *and*, or prepositions such *as to*, *for*, *of*, *from*, *at*, *in*, and *on*, unless they are the first word of a title (e.g., *The King and I*).

Punctuation

Keep the following rules in mind:

- Use a question mark (?) at the end of every question. Use a period (.) at the end of any sentence that is not a question.
- Exclamation marks (!), which indicate strong feelings such as surprise or joy, are generally not used in academic writing.
- Use commas (,) to separate a list of three or more things. (*Aesthetic principles provide a set of criteria for creating and evaluating artistic objects such as painting, music, film, and other art forms.*)
- Use a comma after an introductory word or phrase. (*For example, it has large double doors that are at street level. / Furthermore, the entire library is on one level.*)
- Use a comma before a coordinating conjunction—*and*, *but*, *so*, *yet*, *or*, and *nor*—that joins two sentences. (*Its population in the United States is growing, but experts believe its overall population is declining.*)

- Use an apostrophe (') to show possession. (*The world's fastest mammal is found mainly in east and southwest Africa.*)
- Use quotation marks (" ") to indicate the exact words used by someone else. (*"In biology, if you look at groups with large numbers, there are very few examples where you have a central agent," says Vijay Kumar, a professor of mechanical engineering at the University of Pennsylvania.*)
- Use quotation marks to show when a word or phrase is being used in a special way, such as a definition. (*Marco Dorigo's group in Brussels is leading a European effort to create a "swarmanoid," a group of cooperating robots with complementary abilities.*)

Other Proofreading Tips

- Print out your draft instead of reading it on your computer screen.
- Read your draft out loud. Use your finger or a pen to point to each word as you read it.
- Don't be afraid to mark up your draft. Use a colored pen to make corrections so you can see them easily when you write your next draft.
- Read your draft backwards—starting with the last word—to check your spelling. That way, you won't be distracted by the meaning.
- Have someone else read your draft and give you comments or ask you questions.
- Don't depend on a computer's spell-check. When the spell-check suggests a correction, make sure you agree with it before you accept the change.
- Remember to pay attention to the following items:
  - Short words such as *is, and, but, or, it, to, for, from,* and *so.*
  - Spelling of proper nouns.
  - Numbers and dates.
- Keep a list of spelling and grammar mistakes that you commonly make so that you can be aware of them as you edit your draft.

Watch out for frequently confused words:

- *there, their,* and *they're*
- *its* and *it's*
- *by, buy,* and *bye*
- *your* and *you're*
- *to, too,* and *two*
- *whose* and *who's*
- *where, wear, we're,* and *were*
- *then* and *than*
- *quit, quiet,* and *quite*
- *write* and *right*
- *affect* and *effect*
- *through, though,* and *thorough*
- *week* and *weak*
- *lose* and *loose*
- *accept* and *except*

Research and referencing

Using facts and quotes from journals and online sources will help to support your arguments in a written assignment. When you research information, you need to look for the most relevant and reliable sources. You will also need to provide appropriate citations for these sources; that is, you need to indicate that the words are not your own but rather come from someone else.

In academic writing, it is necessary for a writer to cite sources of all information that is not original. Using a source without citing it is known as **plagiarism**.

There are several ways to cite sources. Check with your teacher on the method or methods required at your institution.

Most institutions use the American Psychological Association (APA) or the Modern Language Association (MLA) format. Here are some examples of the APA format.

Book

Hoy, A. H. (2005). *The book of photography.* Washington, D.C.: National Geographic.

Blog Post

C. Christ. (2013, August 23). How to Save Africa's Elephants [Blog post]. Retrieved from http://intelligenttravel.nationalgeographic.com/2013/08/23/how-to-save-africas-elephants/

Magazine Article

White, M. (June 2011). Brimming Pools. *National Geographic,* 100–115.

Research Checklist

☐ Are my sources relevant to the assignment?

☐ Are my sources reliable? Think about the author and publisher. Ask yourself, "What is the author's point of view? Can I trust this information?" (See also page 154.)

☐ Have I noted all sources properly, including page numbers?

☐ When I am not citing a source directly, am I using my own words? In other words, am I using appropriate paraphrasing, which includes the use of synonyms, different word forms, and/or different grammatical structure? (See page 88 for more on paraphrasing.)

☐ Are my sources up-to-date? Do they use the most recent data available? Having current sources is especially important for fields that change rapidly, such as technology and business.

☐ If I am using a direct quote, am I using the exact words that the person said or wrote?

☐ Am I using varied expressions for introducing citations, such as *According to X, As X says, X says / states / points out / explains . . .?*

Common signal phrases

Making an overview statement

It is generally agreed that . . .
It is clear (from the chart/table) that . . .
Generally, we can see that . . .

Giving supporting details and examples

One/An example (of this) is. . .
For example, . . . / For instance, . . .
Specifically, . . . / More specifically, . . .
From my experience, . . .

Giving reasons

This is due to . . .
This is because (of) . . .
One reason (for this) is . . .

Describing cause and effect

Consequently, . . .
Therefore, . . .
As a result, . . .
As a consequence, . . .
This means that . . .
Because of this, . . .

Giving definitions

. . . which means . . .
In other words, . . .
That is . . .

Linking arguments and reasons

Furthermore, . . . / Moreover, . . .
In addition, . . . / Additionally, . . .
For one thing, . . . / For another example, . . .
Not only . . . but also . . .

Describing a process

First (of all), . . .
Then / Next / After that, . . .
As soon as . . . / When . . .
Finally, . . .

Outlining contrasting views

On the other hand, . . . / However, . . .
Although some people believe (that) . . . , it can also be argued that . . .
While it may be true that . . . , nevertheless, . . .
Despite this, . . . / Despite (the fact that), . . . / Even though . . .

Softening a statement

It seems/appears that . . .
The evidence suggests/indicates that . . .

Giving a personal opinion

In my opinion, . . .
I (generally) agree that . . .
I think/feel that . . .
I believe (that) . . .

Restating/concluding

In conclusion, . . . / In summary, . . .
To conclude, . . . / To summarize, . . .

Reading and Writing Reference

Unit 3

Restrictive and Nonrestrictive Adjective Clauses

There are two types of adjective clauses. One type gives essential information about the noun. These are called **restrictive adjective clauses.** Do not use commas with restrictive adjective clauses.	I saw a photograph **that** illustrated all of Griffiths's aesthetic principles. I read the essay on photography **that** Annie Griffiths wrote.
The other type of adjective clause gives extra, or nonessential, information about the noun. These are called **nonrestrictive adjective clauses.** Commas always set off nonrestrictive adjective clauses.	Photography, **which** is a relatively recent invention, influenced our notions of beauty. Sontag, **who** was a noted essayist, wrote a book on photography. Japonaiserie, **which** is also referred to as Japonism, is an artistic movement from the mid-1800s. The artist, **who/whom** many people consider one of the greatest Impressionists, was influenced by Japanese woodblock prints.

Unit 4

Paraphrasing

When you want to report what someone else wrote, but you don't want to quote the person directly, you can paraphrase. Paraphrasing is using your own words to express another person's idea. Paraphrasing is different from summarizing. For example, when you summarize a paragraph, you restate the main points of the paragraph. When you paraphrase a paragraph, you restate all of the ideas of the paragraph.

Follow these steps to help you paraphrase successfully:

1. Read the original passage that you want to paraphrase several times to make sure that you understand the meaning. Look up any words that you don't understand.

2. Without looking at the original passage, write notes about it on a piece of paper. Don't write complete sentences.

3. Use your notes to write a paraphrase. Don't look at the original passage.

4. Compare your paraphrase with the original passage. Make sure that your paraphrase expresses the same meaning as the original. If your paraphrase looks too much like the original, check your sentence structures and word choices. Make sure that your sentence structures are different from the original. Also, try to use synonyms for the content words (like nouns and verbs) in the original passage.

Here's an example of a paraphrase:

Original Passage:

Between 1960 and 2000, Seoul's population increased from fewer than three million to ten million people. In the same period, South Korea went from being one of the world's poorest countries, with a per capita GDP of less than $100, to being richer than some countries in Europe.

Paraphrase:

The population of Seoul grew a lot between 1960 and 2000. In 1960, there were fewer than three million people in Seoul. By 2000, 10 million people were living there. In 1960, the per capita GDP of South Korea was less than $100, and the country was one of the poorest in the world. However, by 2000, South Korea was wealthier than some European countries.

Unit 7

According to and *say* are the most commonly used reporting verbs/phrases. Following are some additional verbs and phrases to help you vary your style. Consider the meaning you intend to convey when choosing a reporting verb.

according to	emphasize	predict
acknowledge	estimate	propose
admit	explain	recommend
allege	express	report
argue	feel	say
ask	indicate	speculate
assert	insist	state
believe	iterate	stress
claim	maintain	suggest
conclude	mention	think
deny	note	warn
determine	point out	write

Unit 9

Past Simple and Past Participle Forms of Commonly Used Irregular Verbs

become—became—become	eat—ate—eaten	mean—meant—meant
begin—began—begun	fall—fell—fallen	meet—met—met
bend—bent—bent	feel—felt—felt	pay—paid—paid
bet—bet—bet	fight—fought—fought	put—put—put
bite—bit—bitten	find—found—found	quit—quit—quit
bleed—bled—bled	fly—flew—flown	read—read—read
blow—blew—blown	forget—forgot—forgotten	run—ran—run
break—broke—broken	get—got—got	say—said—said
bring—brought—brought	give—gave—given	see—saw—seen
build—built—built	go—went—gone	send—sent—sent
burn—burned/burnt— burned/burnt	grow—grew—grown	sleep—slept—slept
buy—bought—bought	have—had—had	speak—spoke—spoken
catch—caught—caught	hear—heard—heard	spend—spent—spent
choose—chose—chosen	hide—hid—hidden	stand—stood—stood
come—came—come	hold—held—held	steal—stole—stolen
cost—cost—cost	hurt—hurt—hurt	take—took—taken
cut—cut—cut	keep—kept—kept	teach—taught—taught
deal—dealt—dealt	know—knew—known	tell—told—told
dive—dove—dove	lead—led—led	think—thought—thought
do—did—done	leave—left—left	understand—understood—understood
draw—drew—drawn	lie—lay—laid	wear—wore—worn
drink—drank—drunk	lose—lost—lost	win—won—won
drive—drove—driven	make—made—made	write—wrote—written

Vocabulary Index

*These words are on the Academic Word List (AWL). The AWL is a list of the 570 most frequent word families in academic texts. The list does not include words that are among the most frequent 2,000 words of English. For more information on the AWL, see http://www.victoria.ac.nz/lals/resources/academicwordlist/.

Academic Literacy Skills Index

Critical Thinking

Reading Skills/Strategies

Vocabulary Skills

Writing Skills

Visual Literacy

Test-Taking Skills

Language for Writing

Acknowledgments

The authors and publisher would like to thank the following reviewers for their help during the development of this series:

UNITED STATES AND CANADA

Gokhan Alkanat, Auburn University at Montgomery, AL; Nikki Ashcraft, Shenandoah University, VA; Karin Avila-John, University of Dayton, OH; John Baker, Oakland Community College, MI; Shirley Baker, Alliant International University, CA; Michelle Bell, University of South Florida, FL; Nancy Boyer, Golden West College, CA; Kathy Brenner, BU/CELOP, Mattapan, MA; Janna Brink, Mt. San Antonio College, Chino Hills, CA; Carol Brutza, Gateway Community College, CT; Sarah Camp, University of Kentucky, Center for ESL, KY; Maria Caratini, Eastfield College, TX; Ana Maria Cepero, Miami Dade College, Miami, FL; Daniel Chaboya, Tulsa Community College, OK; Patricia Chukwueke, English Language Institute – UCSD Extension, CA; Julia A. Correia, Henderson State University, CT; Suzanne Crisci, Bunker Hill Community College, MA; Lina Crocker, University of Kentucky, Lexington, KY; Katie Crowder, University of North Texas, TX; Joe Cunningham, Park University, Kansas City, MO; Lynda Dalgish, Concordia College, NY; Jeffrey Diluglio, Center for English Language and Orientation Programs: Boston University, MA; Scott Dirks, Kaplan International Center at Harvard Square, MA; Kathleen Dixon, SUNY Stony Brook - Intensive English Center, Stony Brook, NY; Margo Downey, Boston University, Boston, MA; John Drezek, Richland College, TX; Qian Du, Ohio State University, Columbus, OH; Leslie Kosel Eckstein, Hillsborough Community College, FL; Anwar El-Issa, Antelope Valley College, CA; Beth Kozbial Ernst, University of Wisconsin-Eau Claire, WI; Anrisa Fannin, The International Education Center at Diablo Valley College, CA; Jennie Farnell, Greenwich Japanese School, Greenwich, CT; Rosa Vasquez Fernandez, John F. Kennedy, Institute Of Languages, Inc., Boston, MA; Mark Fisher, Lone Star College, TX; Celeste Flowers, University of Central Arkansas, AR; John Fox, English Language Institute, GA; Pradel R. Frank, Miami Dade College, FL; Sherri Fujita, Hawaii Community College, Hilo, HI; Sally Gearheart, Santa Rosa Jr. College, CA; Elizabeth Gillstrom, University of Pennsylvania, Philadelphia, PA; Sheila Goldstein, Rockland Community College, Brentwood, NY; Karen Grubbs, ELS Language Centers, FL; Sudeepa Gulati, Long Beach City College, Torrance, CA; Joni Hagigeorges, Salem State University, MA; Marcia Peoples Halio, English Language Institute, University of Delaware, DE; Kara Hanson, Oregon State University, Corvallis, OR; Suha Hattab, Triton College, Chicago, IL; Marla Heath, Sacred Heart University and Norwalk Community College, Stamford, CT; Valerie Heming, University of Central Missouri, MO; Mary Hill, North Shore Community College, MA; Harry Holden, North Lake College, Dallas, TX; Ingrid Holm, University of Massachusetts Amherst, MA; Katie Hurter, Lone Star College – North Harris, TX; Barbara Inerfeld, Program in American Language Studies (PALS) Rutgers University/New Brunswick, Piscataway, NJ; Justin Jernigan, Georgia Gwinnett College, GA; Barbara Jonckheere, ALI/CSULB, Long Beach, CA; Susan Jordan, Fisher College, MA; Maria Kasparova, Bergen Community College, NJ; Maureen Kelbert, Vancouver Community College, Surrey, BC, Canada; Gail Kellersberger, University of Houston-Downtown, TX; David Kent, Troy University, Goshen,

AL; Daryl Kinney, Los Angeles City College, CA; Jennifer Lacroix, Center for English Language and Orientation Programs: Boston University, MA; Stuart Landers, Missouri State University, Springfield, MO; Mary Jo Fletcher LaRocco, Ph.D., Salve Regina University, Newport, RI; Bea Lawn, Gavilan College, Gilroy, CA; Margaret V. Layton, University of Nevada, Reno Intensive English Language Center, NV; Alice Lee, Richland College, Mesquite, TX; Heidi Lieb, Bergen Community College, NJ; Kerry Linder, Language Studies International, New York, NY; Jenifer Lucas-Uygun, Passaic County Community College, Paterson, NJ; Alison MacAdams, Approach International Student Center, MA; Julia MacDonald, Brock University, Saint Catharines, ON, Canada; Craig Machado, Norwalk Community College, CT; Andrew J. MacNeill, Southwestern College, CA; Melanie A. Majeski, Naugatuck Valley Community College, CT; Wendy Maloney, College of DuPage, Aurora, IL; Chris Mares, University of Maine – Intensive English Institute, ME; Josefina Mark, Union County College, NJ; Connie Mathews, Nashville State Community College, TN; Bette Matthews, Mid-Pacific Institute, HI; Richard McDorman, inlingua Language Centers (Miami, FL) and Pennsylvania State University, Pompano Beach, FL; Sara McKinnon, College of Marin, CA; Christine Mekkaoui, Pittsburg State University, KS; Holly A. Milkowart, Johnson County Community College, KS; Donna Moore, Hawaii Community College, Hilo, HI; Ruth W. Moore, International English Center, University of Colorado at Boulder, CO; Kimberly McGrath Moreira, University of Miami, FL; Warren Mosher, University of Miami, FL; Sarah Moyer, California State University Long Beach, CA; Lukas Murphy, Westchester Community College, NY; Elena Nehrebecki, Hudson Community College, NJ; Bjarne Nielsen, Central Piedmont Community College, NC; David Nippoldt, Reedley College, CA; Nancy Nystrom, University of Texas at San Antonio, Austin, TX; Jane O'Connor, Emory College, Atlanta, GA; Daniel E. Opacki, SIT Graduate Institute, Brattleboro, VT; Lucia Parsley, Virginia Commonwealth University, VA; Wendy Patriquin, Parkland College, IL; Nancy Pendleton, Cape Cod Community College, Attleboro, MA; Marion Piccolomini, Communicate With Ease, LTD, PA; Barbara Pijan, Portland State University, Portland, OR; Marjorie Pitts, Ohio Northern University, Ada, OH; Carolyn Prager, Spanish-American Institute, NY; Eileen Prince, Prince Language Associates Incorporated, MA; Sema Pulak, Texas A & M University, TX; Mary Kay Purcell, University of Evansville, Evansville, IN; Christina Quartararo, St. John's University, Jamaica, NY; James T. Raby, Clark University, MA; Anouchka Rachelson, Miami-Dade College, FL; Sherry Rasmussen, DePaul University, IL; Amy Renehan, University of Washington, WA; Daniel Rivas, Irvine Valley College, Irvine, CA; Esther Robbins, Prince George's Community College, PA; Bruce Rogers, Spring International Language Center at Arapahoe College, Littleton, CO; Helen Roland, Miami Dade College, FL; Linda Roth, Vanderbilt University English Language Center, TN; Janine Rudnick, El Paso Community College, TX; Paula Sanchez, Miami Dade College – Kendall Campus, FL; Deborah Sandstrom, Tutorium in Intensive English at University of Illinois at Chicago, Elmhurst, IL; Marianne Hsu Santelli, Middlesex County College, NJ; Elena Sapp, INTO Oregon State University, Corvallis, OR; Alice Savage, Lone Star College System: North Harris, TX; Jitana Schaefer, Pensacola State College, Pensacola, FL; Lynn Ramage Schaefer, University of Central Arkansas, AR; Ann Schroth, Johnson & Wales University, Dayville, CT;

Margaret Shippey, Miami Dade College, FL; Lisa Sieg, Murray State University, KY; Samanthia Slaight, North Lake College, Richardson, TX; Ann Snider, UNK University of NE Kearney, Kearney, NE; Alison Stamps, ESL Center at Mississippi State University, MI; Peggy Street, ELS Language Centers, Miami, FL; Lydia Streiter, York College Adult Learning Center, NY; Steve Strizver, Miami Beach, FL; Nicholas Taggart, Arkansas State University, AR; Marcia Takacs, Coastline Community College, CA; Tamara Teffeteller, University of California Los Angeles, American Language Center, CA; Adrianne Aiko Thompson, Miami Dade College, Miami, FL; Rebecca Toner, English Language Programs, University of Pennsylvania, PA; Evina Baquiran Torres, Zoni Language Centers, NY; William G. Trudeau, Missouri Southern State University, MO; Troy Tucker, Edison State College, FL; Maria Vargas-O'Neel, Miami Dade College, FL; Amerca Vazquez, Miami Dade College, FL; Alison Vinande, Modesto Junior College, CA; Christie Ward, IELP, Central CT State University, Hartford, CT; Colin Ward, Lone Star College - North Harris, Houston, TX; Denise Warner, Lansing Community College, Lansing, MI; Rita Rutkowski Weber, University of Wisconsin – Milwaukee, WI; James Wilson, Cosumnes River College, Sacramento, CA; Dolores "Lorrie" Winter, California State University Fullerton, Buena Park, CA; Wendy Wish-Bogue, Valencia Community College, FL; Cissy Wong, Sacramento City College, CA; Sarah Worthington, Tucson, AZ; Kimberly Yoder, Kent State University, ESL Center, OH.

ASIA

Nor Azni Abdullah, Universiti Teknologi Mara; Morgan Bapst, Seoul National University of Science and Technology; Herman Bartelen, Kanda Institute of Foreign Languages, Sano; Maiko Berger, Ritsumeikan Asia Pacific University; Thomas E. Bieri, Nagoya College; Paul Bournhonesque, Seoul National University of Technology; Joyce Cheah Kim Sim, Taylor's University, Selangor Darul Ehsan; Michael C. Cheng, National Chengchi University; Fu-Dong Chiou, National Taiwan University; Derek Currie, Korea University, Sejong Institute of Foreign Language Studies; Wendy Gough, St. Mary College/Nunoike Gaigo Senmon Gakko, Ichinomiya; Christoph A. Hafner, City University of Hong Kong; Monica Hamciuc, Ritsumeikan Asia-Pacific University, Kagoshima; Rob Higgens, Ritsumeikan University; Wenhua Hsu, I-Shou University; Lawrie Hunter, Kochi University of Technology; Helen Huntley, Hanoi University; Debra Jones, Tokyo Woman's Christian University, Tokyo; Shih Fan Kao, JinWen University of Science and Technology; Ikuko Kashiwabara, Osaka Electro-Communication University; Alyssa Kim, Hankuk University of Foreign Studies; Richard S. Lavin, Prefecturla University of Kumamoto; Mike Lay, American Institute Cambodia; Byoung-Kyo Lee, Yonsei University; Lin Li, Capital Normal University, Beijing; Bien Thi Thanh Mai, The International University – Vietnam National University, Ho Chi Minh City; Hudson Murrell, Baiko Gakuin University; Keiichi Narita, Niigata University; Orapin Nasawang, Udon Thani Rajabhat University; Huynh Thi Ai Nguyen, Vietnam USA Society; James Pham, IDP Phnom Penh; John Racine, Dokkyo University; Duncan Rose, British Council Singapore; Greg Rouault, Konan University, Hirao School of Management, Osaka; Simone Samuels, The Indonesia Australia Language Foundation, Jakarta; Yuko Shimizu, Ritsumeikan University; Wang Songmei, Beijing Institute of Education Faculty; Richmond Stroupe, Soka University; Peechaya Suriyawong, Udon Thani Rajabhat University; Teoh Swee Ai, Universiti Teknologi Mara; Chien-Wen Jenny Tseng, National Sun Yat-Sen University; Hajime Uematsu, Hirosaki University; Sy Vanna, Newton Thilay School, Phnom Penh; Matthew Watterson, Hongik University; Anthony Zak, English Language Center, Shantou University.

LATIN AMERICA AND THE CARIBBEAN

Ramon Aguilar, Universidad Tecnológica de Hermosillo, México; Lívia de Araújo Donnini Rodrigues, University of São Paulo, Brazil; Cecilia Avila, Universidad de Xapala, México; Beth Bartlett, Centro Cultural Colombo Americano, Cali, Colombia; Raúl Billini, Colegio Loyola, Dominican Republic; Nohora Edith Bryan, Universidad de La Sabana, Colombia; Raquel Hernández Cantú, Instituto Tecnológico de Monterrey, Mexico; Millie Commander, Inter American University of Puerto Rico, Puerto Rico; José Alonso Gaxiola Soto, CEI Universidad Autonoma de Sinaloa, Mazatlán, Mexico; Raquel Hernandez, Tecnologico de Monterrey, Mexico; Edwin Marín-Arroyo, Instituto Tecnológico de Costa Rica; Rosario Mena, Instituto Cultural Dominico-Americano, Dominican Republic; Elizabeth Ortiz Lozada, COPEI-COPOL English Institute, Ecuador; Gilberto Rios Zamora, Sinaloa State Language Center, Mexico; Patricia Veciños, El Instituto Cultural Argentino Norteamericano, Argentina; Isabela Villas Boas, Casa Thomas Jefferson, Brasília, Brazil; Roxana Viñes, Language Two School of English, Argentina.

EUROPE, MIDDLE EAST, AND NORTH AFRICA

Tom Farkas, American University of Cairo, Egypt; Ghada Hozayen, Arab Academy for Science, Technology and Maritime Transport, Egypt; Tamara Jones, ESL Instructor, SHAPE Language Center, Belgium; Jodi Lefort, Sultan Qaboos University, Muscat, Oman; Neil McBeath, Sultan Qaboos University, Oman; Barbara R. Reimer, CERTESL, UAE University, UAE; Nashwa Nashaat Sobhy, The American University in Cairo, Egypt; Virginia Van Hest-Bastaki, Kuwait University, Kuwait.

AUSTRALIA

Susan Austin, University of South Australia; Joanne Cummins, Swinburne College; Pamela Humphreys, Griffith University.

Special thanks to Annie Griffiths, Stephen S. Hall, Peter Miller, Kees Veenenbos, Michael Whelan, and Daisy Zamora for their kind assistance during the book's development.

This series is dedicated to Kristin L. Johannsen, whose love for the world's cultures and concern for the world's environment were an inspiration to family, friends, students, and colleagues.

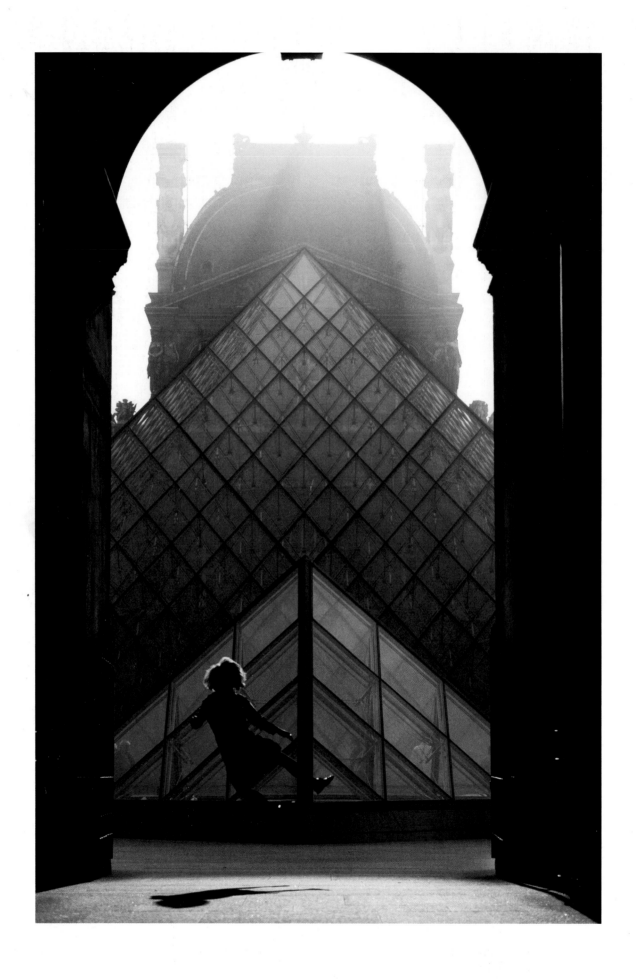